The Family Quarrel A Journey Through The Years Of The Revolution

Elswyth Thane

Nabu Public Domain Reprints:

You are holding a reproduction of an original work published before 1923 that is in the public domain in the United States of America, and possibly other countries. You may freely copy and distribute this work as no entity (individual or corporate) has a copyright on the body of the work. This book may contain prior copyright references, and library stamps (as most of these works were scanned from library copies). These have been scanned and retained as part of the historical artifact.

This book may have occasional imperfections such as missing or blurred pages, poor pictures, errant marks, etc. that were either part of the original artifact, or were introduced by the scanning process. We believe this work is culturally important, and despite the imperfections, have elected to bring it back into print as part of our continuing commitment to the preservation of printed works worldwide. We appreciate your understanding of the imperfections in the preservation process, and hope you enjoy this valuable book.

The Family Quarrel

Elswyth Thane's new book is a fresh approach to the Revolutionary War and a deftly written, absorbing chronicle of one whole phase of the Revolution—the battles fought in the South which led to the surrender at Yorktown and which have been curiously neglected by most historians.

Guiding the author's hand is a vivid sourcebook, the almost forgotten *Pictorial Field Book of the Revolution* by Benson Lossing, a writer-artist who more than a century ago visited every important Revolutionary setting, driving a horse and wagon and sketching as he went.

By ELSWYTH THANE

Fiction

- RIDERS OF THE WIND
- ECHO ANSWERS
- CLOTH OF GOLD
- HIS ELIZABETH
- BOUND TO HAPPEN
- QUEEN'S FOLLY
- TRYST
- REMEMBER TODAY
- FROM THIS DAY FORWARD
- MELODY
- THE LOST GENERAL
- LETTER TO A STRANGER

The Williamsburg Novels

- DAWN'S EARLY LIGHT
- YANKEE STRANGER
- EVER AFTER
- THE LIGHT HEART
- KISSING KIN
- THIS WAS TOMORROW
- HOMING

Non-Fiction

- THE TUDOR WENCH
- YOUNG MR. DISRAELI
- ENGLAND WAS AN ISLAND ONCE
- THE BIRD WHO MADE GOOD
- RELUCTANT FARMER
- THE FAMILY QUARREL

Plays

- THE TUDOR WENCH
- YOUNG MR. DISRAELI

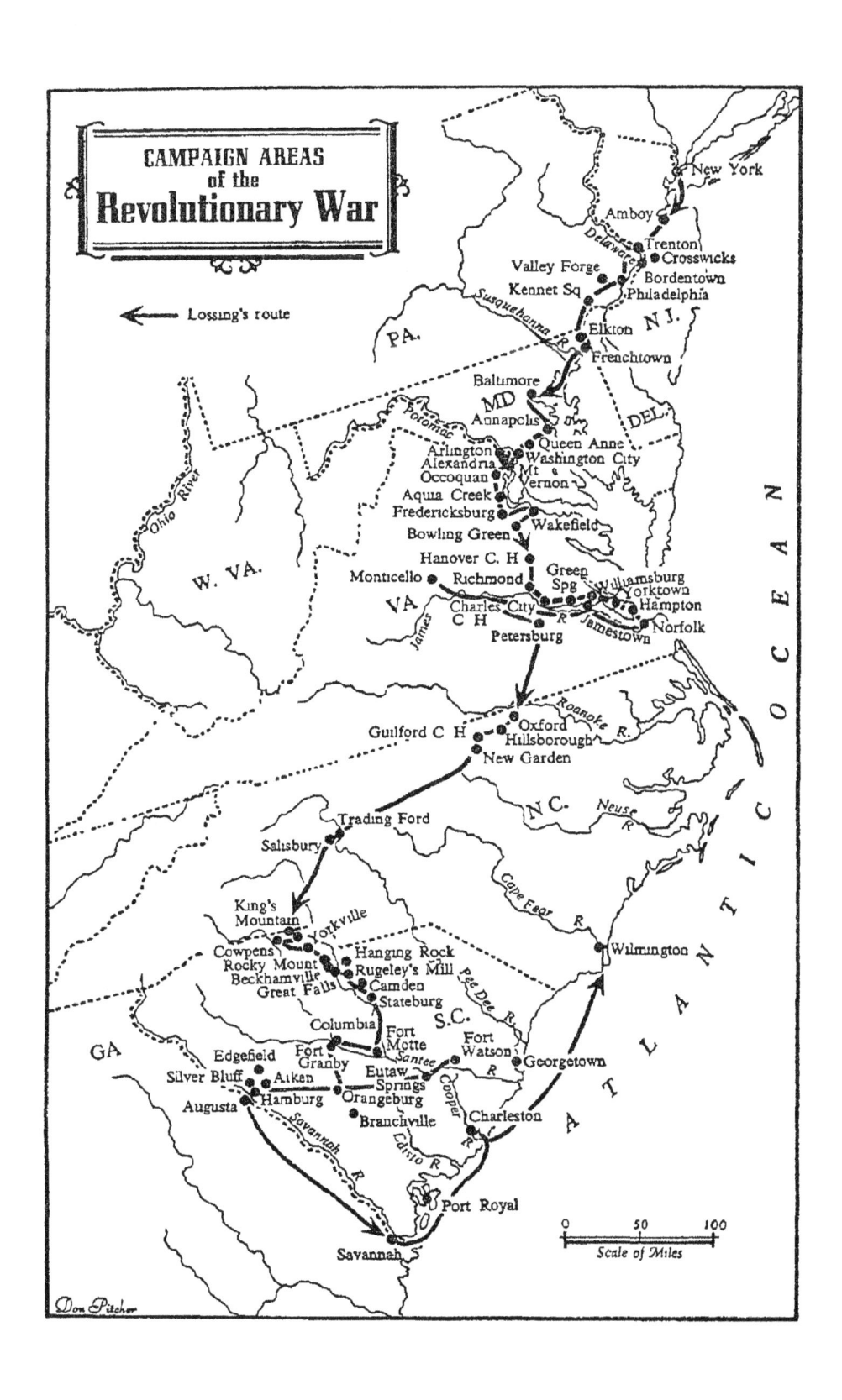

CAMPAIGN AREAS of the Revolutionary War

The Family Quarrel

A JOURNEY THROUGH THE
YEARS OF THE REVOLUTION

by
ELSWYTH THANE

Illustrations from Benson Lossing's
Pictorial Field Book of the Revolution

DUELL, SLOAN AND PEARCE
New York

COPYRIGHT © 1959 BY ELSWYTH THANE

All rights reserved No part of this book in excess of five hundred words may be reproduced in any form without permission in writing from the publisher.

First edition

Library of Congress Catalogue Card Number 59-5562

MANUFACTURED IN THE UNITED STATES OF AMERICA

VAN REES PRESS • NEW YORK

For
Florence Wren

Contents

I.	The Project	3
II.	The Start — Amboy — Crosswicks — Bordentown — Trenton	10
III.	Philadelphia to Valley Forge	35
IV.	Kennet Square — Elkton — Frenchtown — Baltimore — Annapolis	60
V.	Queen Anne — Washington City — Arlington — Alexandria — Mount Vernon — Pohick — Occoquan	67
VI.	Aquia Creek — Fredericksburg — Wakefield — Bowling Green — Hanover Courthouse	91
VII.	Richmond — Westover — Charles City Courthouse — Sherwood Forest — Green Spring — Jamestown	102
VIII.	Jamestown to Williamsburg	125
IX.	Yorktown	138
X.	Hampton — Great Bridge — Norfolk — City Point — Monticello — Petersburg — Oxford — Hillsborough — Guilford Courthouse — New Garden — Trading Ford — Salisbury — King's Mountain — The Cowpens	153

CONTENTS

XI. Cherokee Ford — Yorkville — Fishing Creek — Beckhamville — Great Falls — Rocky Mount — Hanging Rock — Stateburg — Rugeley's Mill — Saunder's Creek — Camden — Hobkirk's Hill . . 186

XII. High Hills of Santee — Stateburg — Fort Motte — Columbia — Fort Granby — 96 — Orangeburg — Eutaw Springs 226

XIII. Eutaw Springs — Fort Watson — Pond Bluff . . . 254

XIV. Branchville — Aiken — Edgefield — Silver Bluff — Hamburg — Augusta — Savannah . . . 266

XV. Port Royal — Charleston — Wilmington . . . 282

Index 299

The Family Quarrel

"Let this ever be considered as a *family quarrel*, *disgraceful* and *ruinous*, into which we are innocently plunged by intolerable oppression, and which we are sincerely disposed to appease and reconcile, whenever the good Providence of God shall put it in our power, consistent with the preservation of our just rights."

JAMES DUANE
Delegate from New York to the
Continental Congress in the
summer of 1775

I

The Project

THIS book is about the American Revolution, in 1775–83. It's about the places where the Revolution happened, and the people it happened to. It's about a journey that one man took, within living memory of the war, to see for himself and to record what the men who made the Revolution had seen at that time. It's about that man, whose name was Benson Lossing, and who says in the Preface to his two-volume account of his tour:

"I knew that the men of old were fast fading away, and that relics associated with their trials and triumphs would soon be covered up forever. I felt shame such as every American ought to feel on seeing the plough levelling the breastworks where our fathers bled, and those edifices containing the council chambers of men who planned the attack, the ambuscade, or the retreat, crumbling into utter ruin.

"To delineate with pen and pencil what is left of the physical features of that period and to rescue from oblivion the mementoes which another generation will appreciate; and a desire to place the result in an enduring form before my countrymen, has given birth to these pages."

Lossing was a natural scholar, who had been orphaned at twelve, when he was apprenticed to a watch-maker at Poughkeepsie. By the time he was twenty-two he had become joint editor of the local paper, and at thirty-five he was making a living in New York as a writer, editor, and professional wood-engraver, with a published volume in the *Harper's Family Library*. Probably by sheer enthusiasm he talked somebody at Harper's into advancing funds for his great project. He must have been a very disarming man. It shows in his own words, as well as in his achievement. "To collect the pictorial and other materials for this work," he says, when after about five years he has done so, "I travelled more than eight thousand miles and visited every important place made memorable by the events of the war; yet in all that long and devious journey, from New England to Georgia, with no passport to the confidence and no claim to the regard of those from whom information was sought, and communing with men of every social and intellectual grade, I never experienced an unkind word or cold repulsion of manner."

It was for its time an unusual idea which he had conceived, more than a generation ahead of the motorized tourist, as he was more than a generation behind the Revolution. And the book he wrote is in its way Lossing himself, acute, benign, and inquisitive on every page. But that's only the top of it, as *Skippy* said while gazing at the ocean. It is also the sound of guns on a spring morning at Guilford Courthouse. It is the swamps and slashes of the Carolinas where Marion rode, and the eerie silence of the great rocks in the forest where Sumter dodged and raided and hid. It is deserted Jamestown, with its broken church and crooked tombs, and little old Williamsburg nearly a century before the magnificent Rockefeller Restoration began. It is chance meetings with men whose fathers had starved and shivered in the ragged colonial ranks because they believed in a general named Washington, whom many of them never set eyes on; and with aged women who as little girls had run shrieking from the clanking cavalry of their own side.

When Lossing set out southward in the autumn of 1848 with his notebooks and pencils, it was just sixty-seven years since Cornwallis had surrendered at Yorktown. Travelling alone in a dearborn wagon drawn by a "strong, good-natured horse" named Charley, he touched the Revolution at only one remove. A hundred years later, we in a motor car can follow the line he drew on the map and so touch the eighteenth century ourselves. We can take a photograph from where he stood to sketch Sumter's Hanging Rock—of the same view almost unaltered. Or where he found only fence-rails and falling snow at Guilford Courthouse, we will find a reconstructed battlefield with markers and a museum and an electric map of the action, and a friendly Ranger in attendance. At Williamsburg he sketched the real Apollo Room at the Raleigh Tavern just as "modernization" destroyed its original outlines. Ten years after his visit the Raleigh burned down entirely, and has now been rebuilt at enormous expense—as it was *before* he saw it. So time shifts and interlocks and frames pictures for us today.

Even then, in an age with fewer distractions and less easy entertainment, a writer with any sort of serious intent was dogged by the dread of dullness and the suspicion that readers hate to be required to think. Even then, he cast about for window-dressing, and endeavored to ice the cake, with the comment. "As my journey was among things and scenes hallowed to the feelings of every American, I felt a hope that a record of the pilgrimage, interwoven with the facts of past history, would attract the attention of many who could not be otherwise decoyed into the apparently arid domain of mere history. I accordingly determined to make the record of the tour to the localities of the Revolution a leading feature of the work."

So his book was not "mere" history, and neither is this one. There are recent texts aplenty for the immense over-all coverage of the conflict. There will be no attempt here to examine its profound political significance, arising from the collision between new ideas and old tyrannies, or the interplay of diplomacy and military action which embarrassed the British Government and brought French troops to Washington's aid. The American Revolutionary War is perhaps unique in that it was not only won decisively on the field, but in its basic conception has stayed won—America is still a free and independent country. And yet the same war is still being fought all over the world, wherever the ideas embodied in the American declaration of human rights and beliefs are being challenged and suppressed. And so the story of the American Revolution is still vital and inspiring and always new, and the men and women who lived it are still vivid and dear.

The names are not new—Washington, alone on his pinnacle, in no need of adjectives; fire-eating Wayne, Quaker Greene, jolly Knox, grim Steuben, poor De Kalb, granny Gates, Marion the Swamp-fox, Game-cock Sumter, and the man Arnold who gave his own name forever to treachery. The deeds have all been told—Trenton, Valley Forge, Camden, the Cowpens, Fort Motte, Charleston, Savannah, Yorktown. Even the painted likenesses are familiar—the soldier-artist Peale imposed on Washington for sittings in the middle of the Monmouth campaign and at Valley Forge; Gilbert Stuart painted Knox with his maimed hand folded on the muzzle of a cannon.

But what kind of men were they, outside the history books? What kind of men, around their scanty camp-fires, in their scribbled diaries and their private letters home, and in the eyes of their devoted women folk who often shared the hardships of the winter headquarters? Because that is the kind of men we need still, need *now*. How did they think, and what did they say at the time; how did they brace themselves to the ordeal, and what were the conditions of their daily lives as they stuck it out to the end they never lost sight of—which was victory. This is a book of personalities and places. Its content is emotional and visual, rather than philosophical and didactic. The little things, not the *quod erat demonstrandum*. The heart, not the head. This is the "mere" book, but Lossing's use of the word is illuminating.

Because there is already so much more recent material available on Washington's own campaigns around Manhattan and Philadelphia, and on the northern battlefields, I have concentrated here on the almost separate war which was fought below the Potomac during 1780–81, and which wore out the British troops under Clinton and Cornwallis and set up the siege and surrender of Yorktown. Many of the commanders, like Greene, Lafayette, and Wayne, had already distinguished themselves under Washington's eye. Others, like the partisans Marion and Sumter, had never been within miles of the Commander-in-chief whom they served so single-mindedly, and were not even present at the Virginia surrender which they had done so much to bring about.

It is hard to remember that these men were Washington's seconds, carrying on a desperate campaign in his absence while he was pinned down by another British army in the New York area. And it was not until Cornwallis had gone to earth at Yorktown that the Commander-in-chief, with Rochambeau and their combined armies, swept down through Williamsburg and shot it out with him.

One quibble which Lossing probably did not encounter when he embarked on his original project is that the Revolution was a war with England—and the world being the way it is today, we don't want to bring all *that* up again. But we tend to forget that at the time it was regarded as a civil war. It was fought by Englishmen in America to maintain the rights which Englishmen had first enunciated in Magna Charta, and which George III in the eighteenth century, like John in the thirteenth, attempted to deny his subjects.

George III was not an Englishman. His only English blood came from a Stuart grandmother six generations back. After the Hanoverians succeeded to the throne of England they continued to marry German princesses, and to live and talk and think like Germans. His ideas of government were mid-European, and many of his English ministers and generals were shocked and embarrassed by his views and their violent expression. Chatham furiously fought them in Parliament, Amherst refused to accept command of the army which was being sent to punish the colonies, Cornwallis himself was reluctant, Burgoyne was not happy, Howe the soldier more than once allowed his advantages to slip away from him, and Howe the admiral, "who was a man of fine feelings," says Lossing, "hesitated long before he would accept the command of the fleet destined to sail against his fellow-subjects in America. In Parliament, a few days before he sailed, he spoke with much warmth upon the horrors of civil war, and declared he knew no struggle so painful as that between an officer's duties as a soldier and a man. If left to his own choice, he should decline serving, but if commanded it became his duty, and he should not refuse to obey."

As for Lord North, who has become the arch-villain and scapegoat of the Parliamentary conflict, his administration "teemed with calamitous events beyond any of the same duration to be found in our annals," according to one of his contemporaries, and Appleton adds, "The American war was its great feature, and North's efforts were principally directed to measures for the coercion of the colonies.... But although he did not waver in his opinion as to the right of Parliament to tax the colonies, he entertained serious doubts as to the expediency of continuing the war during the last four years of his administration, and was induced to persevere only through regard to the wishes of George III." His wife recorded that later in life he would "deeply reproach himself for having at the earnest desire of the King remained in administration after he thought that peace ought to have been made with America."

We are accustomed to hearing about self-determination now. We recognize that colonies grow up, just as children grow up. Nowadays the sceptred isle of Britain gracefully acknowledges her separate Dominions. But in the eighteenth century it was truly revolution when a community, or a family, announced its intention of seceding from the parental rooftree. There was no precedent; that had to be born here. One must consider the repercussions in the minds of men all over the world. One must remember the sanctity of thrones, and the then almost unquestioned prerogative of kings to rule as they saw fit. Charles I's death on the scaffold did not establish a precedent. It did not lead to Louis XVI's, except by way of the State House at Philadelphia. Even the colonists were themselves incredulous of their own trend of thought, as the stupendous idea of Independence finally became articulate.

They wanted desperately to believe that the Throne would see reason. The First Continental Congress adjourned in 1774 with a respectful petition, to which George III replied furiously that he considered the New England governments in a state of rebellion, and that "blows must now decide whether they are to be subject to this country or independent." So it was really the King himself who first used the awful word.

At Bunker Hill in June, 1775, the colonists' intentions were made clear to his Majesty, though the Declaration was not spelled out for him till a whole year later. Meanwhile he made his ultimate, irretrievable blunder, which was the hiring of a German army of mercenaries to fight on American soil. Once he had brought in his outsiders, no reconciliation was possible. The colonists then sought a foreign alliance of their own. More from a willingness to see an old enemy humbled than from sympathy with colonial liberty, France stepped in on the side of the Americans, and the combat became mortal. But liberty was catching. Soon it spread to France.

"I have aimed to view men and events with an impartial eye," says Lossing, "censuring friends when they deserved censure and commending enemies when truth and justice demanded the tribute. The historical events recorded were those of a family quarrel concerning vital principles in jurisprudence; and wisely did a sagacious English statesman console himself, at the close of the war, with the reflection: 'We have been subdued, it is true, but thank Heaven the brain and muscle which achieved the victory were nurtured by English blood, Old England, upon the Island of Great Britain, has been beaten only by Young England, in America.'"

II

The Start

A HARD childhood, a chancy income, an early marriage and its responsibilities might have had a sobering effect on a man, but Lossing's volatile spirits always gleam through the rather ponderous style which was the fashion in his day. Only an optimist could have conceived and undertaken his self-imposed task, on borrowed money. And one wonders how much money he actually had in his possession as he set out on this long journey to the South, which was to take him as far as Savannah before he turned homeward. He was thirty-five, he must have been in rugged health, no doubt his wife had encouraged him, he was being paid to do a job he had himself invented—surely a fortunate man, and well aware of it.

"On the 22d of November, 1848," he records with an almost visible effort not to sound excited, "I left New York to visit the Southern portions of the old Thirteen States, made memorable by the events of the War for Independence. Aware of the lack of public facilities for travel below the Potomac, and not doubting that many of the localities which I intended to visit were far distant from public highways, I resolved to journey with my own conveyance, with an independence and thoroughness not vouchsafed by steam or stage-drivers.

"I purchased a strong, good-natured horse, harnessed him to a light dearborn wagon, stowed my luggage under the seat, and taking the reins on a bright and balmy afternoon departed on a *drive* of nearly fourteen hundred miles. The wisdom of my resolve was a hundred times made manifest, for in some portions of the South, horse, mule or ox could not have been procured to convey me to places of interest lying scores of miles apart, and scores of miles away from stage-routes.

"It was a lonely journey; sometimes among mountains, sometimes through swamps, sometimes through vast pine forests and over sandy plains.... It was to me a journey of great interest, and the dreary days passed in riding from one hallowed locality to another were all forgotten when sitting down, pencil in hand, in the midst of some arena consecrated by patriotism and love of country. Then glorious associations would crowd thickly upon the memory, and weariness and privations would be forgotten. I shall endeavor to impart to my readers some of the pleasures and profits of this Southern journey, extended after leaving my horse and wagon at Camden in South Carolina, to nearly four hundred miles further.

"I left New York at three o'clock in the afternoon on the steamboat *Transport*, of the Camden and Amboy Railroad Company. We passed out at the Narrows at four o'clock between Forts Hamilton and Lafayette, and, traversing Raritan Bay, reached South Amboy at twilight, where I remained until morning. I left Amboy for Trenton by way of Crosswicks before sunrise. The air was clear and frosty; the pools by the roadside were skimmed with ice, and the fields and fences were white with hoar frost. The deep sand of the road made the travelling heavy, yet before the sun was fairly up my strong horse had taken me half the way to Spottswood, ten miles distant.

"During my brief tarry of an hour and a half at Crosswicks I visited the venerable Mrs. Idell, who was eighty-three years old. She clearly remembered the advent of the Americans there, after the battle of Trenton. She lived with her brother, two or three miles from the meeting-house. Twelve American officers on horseback took possession of his house, while himself and family were in meeting. The parlor was filled with equestrian accouterments, and she and two other children 'almost lost their wits by fright.' The old lady was strong in mind but feeble in body when I saw her, yet she was able to sit in their plain old house of worship every meeting day.

"I left Crosswicks at four o'clock, and arrived at Trenton at sunset. It was a pleasant drive of eight miles through a fertile country, the well-filled barns and the numerous haystacks denoting bountiful harvests. I passed a little northward of Bordentown, and had an occasional glimpse of its spires above the brown tree-tops. As we may not approach so near this pleasant village again, let us slacken our pace a little as we go over the crown of the hill, from whence the vane of the church is visible, and consider its Revolutionary history."

A timely pause in his journey is Lossing's usual lead-in to one of his lively and well-documented accounts of the events which had taken place in his immediate surroundings. He went to enormous trouble after his return home to accumulate the material to go with the sketches he had made on the spot, sometimes under an umbrella held by a friendly stranger, in all kinds of weather and in whatever state of hunger or fatigue he came upon something of interest. Not only his thoroughness and industry, but his available sources seem remarkable. And he had a way of embedding in his footnotes incidents which would seem worthy of a place in the main text.

Bordentown changed hands several times during the war, and it was during a raid by the British while they held Philadelphia in '78 that the following cameo was enacted. It opens vistas of further speculation to the reader, but is related by Lossing with a dry period and no comment. The British officers in charge of the marauding soldiery "dined at the house of Francis Hopkinson, one of the signers of the Declaration of Independence, who with his family was absent at the time. A young lady, eighteen years old, named Mary Comely, provided the dinner for them. While they were dining she was informed that the soldiers were robbing the houses of her mother and grandmother, on the opposite side of the street. She went in and stealthily cut a piece from the skirt of one of the soldier's coats. This she handed to the commander, and by it he detected the thief. By this means the property of her relations and some neighbors were restored."

Naturally the Signer and his family were absent during a British raid, for he was guilty of treason against the Crown, and as a member of Congress had probably at that time accompanied his colleagues on their second hasty departure from Philadelphia within a year. Who was Mary Comely, to be cooking dinner in his house for the British—a servant? But her family had similar houses in the same street. Cut a piece, how? Was the guilty soldier *wearing* the coat at the time? And was there a company parade, to detect the man whose coat lacked a piece? Was his face red? It would have been a bit difficult to fit a missing snippet into the rags and tatters of an American infantryman, but the British uniforms around Philadelphia were respectable and whole. And here we find a British commander—not named—who undertook to control his men and protect the civilian population from wilful looting, when the main objective was army stores and shipping. (The Hessians plundered right and left unrebuked.) The episode is one of Lossing's many glancing stories which leave one roused and questioning, in the familiar childish state of *What happened then?* But Lossing has driven on.

His chronicle is governed by his geographical route rather than by the sequence of events, and writing as he comes to it is likely to put the cart before the horse, historically. However, at Trenton, at the start of his journey southward, he is in the midst of that dramatic winter of 1776, the second of the eight war winters, when New Jersey was the scene of some of the blackest days of the whole conflict. The British were in New York and Newport. After losing the Hudson River forts in November, Washington had been for three weeks on the run, abandoning Hackensack, Newark, New Brunswick, Princeton, and Trenton, one after another, to British occupation. His army had left blankets, tents, rations, even entrenching tools behind in order to take with them the precious arms and ammunition and heavy field-pieces which wet weather could render almost useless. The men endured a daily torment of frostbite, hunger, and fatigue. Cornwallis was so close on their heels that, says Lossing, "often the music of the pursued and the pursuers would be heard by each other, yet no action occurred."

Although Trenton lies outside the Southern campaign, it saw one of the most decisive days of the war, and is worth a brief excursion from the main theme of this volume. Also it is the only time, until we reach Yorktown, when we shall encounter Washington in action. Only two of his letters to Martha have survived her destructive passion for privacy, but it is impossible to read even his more impersonal communications, and the daily accounts of him by the men who knew him best, without falling a little in love with him. The Virginia general on the tall horse who wept with rage at Kip's Bay when his men broke and ran, who cursed the leaves off the trees at Monmouth when Charles Lee let him down, whose cheeks shone wet with tears when he visited his sick and dying at Valley Forge, and who danced the minuets with Lucy Knox at the little balls they gave when the wives arrived at winter headquarters to keep them company, is not the austere wax-works figure which the legend of his greatness has somehow counterfeited. His men revered and loved him, aides and privates alike. Considering what he asked of them, and what they endured out of their belief in him, one can hardly doubt him now. And it was at Trenton that he demonstrated his right to their devotion, and the legend began.

On December 7th of 1776 he got his ragged, starving, exhausted army out of Trenton and across the icy Delaware, the last boatload arriving on the Pennsylvania shore around midnight, as the first British division marched in at the other end of the little town. He had collected and retained on the Pennsylvania side every boat for miles up and down the Jersey banks, so that Cornwallis could not cross the river in pursuit until it froze solid, or until he built new boats. A more energetic enemy determined to win his campaign might have done just that, out of the wooden houses and fences of Trenton village. But it was winter time, and Howe and Cornwallis were accustomed from boyhood to wars which obeyed the rules, and they considered the Americans disposed of, perhaps permanently. They put out a chain of cantonments eighty miles long, from Staten Island to Princeton, to be manned chiefly by the Hessians, and on December 13th Cornwallis returned to General Howe's headquarters in New York. He had an ailing wife in England, and intended to take several months' leave at home.

Lord Cornwallis's wife's enchanting maiden name was Jemima Tullekens Jones, and she was the well-dowered daughter of a colonel in the 3d Guards. They were married in 1768, and an only son was born in '74. Jemima must have been very much in love with his lordship (who was a fine figure of a man with great charm of manner and a gallant record in the Seven Years War), for she maintained that she would die of a broken heart if he went away to the service. He had succeeded to his father's earldom at twenty-four, and in the House of Lords had steadily opposed the Government's bullying policy towards the colonies. In spite of his Whig sentiments, he was comfortably installed in the sinecure office of Constable of the Tower with the rank of major-general when his orders came to join the equally Whiggish General Howe in America. Unwillingly, against Jemima's tearful objections, he had sailed in the spring of '76 with seven regiments of infantry, and was present with General Clinton at the first attempt to take Charleston, which was beaten off by the defenders. In July he landed on Staten Island just as Howe's New York campaign against Washington began. He will be with us almost all the way, the most vigorous, disinterested, and able officer the British army possessed, though he could never get along with Clinton.

The return to New York of Cornwallis in December, '76, left as senior officer in Jersey a General Grant, whose headquarters were at New Brunswick at the northern end of the cantonment line. "I will undertake to keep the peace in New Jersey with a corporal's guard," he announced recklessly.

During the following weeks Washington crossed and re-crossed the Delaware River several times, but *the* crossing, the one before the battle which was the turning point in his career, if not in the life of the whole new nation, took place at McConkey's Ferry in that famous Christmas snowstorm. It was raining at Trenton when Lossing drove in on a November afternoon seventy-two years later.

"The sun was veiled at its setting by an ominous red vapor that betokened a storm," he relates. "True to the sign, the morning following was lowery, and a chilly east wind made sketching in the open air anything but pleasant. I was busy with my pencil until the rain began to fall at noon. At two o'clock the sun peeped out and smiled so pleasantly that I ordered my horse and started for McConkey's Ferry, now Taylorsville, eight miles above Trenton, the place where

> 'On Christmas Day in seventy-six
> Our gallant troops with bayonets fixed
> To Trenton marched away.'

"A noble bridge, six hundred feet long, here spans the river. The bridge is of timber, the piers of solid masonry, with an icebreaker on the upper side. The view here given is from below the bridge on the Pennsylvania side, looking northeast, and exhibits the Jersey shore at the precise point where the American army landed. Mr. Taylor, an old resident of the place, pointed out the spot on each side of the river where a log-house stood at the time. The one on the Pennsylvania side was upon the site of the Temperance House in Taylorsville; that upon the Jersey side was exactly at the end of the bridge."

The only bridge available to Washington was one of overloaded open boats, buffeted by great jagged cakes of floating ice, and shipping water which froze stiff on the inadequate clothing of the huddled men, who had wrapped the firing-pans of their muskets with greasy rags to keep their priming-powder dry, while their wet fingers froze fast to the gun-barrels. Nowadays at a place called Washington's Crossing there is a State Park, and an old white-painted Inn with green shutters, and the Ferry House has been preserved pretty much as it was built in 1757. It is possible to descend a grassy slope past a stone marker with a tablet, and stand at the edge of the water at the approximate point where Washington must have stepped into the boat to leave the Pennsylvania shore. Such a pause is recommended as an exercise in imagination. The river does not look very wide, on a sunny autumn day. Down stream is the unimpressive iron bridge, only two lanes wide, which has replaced the one Lossing saw.

The General's decision to re-cross the river had been taken in cold blood, alone, in some unfathomable secret agony of faith or desperation—alone in his upstairs bedroom at the headquarters at Keith's farm-house in what might have been the darkest hour he knew throughout the war, with no real success so far to sustain a belief in himself. The house which sheltered him then was a comfortable stone building belonging to the local tax collector. His window looked out at the back towards the spring-house and the bleak slope of the hill, under the bare branches of a fine elm tree. All the news was calamitous—Newport in Rhode Island had been occupied by Clinton, as a convenient British sea-base—Charles Lee, who had not then proved himself a liability, had recently been taken prisoner, as had two of Washington's aides, Graydon and McHenry, separately. It was from this farm-house headquarters on December 18th that he wrote his favorite brother, John Augustine Washington, who lived not far from Mount Vernon in Virginia: "I have no doubt but that General Howe will still make an attempt upon Philadelphia this winter.... In a word, my dear sir, if every nerve is not strained to recruit the new army with all possible expedition, I think the game is pretty near up...."

Something had to be done, and quickly. Alone in the back bedroom he had made up his mind. Although with his usual courtesy to his subordinates he called a Council of his officers on the evening of December 24th, it was plain to them then that his decision was already made, and no objections were raised.

On that Christmas morning, therefore, he committed himself and his army to the great enterprise. For the march on Trenton the men were to carry three days' cooked rations—three days as spartanly conceived by an always hard-pressed commissary—and forty rounds of ammunition. Each officer was required to provide himself with a piece of white paper stuck in his hat for a field-mark —in a snowstorm. The countersign, which Washington wrote out in his own hand, was *Victory or Death.*

It was a grim Christmas for the American side, whatever they did, wherever they were. On the day before Cornwallis had turned back to New York, the Continental Congress in session in Philadelphia had hastily loaded their papers and belongings into wagons and taken refuge at Baltimore. This was the first of their two flights from the capital, and the British would have been on the whole cordially received if they had chosen to spend Christmas there, for its large Tory population were crowing, and the patriots were close to panic. But the British stayed cosy in New York, and the Hessian celebration of the holidays, featuring a popular local discovery of theirs called apple-jack, which any German could pronounce, got well under way at Trenton.

Washington's actual orders for the day are hair-raising to contemplate even now. To cold, ill-fed, homesick men at the bitter end of a long licking, they must have seemed the last straw. See what he expected of them. They were to be got back across the half-frozen river again, no matter how; they were to march eight miles along slippery, rutted roads in a snowstorm at night, and attack trained professional soldiers solidly ensconced in a comfortable village with dry ammunition and their field-pieces parked—attack *by surprise*. This is part of what was read out to them by their officers, very early on Christmas morning:

"Each brigade to be furnished with two good guides, and to have with them a detachment of the artillery without cannon, provided with spikes and hammers to spike up the enemy's cannon in case of necessity, or to bring them off if it can be effected, the party to be provided with drag-ropes for the purpose of dragging off the cannon.

"Immediately upon their debarkation, the whole is to form and march in subdivision from the right. A profound silence to be enjoined, and no man will quit his ranks on pain of death.... General Stephen will appoint a guard to form a chain of sentries round the landing-place at a sufficient distance from the river to permit troops to form, this guard not to suffer any person to go in or come out, but to detain all persons who attempt either. This guard to join their brigade when the troops are all over....

"General Stephen is to attack and force the enemy's guards and seize any such posts as may prevent them from forming in the streets, and in case they are annoyed from the houses to set them on fire...."

How does this sound to a man who took part in a more recent crossing of a somewhat wider body of water, to disembark on Omaha Beach? Like something for toy soldiers on the nursery floor? Or are not all such requirements, in terms of pre-dawn courage, equally spine-stiffening?

One of Washington's Staff officers had the presence of mind to take notes in his pocket-diary as the day wore on: "They make a great deal of Christmas in Germany," he wrote that morning, "and no doubt the Hessians will drink a great deal and have a dance tonight. They will be sleepy tomorrow morning. Washington will set the tune for them about daybreak. The rations are cooked. New flints and ammunition have been distributed. The regiments have had their evening parade, but instead of returning to their quarters are marching towards the ferry. It is fearfully cold and raw, and a snow-storm setting in. The wind is northeast and beats in the faces of the men. It will be a terrible night for the soldiers who have no shoes. Some of them have tied old rags around their feet; others are barefoot, but I have not heard a man complain."

It took nine hours to get the army over the river; the men first, then the horses—that must have been the liveliest part of it—and last the precious artillery. Silence, of course, became a myth. The rising wind, the ice chunks in the river knocking the boats about, the horrified horses plunging and squealing, the profane and prayerful men who stumbled and fell and groped in the bitter dark, made it almost impossible for even the necessary words of command to be heard. Washington, like everybody else, was laboring under a heavy cold, and wore a piece of woollen tied round his neck. He was soon too hoarse to compete with the elements, and it was the booming bass voice, already famous in the army, of the artillery's Colonel Knox which guided the men to the river bank and into the boats on the Pennsylvania side.

After he had himself crossed in the same boat with Washington, Knox stood beside the Commander-in-chief at the water's edge and hallooed the boats ashore at the Jersey landing-place. He was a big burly man of great good-nature, and doubtless no one laughed louder when Washington with a rare sense of timing unbent to make a rude army-type joke at his expense while their boat was being fought through the ice-blocks and the swift current on the way over. "Shift your weight, Knox, and trim the boat," the great man is supposed to have said, in effect. It was a small jest, but it grew in savor as it was passed along, and it relieved the tension as it was meant to do.

The men did their best to obey orders shouted by officers they could not see, and once safely ashore themselves imagined that they heard cries for help from their friends still on the way—or was it the wind?—imagined boats stove in by the grinding ice, boats carried away down stream and lost forever with their numbed and helpless cargoes. . . .

When Washington's horse was brought over to him he mounted and rode among them, with a husky word of encouragement here and there, while relief and confidence spread outward from him in widening circles—Look, right behind you, on the left—it's *him*—they've got his horse across to him, anyway—he knows what he's about, look—he's here—*he's here*. . . . And they straightened against the wind, and dressed their lines in the dark, to do him proud. Liberty, yes. Victory, oh, yes. But those were words. Washington they could see, could touch, if they had dared. Washington was *there*.

Then the artillery horses arrived, gaunt and wet and bewildered, but obedient to the hands and voices they knew. And then the guns came, lunging into the drag-ropes or else dead-weight against them, till the horses were put to again, and took the strain. A Delaware captain recorded mildly that "It was only with the greatest care and labor that the horses and artillery could be ferried over the river." To our everlasting surprise not a boat capsized, not a man or a cannon was lost in that nine hours of pandemonium. The Staff officer's blow-by-blow account kept in his damp pocket-diary was continued on the Jersey shore:

"Dec. 26, 3 A.M. I am writing in the ferry house. The troops are all over, and the boats have gone back for the artillery. We are three hours behind the set time. Glover's men have had a hard time to force the boats through the floating ice with the snow drifting in their faces. I have never seen Washington so determined as he is now. He stands on the bank of the river, wrapped in his cloak, superintending the landing of his troops. He is calm and collected, but very determined. The storm is changing to sleet, and cuts like a knife. The last cannon is being landed, and we are ready to mount our horses."

The sentries were called in. "Shoulder your firelocks!" was given. Silence now, in the ranks. They moved off, shepherded by their officers, those dim, comforting shapes on horseback with the snow lying white in the folds of their cloaks—the creak of saddle leather, the ring of horses' shoes on rock and rut, the rumble and bump of the gun-carriages, the hard breathing of the men, the low, reassuring commands, all swallowed by the roar of the storm. No turning back now, no falling out, no lagging behind. Forward into a murky dawn which would reveal their presence too soon. They had to go on, but they knew they were a forlorn hope, and they knew the usual fate of forlorn hopes, which was to be cut to pieces in brief, inconspicuous glory. When they came back to the boats that waited round the ferry under guard, how many of them would cross the river again to the Pennsylvania side?

At Birmingham, beyond the Bear Tavern, they were allowed a brief halt for breakfast from the cooked rations they carried in their knapsacks. Washington ate without dismounting. Some of the men fell asleep in their tracks and were roused with difficulty. Again he was among them on the tall brown horse, calm and collected, wrapped in thought as in his long blue cloak. "Press on, boys—press on," he urged them gently, and they stumbled after him again.

There was a man named Paine, attached to General Greene's staff as volunteer aide—he had written a thing that summed it all up for them. They had clustered round their officers to hear it read out loud in the Pennsylvania camp, only a few days ago, and they had tried ever since to remember just how it went, piecing it together round their fires, a bit here, a bit there, arguing over the words he had used, but never the ideas. Paine knew. Paine had said it all for them. Paine was very bracing. "The summer soldier and the sunshine patriot," he had written, using a drum-head for a writing-desk at Newark on the way down, "will in this crisis shrink from the service of their country; but he that stands it *now*, deserves the love and thanks of every man and woman...."

They stood it now, tramping towards Trenton, and the wind was everywhere, in their faces holding them back, behind them, whipping their frozen rags forward, and their feet left bloody tracks in the new snow. "By perseverance and fortitude we have the prospect of a glorious issue," Paine had told them, bent above the drum on the windward side of a smoky camp-fire. "By cowardice and submission, the sad choice of a variety of evils.... It matters not

THE START

where you live—" And this part they remembered well. "—or what rank of life you hold, the evil or the blessing will reach you all." Then they rather lost him, except for something about slavery without hope, and a ravaged country, and homes being turned into bawdy houses for Hessians, and a future generation with doubtful fathers. . . . But there was one sentence none of them had forgotten —the first one. And as they lurched along the road to Trenton the company wit glanced round in the growing light and saw no mounted authority near by. "'These are the times that try men's souls!'" he quoted in a rasping whisper, and the easy snickers of men lightheaded with hunger and nervous strain carried the echoed words along the files.

"Dec. 26. Noon," says the Staff officer's diary. "It was nearly four o'clock when we started. At Birmingham a man came with a message from General Sullivan that the storm was wetting the muskets and rendering them unfit for service. 'Tell General Sullivan,' said Washington, 'to use the bayonet. I am resolved to take Trenton.'"

And take it he did, cutting up the Hessians there and scattering them as far as New Brunswick, besides taking nearly a thousand prisoners—the first time he had been in a position to take prisoners since the war began. The Hessians were just as drunk and demoralized by their holiday festivities as he had hoped. Colonel Rall, who was in command and who thought so little of what he called Washington's "country clowns" that he did not see to his defences, was with difficulty got out of bed after the firing had reached the very streets of the town amid shrill astonished shouts of *"Der Feind!"* and *"Heraus!"* and *"Was ist?"*

"Washington gave the order to advance," the Staff officer's diary continues, "and we rushed on to the junction of King and Queen Streets. Forrest wheeled six of his cannon into position to sweep both streets. The riflemen under Colonel Hand went upon the run through the fields on the left to gain possession of the Princeton road. The Hessians were just ready to open fire with two of their cannon when Captain Washington and Lieutenant Monroe with their men rushed forward and captured them. We saw Rall come riding up the street from his headquarters, which were at Stacey Potts' house. We could hear him shouting in Dutch, 'My brave soldiers, advance!' His men were frightened and confused, for our men were firing upon them from fences and houses and they were falling fast. Instead of advancing they ran into an apple orchard. The officers tried to rally them, but our men kept advancing and picking off the officers. It was not long before Rall tumbled from his horse and his soldiers threw down their arms and gave themselves up as prisoners.

"While this was taking place, Colonel Stark from New Hampshire was driving Knyphausen's men pell mell through the town. Sullivan sent a portion of his troops to seize the bridge and cut off the retreat of the Hessians towards Bordentown. Sullivan's men shot the artillery horses and captured two cannon attached to Knyphausen's regiment."

This is the first appearance of the Commander-in-chief's young kinsman, William Washington, who turns up again in the Carolinas; and of James Monroe, who at eighteen had left the College at Williamsburg to join the army, and who would be elected President exactly forty years later. It was Captain Alexander Hamilton's artillery company whose two guns were posted at the top of King Street, where the Battle Monument now stands. He was not yet twenty-one, and had been seen to pat his cherished brass cannon as though they were horses, and was said to think more of them than of his men, all of whom were older than he was.

Accustomed as we are to think of the men who made the Revolution as forefathers, and forgetting that eight whole years lay between Yorktown and Washington's first inauguration as President, we can be surprised at how young they were when the fighting began. Washington was forty-three when he set out for Cambridge in June of '75 to take command of the colonial army. Knox was twenty-five, William Washington was twenty-four, Greene was thirty-three, Sullivan thirty-five. Lafayette, when he arrived at Philadelphia in '77, had not yet passed his twentieth birthday. Many of the British officers had already seen service in Europe in the Seven Years War, and General Howe was pushing fifty, but both Clinton and Cornwallis were only thirty-seven, and the terrible Tarleton was twenty-two.

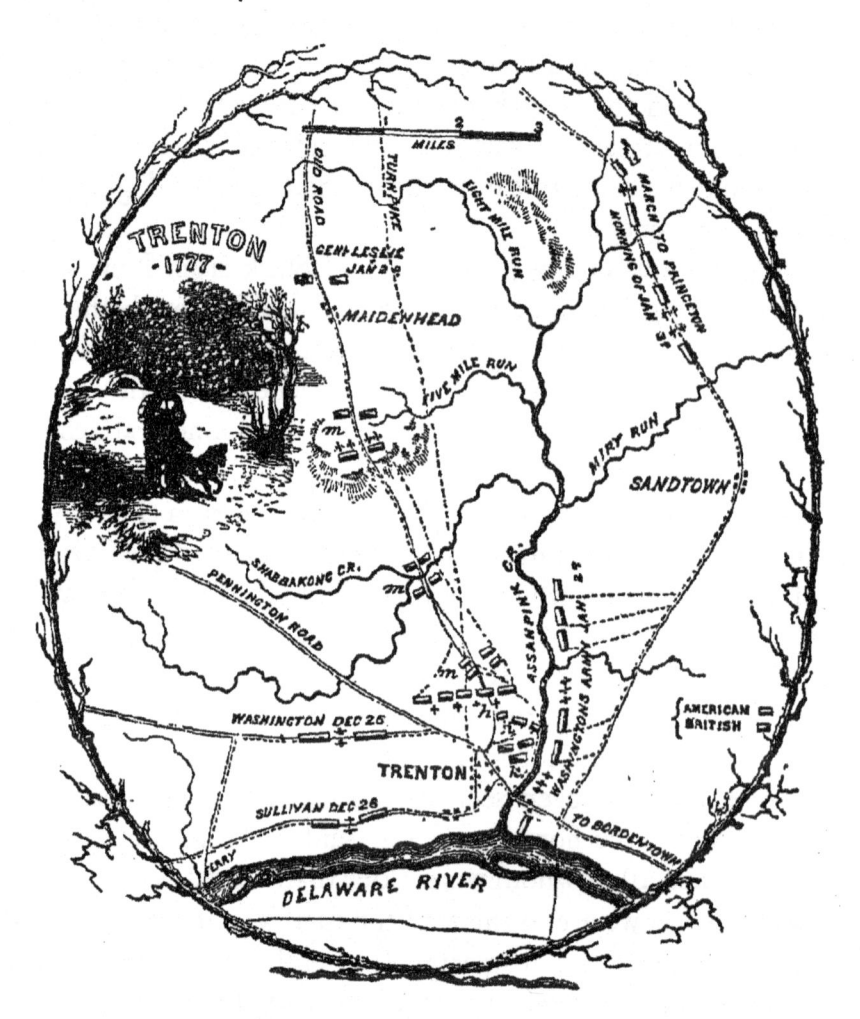

Rall's wound was mortal, and he was carried back to his quarters on a pew taken from the Methodist Church. The Staff officer resumes: "Dec. 26, 3 P.M. I have just been with General Washington and Greene to see Rall. He will not live through the night. He asked that his men might be kindly treated. Washington promised that he would see they were well cared for.

"Dec. 27, 1776. Here we are back at our camp with the prisoners and supplies. Washington is keeping his promise. The [Hessian] soldiers are in the New Town Meeting-house and other buildings. He has just given directions for tomorrow's dinner. All the captured officers are to dine with him. He bears the Hessians no malice, but says they have been sold by their Grand Duke to King George and sent to America, when if they could have their own way they would be peaceably living in their own country."

"This is a copy," Lossing explains, "by permission, of a picture by Flagg, in the possession of Joseph C. Potts, Esq. of Trenton. On the right is seen Generals Washington and Greene; in the center is Mrs. Potts, and near her stands her husband. On the left Colonel Rall reclines upon a couch, and behind him, supporting his pillow, is his servant. I was informed that the portrait of Rall was painted from a description given by a person who knew him, and who pronounced the likeness good, as he remembers him."

Likeness, maybe, but as Colonel Rall had been badly shot to pieces with three wounds, and must have been immediately undressed and got to bed by the Pottses, who were Quakers and who nursed him devotedly, the picture lacks some realism.

"It is a glorious victory," the diary concludes with reasonable exultation. "It will rejoice the hearts of our friends everywhere, and give new life to our hitherto waning fortunes. Washington has pounced upon the enemy like an eagle upon a hen, and is safe once more this side of the river.... If he does nothing more, he will live in history as a great military commander."

History has not disputed it, although Washington had prudently withdrawn back across the river the same night. His total losses were two privates who froze to death. Both William Washington and Monroe had received minor wounds in their fight for the guns. The Hessians had lost six officers and about thirty men killed, besides the wounded and the prisoners who were hunted down in the houses and barns and secured.

When the American troops realized that they had actually done it, when they saw through the haze of sleet and powder-smoke the surrendered swords and colors in the hands of their own generals Stirling and St. Clair, and the crowds of hung-over Hessians in their ridiculous pigtails and leggings asking for quarter, they began to cheer themselves loudly; and then they cheered their officers, and having started they got a kind of hysteria and couldn't stop cheering and throwing their hats into the air, which was full of wind-borne headgear causing added confusion. They had won. The Hessians could be had. They cheered until they set Washington laughing, and until he sent to say it was enough. The whole battle in the town had not lasted two hours, and the enemy had not succeeded in murdering a single one of them. They dined better than they had done for weeks, on the Hessians' Christmas left-overs, and some of them found a drop of something in which to drink to Victory. Tired as they were by early afternoon, the road back to the ferry didn't seem so long as it had when they came in. Their hearts were lighter now than their heads had been.

"Rall's defeat is a most unfortunate business," wrote General Grant at New Brunswick to Hessian Colonel Donop at Bordentown on the 27th, with noticeable restraint. The Hessians claimed that the sleet had made their muskets useless and they couldn't get at the Americans with the bayonet because there was so much lead flying. But their weapons had been under cover until their drums beat to arms, while the Americans had kept theirs wrapped and dry all night all the way through a blizzard, and were able to fire a few rounds before the touch-holes clogged up and the flints refused to spark—after which they went to the bayonet, and without being told. Some of Washington's men had marched about forty miles since Christmas afternoon, and all had gone sleepless for twenty-four hours. A captain from Connecticut recorded that on returning to his quarters in Pennsylvania after the battle he sat down to a meal and fell from his chair to the floor with weariness, awaking some hours later with the spoon still in his hand.

Philadelphia was in an uproar that night, all the bells ringing, and the patriots running to General Putnam's camp for confirmation of the intoxicating rumor that Washington had finally won a battle; the Tories were truculent and unbelieving, so that some private wars were fought in the streets. Washington, back at his supply base at Newtown on the Pennsylvania side, four miles further inland from Keith's house, wrote out one of his least emphatic reports to the Congress then residing at Baltimore: "I have the pleasure of congratulating you upon the success of an enterprise which I had formed against a detachment of the enemy lying at Trenton, which was executed yesterday morning...."

The mortification of the British command in New York can be imagined, when the news was conveyed to them by a Hessian Captain Baum, who with a Captain von Schimmelpfennig and a few of their men had escaped capture via Crosswicks Creek and reported to General Grant, and were in consequence required by him to report at Headquarters. Howe sent a frantic recall to Cornwallis, who had gone aboard a ship with his baggage and was on the point of sailing for his proposed leave in England, and Cornwallis rushed back to Jersey to give General Grant a wigging and himself lead a march on Trenton, perhaps on to Philadelphia. Both Howe and Cornwallis must have been furious with the provincial general, who should have recognized that it was not the thing to campaign in the winter time.

It was then that Washington made his famous flanking move, and on January 3d struck at Princeton *behind* the British army, and got away to Morristown, where he established his winter quarters. The fact that he could not hold either Trenton or Princeton did not diminish the fact that he had made an ass out of Cornwallis and his fancy soldiers in scarlet coats.

The reaction of the German princelings to the defeat at Trenton was prompt and terrible. The Landgrave of Hesse-Cassel wrote to von Knyphausen who was at British Headquarters in New York: "Nothing but an utter disregard of all drill and discipline could have caused this disgrace. The death of Colonel Rall has taken him away from my wrath, which he so well deserved in allowing himself in so inexcusable a way to be surprised."

The Teutonic temper improved very little during the next one hundred and sixty-odd years, as a man named Rommel learned from a man named Hitler. If you were a German officer, and failed, you were better dead.

The Crown's use of foreign mercenaries, generically known as Hessians, created almost as much indignation at home in England as it did in America, and there had been vehement debate in the House of Commons. In the Lords, the Earl of Coventry was far-sighted enough to advise that Britain should abandon "wild schemes of coercion" and avail herself wisely of the "profits of an extensive commerce and the strong support of a firm and friendly alliance for mutual defence and assistance."

But the obstinate North Ministry had a majority obedient to the King's wishes, and the British Government therefore agreed to pay something around seven hundred thousand dollars for the use of the foreign fighting machines. This worked out at roughly thirty-six dollars a head, double for each man killed, and three wounded to count as one killed. Even the British regulars resented the intrusion of foreign hirelings into their war, and soon the German troops had to be kept entirely separate. They were on the whole a great disappointment to their English masters, a majority of them being dirty and stupid and brutal, and many a stubborn Tory turned patriot overnight out of sheer fury at their behavior.

There is one more eye-witness who should be briefly heard before we leave Trenton in the dearborn wagon bound for Philadelphia. The ebullient Colonel Knox, whose lung power had been so useful during the crossing at McConkey's Ferry, and whose well-served cannon had raked the streets of Trenton that December morning, wrote to his wife from the headquarters at Newtown, in Pennsylvania, on the 28th: "The attack on Trenton was a most horrid scene to the poor inhabitants. War, my Lucy, is not a humane trade, and the man who follows it as such will meet with his proper demerits in another world. The hurry, fright, and confusion of the enemy was not unlike that which will be when the last trump shall sound. They endeavored to form in the streets, the heads of which we had previously the possession of with cannon and howitzers, and these, in the twinkling of an eye cleared the streets. The backs of the houses were resorted to for shelter. These proved ineffectual; the musketry soon dislodged them. Finally they were driven through the town into an open plain beyond. Here they were formed in an instant. During the contest in the streets measures were taken for putting an entire stop to their retreat by posting troops and cannon in such passes and roads as was possible for them to get away by. The poor fellows after they were formed on the plain saw themselves completely surrounded, the only resource left was to force their way through numbers unknown to them. The Hessians had lost part of their cannon in the town; they did not relish the prospect of forcing, and were obliged to surrender on the spot. . . .

"His Excellency the General has done me the unmerited great honor of thanking me in public orders in terms strong and polite. This I would blush to mention to any other than to you, my dear

Lucy; and I am fearful that even my Lucy may think her Harry possesses a species of little vanity in doing it at all...."

His Lucy was a stout, talkative, good-hearted woman who became one of the most brilliant hostesses of the Washington administration. She was the cherished daughter of a wealthy Boston family which had objected violently to what they considered an unsuitable marriage. Lossing says: "Knox was a young Whig bookseller in Boston and Miss Lucy Flucker, who possessed considerable literary taste, became acquainted with him while visiting his store to purchase articles in his line. A sympathy of taste, feeling, and views produced mutual esteem, which soon ripened into love. Her friends looked upon her as ruined in prospects of future social esteem and personal happiness, in wedding one who had espoused the cause of rebellion; but many of those friends when the great political change took place were outcasts and in poverty, while Lucy Knox was the center of the first social circle in America."

The "London Bookstore" in Boston's Cornhill was a fashionable morning lounge during the uneasy early '70's, even for the officers of the British garrison and their Tory lady friends. On its shelves Lucy would have found *Don Quixote, The Vicar of Wakefield, Pamela, Clarissa, Tom Jones, Tristram Shandy, Peregrine Pickel, Robinson Crusoe*—all of which appear on Knox's stock list for '72, ordered from Longmans in London. Her family was staunchly Loyalist, and her only brother was a lieutenant in the British army. Her parents compelled her to choose between them and an insignificant tradesman who was furthermore an officer in the provincial militia. Lucy chose, and married him at eighteen—he was twenty-four—not long before the shots were fired at Lexington and Concord. Her parents never forgave her, and finally took ship to England.

The natural born gunner who became Washington's artillery commander might have lived out a peaceful life as an intellectual shop-keeper, but for the war. He was anything but bookish in the field, but he wrote some of the most delightful letters of an articulate generation, out of his single-hearted devotion to his round, pretty Lucy who had entrusted her life to him with such high spirits against such odds. Earlier that year, before the long retreat across Jersey began, he wrote to her from New York words which have never dated: "We want great men who when fortune frowns will not be discouraged. God will I trust in time give us those men. The Congress will ruin everything by their stupid parsimony and they begin to see it. It is, as I have always said, misfortunes that must raise us to the character of a *great people*. One or two drubbings will be of service to us; and one severe defeat to the enemy, ruin. We must have a standing army. The militia get sick, or think themselves so, and run home; and wherever they go they spread a panic." He always finished with his unabashed, outgoing tenderness for her. "It is now past twelve o'clock, therefore I wish you a good night's repose, and I will mention you in my prayers.... Those people who love as you and I do never ought to part." In May, '77, after the birth of her second child at home in Boston, he wrote from the midst of the Jersey skirmishing around Middlebrook headquarters: "Though your parents are on the opposite side from your Harry, yet it's very strange that it should divest them of humanity. Not a line! My God! What stuff is the human heart made of! Although your father, mother, sister, and brother have forgotten you, yet, my love, your Harry will ever esteem you the best boon of heaven."

Knox had been Washington's constant companion and mainstay since the Cambridge days in '75, and his cheery spirit and belief in ultimate success always heartened his hard-pressed chief. "A man of understanding, gay, sincere, and honest," wrote de Chastellux, who accompanied Rochambeau to America in 1780 and kept a record of his impressions. "It is impossible to know without esteeming him, to see without loving him." Knox had lost two fingers in the explosion of a fowling-piece before the war began, and when engaged in conversation he used to wind and unwind the black silk handkerchief he wore wrapped around his mutilated hand, "but not," says another contemporary, "so as to show its disfigurement.... His voice was strong, and no one could hear it without feeling that it had been accustomed to command. He said that he had through life left his bed at dawn, and had always been a cheerful and happy man. He was accustomed to use very forceful language on occasion."

Lucy was usually at winter Headquarters, where "her spirit and gaiety encouraged the soldiers to endure hardships that they saw her bear with patience," says Appleton. "Not only her husband, but General Washington relied on her judgment in affairs of moment, while in social and ceremonial matters she was the arbiter of the army, and afterwards the chief adviser of Mrs. Washington in New York and Philadelphia." During the celebration of the first anniversary of the French alliance she managed to give a party on next to nothing at artillery headquarters at Pluckemin in Jersey, in the spring of '79—dinner was served at four o'clock, and for dessert the servants strewed the cloth with cherries and strawberries. Then there were fireworks, and a ball, at which General Washington with Lucy "danced down twenty couples." She bore her husband twelve children, only three of whom survived into maturity. One little daughter died and was buried during the hot summer weather at Pluckemin. General Greene's second son Nat was born during the dreadful second winter at Morristown, but *he* lived to be almost a hundred.

Lucy was a bit outspoken for a diplomatic hostess and she became more so by the time Washington was President and his ex-artilleryman was Secretary at War. "Mrs. Knox had a taste for the management and show of public life, and was a leader of the *ton* in the social circles at the seat of government," says Mrs. Ellet. "Her society was much sought by men of taste and talent, while the unreserved expression of her opinions to those with whom she conversed sometimes displeased persons who could not appreciate the independence of an original and intelligent mind." "Mrs. Knox, fat, lively, if somewhat interfering, was a general favorite," is a less tactful comment.

They were always a devoted couple, and it was a remarkably happy marriage, enlivened by many a domestic tempest which left no hard feelings. There is on record an occasion at their home in Maine some time after the war, where after considerable misunderstanding about the use of a favorite mount which Lucy considered her exclusive property, her never meek or mild Harry addressed a servant within the hearing of an amused concourse of guests: "John, put Mrs. Knox's horse back in the stable and do not take it out again until God Almighty, or Mrs. Knox, tells you to."

III

Philadelphia to Valley Forge

So the British did not march into Philadelphia in '76, but the Hessians did, as prisoners paraded with their captured arms and banners, on their way to a camp near Lancaster. And now that they were weaponless and beaten, it could be seen that their gaudy uniforms were not warm enough and their boots not stout enough for winter duty. Even so, they were better clad than their grinning guards (many of whom were without any shoes at all) and their pigtails were plastered with tallow and flour and their mustaches were blackened with soot. Philadelphia had been saved, and just in time. By the middle of January the enemy at Trenton, if left undisturbed, could have crossed the Delaware on solid ice and pillaged a defenceless city. Without waiting for the river to freeze, Washington had crossed and re-crossed it four times, and inflicted lasting damage on the professionals.

Seventy-two years behind the Hessian prisoners, Lossing and his horse Charley took the road from Trenton to Philadelphia.

"The sun was shining in its noontide glory when I crossed the great Trenton bridge over the Delaware to Morrisville, and reined my horse to the right into the Falsington road for Philadelphia, twenty-eight miles distant. Unlike a summer rain, the storm had developed no new beauties in the fields and orchards, but 'a mantle dun' continued to overspread the landscape, and a cold north wind was heralding the approach of winter.

"I was now in the fertile region of 'old Bucks' in Pennsylvania, and with a loose rein traversed the gentle undulating country over which the Continental battalions often marched and countermarched. The mind, laden with the associations of the place and hour, kept me such entertaining company that the sun went down, and I entered the suburban district of Kensington in the northern liberties of Philadelphia before I was fairly conscious that a dozen miles had been travelled. It was but little more than four hours journey with my strong and vigorous horse.

"Passing through a portion of Kensington suburb, its mud and wretchedness, its barking dogs and squalling babies, where society seems in a transition state from filth to cleanliness, and consequently from vice to godliness, I wheeled down Second Street amid its glowing shops just as the last hue of daylight faded away. It was Saturday night, a season as welcome to the traveller as a 'cross day' in the calendar to the faithful. I was in Philadelphia, the city of brotherly love; the quiet Sabbath near; a glorious harvest of Revolutionary reminiscences spread out before me, inviting the pensickle to reap for my garner; and the broad and sunny South, its chivalry and its patriotism, beckoning me onward. Busy thought kept sleep at bay till midnight."

Philadelphia's part in the story of the Revolution has been told many times, from the first meeting of the Continental Congress there in September of '74 right through the British occupation and the disastrous frivolity which prevailed after its recovery in June, '78, when Benedict Arnold as its commandant was courting Tory Peggy Shippen, two years before he went on to West Point and his ultimate disaster. With Lossing, we are headed South for the campaign of 1780–81. But it was in Philadelphia during the Second Continental Congress that the Virginia colonel became Commander-in-chief in dramatic circumstances which well became him. With the inverted chronology which Lossing's route naturally imposes, we will now look back to June of '75, eighteen months before the battle at Trenton.

He was a very silent delegate, even as a Burgess in the home Assembly at Williamsburg. Still, it is difficult entirely to efface oneself at six foot three, and he apparently carried also an unconscious personal magnetism which wrought miracles. Everyone at Philadelphia was very much aware of him, that anxious spring of '75, when the fight at Concord Bridge had recently given them all such a turn, and the New England farmers had got the British surrounded at Boston and did not know quite what to do next. "There is something charming to me in the conduct of Washington," John Adams wrote to his wife, of the impressive, untalkative man from Virginia.

They had a couple of generals already, at Cambridge, besieging Boston—Artemus Ward, who was all of forty-eight, and always in bad health; Israel Putnam, in his fifties, who lacked authority. The idea of superseding them came hard to some, especially to the New Englanders, but the Congress knew it must find leaders better qualified. The chief candidates were John Hancock, thirty-eight, wealthy, spirited, elegant, a bit assertive, recently risen to the Presidency of the Congress, and regardless of crippling attacks of gout, aspiring to a more spectacular career; Charles Lee, forty-four, eccentric, conceited, sharp-tongued, not of the Virginia Lees, being British-born, but a veteran of Braddock's disastrous frontier war of 1755, as well as of several European campaigns; Horatio Gates, another Braddock alumnus, also born in England, now married to an heiress and established on a Virginia plantation, seeming elderly in spectacles at forty-seven, but with a very high opinion of himself; Philip Schuyler, a well-to-do aristocrat and one-time Indian-fighter from up Albany way, a sort of Northern Washington, a year younger, but like Hancock always plagued by gout; and—there was Washington, who had been with Braddock too, and who had already been chosen unofficially as commander-in-chief in Virginia, where the new militia companies besought the honor of his presence at their drill and reviews, as his diary showed by such entries as: "Feb. 18, 1775. Went up to Alexandria to meet and exercise the Independent Company." He also notes expenditures from his own funds for powder, colors, and drums for the companies, which he apparently gave as presents; £150 for muskets, £30 for Cartooche Boxes, etc.; and £1.12 for "5 Books—Military."

He had done with a soldier's life, he thought, when he married Martha Custis in '59. He dearly loved his country squire's routine at Mount Vernon, absorbed in his building and planting and household affairs, and he always left it with reluctance. And yet, with the militia drilling on the village greens, and the riflemen streaming in from the frontier, and especially since the shooting at Concord and Lexington, he had had very little choice but to resume the uniform he had never intended to wear in action again—the blue coat faced with scarlet of the Virginia militia, which he had worn under Braddock's command and in which Peale had painted his portrait at Mount Vernon in '72, was now replaced in his own new Fairfax County militia by blue and buff, promptly adopted for his own use.

A great deal has been made of his wearing uniform at the Philadelphia Congress, but it must have seemed only natural to him, for he had already been reclaimed by the militia companies at home in Virginia. Perhaps he wore it to the daily sessions instead of trying to make the speeches which were never easy for him—as silent testimony that he was willing to serve in the only way he felt qualified to be of any use, as a soldier. Probably he had some idea of being sent to the army at Boston to work beside Ward and Putnam, with the same modest rank of colonel he had borne since his retirement sixteen years before.

It was at the Second Congress, and it was a Massachusetts man who nominated the quiet gentleman from Mount Vernon for the highest post in the colonial army, John Adams having seen for himself on the way from Boston to Philadelphia the confusion and lack of command among the amateur troops besieging Boston. If Adams had been merely a local politician he would not have realized so clearly the necessity for drawing the South into what was still regarded by many as a New England war. They were all in it now at the Congress, and to Adams it seemed essential that they should all be in it in the field. Adams knew that the way to bring in the Southern enlistments for service at Boston was to appoint a Southern Commander-in-chief, and he had already chosen his man. Washington's wealth and personal distinction equalled Hancock's, and Hancock was a townsman with nothing to put beside Washington's military experience in the French and Indian wars, his surveyor's eye for terrain, his superb horsemanship and physical endurance, and above all his mysterious, effortless ability to inspire admiration and confidence just by sitting there.

On a muggy morning in the middle of June, '75, John Adams rose in Congress to speak on this matter to which he had already given so much private endeavor. He pointed out the urgent necessity of establishing a Continental army under a unified command before the British got themselves together and scattered the undisciplined forces outside Boston. The room fell very silent as they listened, so that the drone of a myriad flies could be heard around the tall windows.

Some of his hearers guessed his intent, for he had been taking soundings out of doors. Some read it wrong. Charles Lee was not present, of course, but Hancock was, in the President's chair facing them all, and his vulnerable vanity and expectation were very plain to see. Washington sat near the door as usual, serene and silent and retiring, as inconspicuous as a man his size could be, with the golden epaulets gleaming on his blue coat. He had known for some days now that his number was up, and he had done his best to deflect the expressed intention of many of his colleagues to name him for the supreme command, both from a modest conviction that he was inadequate to it, and from his reluctance to leave Mount Vernon and all that it meant to him. But by now he must have begun to feel a certain fatalism. Obviously, he was, however unwillingly, more prepared for what was coming than some others of Adams' hearers.

Adams has left his own account of the scene in his *Autobiography*: "I concluded with a motion, in form, that Congress would adopt the army at Cambridge, and appoint a general; that though this was not the proper time to nominate a general, yet as I had reason to believe this was a point of greatest difficulty I had no hesitation to declare that I had but one gentleman in my mind for that important command, and that was a gentleman whose skill and experience as an officer, whose independent fortune, great talents, and excellent universal character would command the approbation of all America, and unite the cordial exertions of all the colonies better than any other person in the Union; a gentleman from Virginia, who was among us, and very well known to all of us.

"Mr. Washington, who happened to sit near the door, as soon as he heard me allude to him, from his usual modesty darted into the library room. Mr. Hancock, who was our president, which gave me the opportunity to observe his countenance while I was speaking on the state of the colonies, the army at Cambridge, and the enemy, heard me with visible pleasure; but when I came to describe Washington for the commander, I never remarked a more sudden and striking change of countenance. Mortification and resentment were expressed as forcibly as his face could exhibit them. Mr. Samuel Adams seconded the motion, and that did not soften the president's physiognomy at all."

It is difficult to see how Hancock, with no military record whatever, could have taken all that to himself, but the word *Virginia* is said to have struck him like a blow in the face. Odd as it may seem now, there was some debate that day as to Washington's qualifications, though only by a small minority, while the rest sat silent, waiting for the vote to be taken. His tactful retreat from the room left them free of the embarrassment of speaking their minds before him, however, and the Hancock men at once tried to plead that the New England troops would not accept a Southerner. Some one else pointed out that Charles Lee spoke French, Spanish, and Italian—though at that time it might have seemed a superfluous accomplishment for a General of the American army. Then one of Ward's friends spoke a eulogy of him. Congress adjourned in the afternoon without having taken a vote.

The next day, in order to leave the floor quite free for further discussion, Washington did not appear in the hall. Adams finishes his account with tantalizing brevity: "In the meantime," he says, "plans were taken out of doors to obtain a unanimity, and the voices were generally so clearly in favor of Washington that the dissenting members were persuaded to withdraw their opposition, and Mr. Washington was nominated, I believe by Mr. Thomas Johnson of Maryland, unanimously elected, and the [Cambridge] army adopted."

The same unanimity did not prevail during the election of his subordinates which followed. That tussle ended with four major-generals—Ward, Lee, Schuyler, and Putnam—and eight brigadiers. The major-generals were to be paid $166 a month, which was considered extravagant, and Washington as Commander-in-chief was to be allowed $500 a month for pay and expenses.

He could not have been surprised when they emerged about dinner time and addressed him as "General" and, yes, congratulated him on having been chosen for a task of such fantastic proportions. His laconic diary shows that he pursued that evening his usual program of dinner at a tavern and a committee meeting. It does not even mention that somewhere during what may well have been a sleepless night he and his fellow Virginia delegate Edmund Pendleton composed and wrote out the necessary speech of acceptance which would be expected of him the next day.

It was the President's duty, which is to say Hancock's, to make the formal announcement to Washington of his appointment, and to desire his acceptance of it. The gentleman from Virginia was in no way triumphant or complacent, it was observed, but looked grave and troubled by the honor they had done him. He rose and made them his formal bow, and standing in his place, according to the minutes of that day's session, read from the paper in his hand one of his rare, unemphatic little speeches: "... I feel great distress from a consciousness that my abilities and military experience may not be equal to the extensive and important trust," he said in part. "However as the Congress desires I will enter upon the momentous duty, and exert every power I possess in their service for the support of the glorious cause.... I beg it may be remembered by every gentleman in the room that I this day declare with the utmost sincerity, I do not think myself equal to the command I am honored with.... As to pay, I beg leave to assure the Congress that as no pecuniary consideration could have tempted me to accept this arduous employment, at the expense of my domestic ease and happiness, I do not wish to make any profit from it; I will keep an exact account of my expenses; those I doubt not they will discharge, and that is all I desire."

Even the skeptics were moved by his simplicity, his deep but dignified humility. It was plain to them all that they had by some miracle chosen right. With his General's commission thereupon granted, Congress pledged itself in return to "maintain and assist him, and adhere to him, the said George Washington, Esq., with their lives and fortunes."

No one had made less effort to secure the nomination than Washington, and certainly no one desired it less. But he did not look back, once it had happened, did not even indulge himself by a brief return to Mount Vernon for family farewells and to make arrangements for what might be a long absence, though he had left there in May merely to attend a Congress, not to fight a war. Instead, he wrote some letters, and his diary suddenly ceased for five years. There is no indication that he intended the entry of June 19th to be the last for almost the duration of the war. He noted down as usual where he had dined and where he spent the evening, and then closed the book.

To the brother he called "Jack," who was four years younger than himself, he often wrote with touching frankness of his secret misgivings and anxieties—because a man must let himself go somewhere. Unlike Martha, John Augustine preserved the letters, perhaps for his son Bushrod whom Washington was to name as his heir after Martha. "I am now to bid adieu to you and to every kind of domestic ease, for a while," he broke the news to Jack of his appointment. "I am embarked on a wide ocean, boundless in its prospect, and in which perhaps no safe harbor is to be found. I have been called upon by the unanimous voice of the Colonies to take command of the Continental army; an honor I have neither sought after nor desired, as I am thoroughly convinced that it requires greater abilities and much more experience than I am master of, to conduct a business so extensive in its nature, and arduous in its execution.... I am now commissioned a General and Commander-in-Chief of all the forces now raised, or to be raised, for the defence of the United Colonies. That I may discharge the trust to the satisfaction of my employers is my first wish; that I shall aim to do it, there remains little doubt of. How far I shall succeed, is another point.... I shall hope that my friends will visit and endeavor to keep up the spirits of my wife, as much as they can, as my departure will, I know, be a cutting stroke upon her; and on this account alone I have many disagreeable sensations. I hope you and my sister (although the distance is great) will find as much leisure this summer as to spend a little time at Mount Vernon. My sincere regards attend you both, and the little ones, and I am your most affectionate brother...."

To Martha, in one of the two letters she allowed to survive her, he said: "You may believe me, my dear Patsy, when I assure you in the most solemn manner that so far from seeking this appointment, I have used every endeavor in my power to avoid it, not only from my unwillingness to part with you and the family, but from a consciousness of its being a trust too great for my capacity, and that I should enjoy more real happiness in one month with you at home than I have the most distant prospect of finding abroad, if my stay were to be seven times seven years. But as it has been a kind of destiny, that has thrown me upon this service, I shall hope that my undertaking it is designed to answer some good purpose...."

The second letter to Martha, written during his last crowded day in Philadelphia, is taut with the pressure which had been put upon him, but determinedly serene. It is probable that he always hid from her, in all those lost pages, the worst of the apprehension and despair which he allowed brother Jack to share with him. "My dearest." he wrote hurriedly amid the bustle of aides and Congressmen. "As I am within a few minutes of leaving this city, I would not think of departing from it without dropping you a line, especially as I do not know whether it may be in my power to write again until I get to the camp at Boston. I go fully trusting in that Providence which has been more bountiful to me than I deserve, and in full confidence of a happy meeting with you sometime in the fall. I have no time to say more, as I am surrounded with company to take leave of me. I return an unalterable affection for you which neither time nor distance can change; my best love to Jack and Nelly, and regard for the rest of the family; conclude me with the utmost truth and sincerity,

Yr. entire,

G. WASHINGTON"

He did not see Mount Vernon again for six years. But Martha joined him at Headquarters every winter, and even took her son Jacky Custis and his young wife to Cambridge with her as a treat. He had not belittled to her the dangers and inconveniences of that first and longest journey and the life she would find at the end of it—nearly a thousand miles from her sister's house near Williamsburg where she was visiting when what he called his "invitation" to join him reached her. Winter was coming on, and she had never been north of Alexandria in her life. But she went to him without delay, and each year after that, throughout the war, as soon as his winter Headquarters were established.

"Every person seems cheerful and happy here," she was able to write to a friend at Alexandria soon after she arrived in Cambridge. "Some days we hear a number of cannon and shells from Boston and Bunker Hill, but it does not seem to surprise anybody but me. I confess I shudder every time I hear the sound of a gun ... but I endeavor to keep my fears to myself as well as I can...." She went to him, and she stayed with him, through gunfire, and smallpox and short rations and bitter cold and crowded, comfortless quarters, and uncertainty and near despair, during eight wartime winters, until that final joyful Christmas homecoming to Mount Vernon in 1783.

Nobody from Virginia had ever heard of Bunker Hill on the June day in '75 when Washington rode out from Philadelphia for Boston with his little escort of new-made generals and aides. But twenty miles along the road they met the dusty messenger who carried news of a battle which had been fought without him, on the 17th.

The British had won it, in that they remained in possession of the hill. The Americans had run out of powder and then they fought the British bayonets with clubbed muskets and rocks, before giving way into retreat. Their casualties were less than five hundred, and they had demonstrated to both the British and their new Commander-in-chief that raw colonial recruits could stand fire, could fight with spirit and courage against drilled professional soldiers, and exact a heavy toll.

There was no way for Washington to know then that the British were badly shaken by their appalling losses, which included ninety-two officers, and that General Howe, who had led three charges himself, had seen every man of his staff of twelve shot down around him, so that his own white buckskin breeches and silk stockings were splashed with the blood of his officers. At one time during the action, which lasted two hours, his face was running with tears, perhaps from the sting of powder-smoke and perspiration in his eyes. And he received such a shock at the slaughter of his disciplined troops as to account for his disinclination thereafter ever to risk a frontal attack on the American forces. Howe had courage to match his men, who advanced doggedly over the bodies of their comrades. Clinton joined the fight midway with a small reinforcement. Burgoyne remained a spectator, and described the engagement as "a complication of horror beyond anything that ever came to my lot to be witness to."

When Lossing set out on that November morning in 1848 to see the sights of Philadelphia, he began with Carpenters' Hall, where the first Congress met in the autumn of '74. He found it "a small, two-story building of somber aspect with a short steeple, and all of a dingy hue." To his further distress, its front was defaced by an auctioneer's sign, and its pillared hall had become merely a storage house for the mean merchandise awaiting the hammer. Only a few years after his visit, the building was rescued from this desecration by the Carpenters' Company itself, repaired with loving care, and ceremoniously opened in 1857 as the historic shrine it has remained.

"The building is constructed of small imported bricks, each alternate one glazed, and darker than the other, giving it a checkered appearance. Many of the old houses of Philadelphia were built of like materials. It was originally erected for the hall of meeting for the society of house-carpenters of Philadelphia. It stands at the end of an alley leading south from Chestnut Street between Third and Fourth Streets."

Lossing continued up Chestnut Street to the State House, where the Second Congress had convened in May, '75. There he was gratified to find that the room in which they had sat, with its tall windows, twin fireplaces, and handsome glass chandelier, was kept reverently closed, except to special visitors and occasions. The mahogany chairs which had been used by President Hancock and Secretary Thomson were cherished as souvenirs, and there were portraits of William Penn and Lafayette on the walls. The silent Bell still hung in the tower, where he climbed to visit it. In 1852 it was brought down and put on exhibition in the lower hall.

In that spacious ground-floor room in the State House Washington had heard and accepted his nomination to destiny. And in that room, almost exactly a year later, the great Declaration was made.

"It is now impossible to determine the precise time when aspirations for political independence first became a prevailing sentiment among the people of the colonies," Lossing says. "The thought, no doubt, was cherished in many minds years before it found expression; but it was not a subject for public discussion more than a few months before it was brought before Congress by Richard Henry Lee of Virginia. A few men, among whom were Dr. Franklin, Samuel Adams, Patrick Henry, and Thomas Paine, seem to have had an early impression that political independence was the only cure for the evils under which the colonies groaned; yet these ideas when expressed met with little favor, even among the most ardent patriots. In the Assembly at Williamsburg on May 15th Virginia instructed her representatives in Congress to *propose* independence; she had a delegate equal to the task.

"On the 7th of June, in the midst of the doubt and dread and hesitation which had brooded over the national assembly, Richard Henry Lee arose, and with his clear, musical voice read aloud the resolution 'That these united colonies are, and of right ought to be, free and independent states; and that all political connection between us and the State of Great Britain is, and ought to be, totally dissolved.'"

This Lee, in contrast to Charles of the same name, was a wealthy Virginia aristocrat, born within a few weeks and a few miles of Washington. He had been educated in England, and was a lawyer and (like Washington) a Burgess at Williamsburg under the last three Royal Governors. Tall and spare, with a Roman profile, he had a formal speaking style which he was suspected of practicing before a mirror, in contrast to Patrick Henry's fluent passion. He had shocked some of his Southern colleagues by his radical views ever since the Stamp Act trouble in '65. But still the Congress were hardly prepared for this drastic resolution, as Mercy Warren, the Boston bluestocking who wrote her own history of her times from personal acquaintance with most of its great men, recorded: "This public and unequivocal proposal," she says, "from a man of his virtue and shining qualities, appeared to spread a kind of sudden dismay. A silent astonishment for a few minutes seemed to pervade the whole assembly; this was soon succeeded by a long debate, and a considerable division of sentiment on the important question."

John Adams, who had certainly expected something of the kind, came to his feet to second the motion—the same John Adams who had forced the issue the year before on the appointment of the Commander-in-chief. And to protect Lee and Adams from possible consequences, such as a halter, Secretary Thomson was directed to omit the names of mover and seconder from the Journals, so that the minutes read: "Certain resolutions respecting independency being moved and seconded, *Resolved*, that the consideration of them be deferred until tomorrow morning."

The next morning a most heated debate began, and the resolutions were deferred again till the first day of July. But "in the mean while, that no time be lost in case the Congress agree thereto, that a committee be appointed to prepare a declaration to that effect," wrote Secretary Thomson. And there sits Thomas Jefferson, aged thirty-three, at work with his pen in his lodgings in Market Street, where he paid thirty-five shillings a week for a bedroom and private parlor. Although Lossing apparently failed to see it, the house was still standing till 1883, when it was thoughtlessly demolished, no attempt being made to preserve it for the nation.

June was always hot and muggy in Philadelphia, and the delegates perspired, yet suffered from such a plague of flying insects from a nearby stable that the windows were kept closed almost to the top against them. At home in his stuffy rooms, Jefferson labored at his desk without his library to hand, drawing on his own memory of Locke, Rousseau, and other past reading for guidance. He accomplished the first draft within two days, and the final clear copy was ready, with amendments by Dr. Franklin and John Adams who were also on his committee, four days before the July 1st deadline.

But it was Richard Henry Lee's resolution for independence, presented June 7th and finally adopted on the 2d of July, that actually severed the colonies from Great Britain. The Declaration itself, which was designed mainly to explain and to justify what was already done, was then debated line by line and almost word by word for two days more, while its author sat silent, fuming, and embarrassed. At the end of that time it was adopted with only a few alterations made.

Lossing has an unusual account of that momentous 4th of July, 1776, when the unanimous vote of the thirteen colonies was given in favor of the great Declaration which pronounced them free and independent states—he may probably have picked it up from local tradition during his stay in the city: "It was two o'clock in the afternoon when the final decision was announced by Secretary

Thomson to the assembled Congress in Independence Hall. It was a moment of solemn interest; and when the Secretary sat down a deep silence pervaded that august assembly. Thousands of anxious citizens had gathered in the streets of Philadelphia, for it was known that the final decision was to be made on that day. From the hour when Congress convened in the morning, the old bellman had been in the steeple. He placed a boy at the door below, to give him notice when the announcement should be made. As hour succeeded hour, the gray-beard shook his head and said, 'They will never do it! they will never do it!' Suddenly a shout came from below, and there stood the blue-eyed boy, clapping his hands and shouting, 'Ring! Ring!' Grasping the tongue of the old bell, backward and forward he hurled it a hundred times, its loud voice 'proclaiming Liberty throughout all the land unto all the inhabitants thereof.' The excited multitude in the streets responded with loud acclamations; and with cannon-peals, bonfires, and illuminations, the patriots held a glorious carnival that night in the quiet city of Penn.

"This gives the appearance of the shorter steeple, which took the place of the stately one taken down in 1774. This was its appearance during the Revolution. A huge clock-case was upon each side of the main building of the State House. The second story was occupied by the Courts; and while the Continental Congress was in session below, the Provincial Assemblies met above."

Here Lossing has made one of his rare errors. His illustration is drawn from an engraving dated about 1800. The steeple was considered dangerously weak as early as 1773, but it was not taken down till '81. A near replica was replaced in 1828, with the addition of the clock-face. In July, 1776, its appearance was approximately what it is today.

As the Southern campaign remains our objective, we will not digress now with Lossing into the battlefields at Brandywine, Germantown, and Monmouth, except for their repercussions in the Capital city. After Washington's successes at Trenton and Princeton at the turn of the year 1776–77, he retired to Morristown in the Jersey hills, and set up winter Headquarters at Freeman's Tavern, with his men in tents and huts, and his officers billeted in the farms and houses around the little town, while Howe spent a comfortable winter in New York. In the spring there were some futile maneuvers and skirmishes, and then another lull, until in July of '77 Howe loaded his army aboard transports at New York and sailed for an unknown destination—some said the Carolina coast. For weeks there was great uneasiness in the American camp. Then in August Howe's fleet turned up in the Chesapeake. His army came ashore below Elkton, and again threatened Philadelphia. Washington was already there, looking at its defences, which were negligible.

To impress the Tory population and hearten the patriots, he decided on a parade through the city on his way out to meet Howe, and issued minute instructions so as to make the best of what little he had to show—"great attention being given by officers to see that the men carry their arms well and are made to appear as decent as circumstances will permit.... Not a woman belonging to the army is to be seen with the troops on their march through the city.... The drums and fifes of each brigade are to be collected in the center of the brigade and a tune for the quick-step to be played, but with such moderation that the men may step to it with ease and without *dancing* along or totally disregarding the music which is too often the case...." They had no uniforms or cockades, but each man stuck a sprig of greenery in his hat in a pathetic attempt at decoration, and some put nosegays in the ends of their gun-barrels. They were beaten at Brandywine on September 11th, and the British were in a position to take Philadelphia at their leisure.

Again, as before Christmas in '76, there was panic in the city, and again Congress departed in haste, this time to York, Pennsylvania. The Tories prepared a welcome, and on the 26th of September, '77, the British finally arrived. Accounts of that day were gathered within living memory, by John Watson, for his *Philadelphia Annals*.

"The grenadiers with Lord Cornwallis at their head led the van when they entered the city," one of the stories runs. "Their tranquil look and dignified appearance left an impression on my mind that the British Grenadiers were inimitable. As I am relating the feelings and observations of a boy only ten years old, I shall mention things perhaps not worth relating; for instance, I went up to the front rank of the Grenadiers when they had entered Second Street, when several of them addressed me thus—'How do you do, young one?—How are you, my boy?' in a brotherly tone, that seems still to vibrate on my ear; then reached out their hands and severally caught mine, and shook it, not with the exulting shake of conquerors, I thought, but with a sympathizing one for the vanquished. The Hessians (those who had not been in Trenton) followed in the rear of the Grenadiers—their looks to me were terrific—their brass caps—their mustachios—their countenances by nature morose, and their music, that sounded better English than they themselves could speak...."

"They looked well, clean, and well-clad," was the recollection of a woman who was required to lodge some British officers during the occupation, "and the contrast between them and our own poor bare-footed and ragged troops was very great, and caused a feeling of despair...."

Howe had established his camp at Germantown, while Cornwallis marched into Philadelphia, and he fought a battle with

Washington there in a fog on October 4th, after which Washington withdrew his army to Whitemarsh and Howe moved his headquarters into the captured city. Cornwallis went home to England on leave from January to May of 1778, and Clinton was left holding New York.

Sir William Howe was an impressively tall, bulky man, of a very dark complexion, whose easy-going, self-indulgent nature made him popular with his officers and men, and was a social asset to the Tory population. His left-handed cousinship with the King, through his mother who was the illegitimate daughter of George I, had not hampered his army career. When he arrived in America he was ten years married without children, and he was soon flaunting a blond American mistress, the famous Mrs. Loring. She and her complaisant husband, who had been made Howe's Commissary of Prisoners with unlimited opportunity for graft, had accompanied Howe from Boston to Halifax to New York to Philadelphia, and were soon established in the mansion called Stenton, which had sheltered Washington before Brandywine, and had caught Howe's eye as his Germantown headquarters.

Mrs. Loring was by now generally known as the Sultana, and whatever the Philadelphia matrons may have called her in private, they had to accept her as the General's official hostess and the first lady of the British army. Howe spent an idle and scandalous winter at Philadelphia, indulging Mrs. Loring's love of gambling, which could not exceed his own, and a mutually extravagant taste for balls and amateur theatricals, while his red-coated officers cut a wide swathe among the Tory belles. Howe's heart was never in the war, which he had always hoped to end by conciliation rather than slaughter if only he could discourage the colonists sufficiently to make them give up, and he considered his present force inadequate in any case—as it was—for any decisive campaign. After Germantown when the news of Burgoyne's surrender at Saratoga arrived—which might have been laid to a lack of co-operation from Howe because of his Philadelphia venture—he had sent in his resignation. While awaiting its acceptance in London he saw no reason for not amusing himself, and the disappointed Tory hotheads made up rude rhymes:

> "Awake, arouse, Sir Billy,
>   There's forage in the plain;
> Ah, leave your little filly,
>   And open the campaign!"

In April of '78 his orders came to turn over his command to Clinton and return to England. He sailed in May without regret—and without Mrs. Loring—and Clinton promptly evacuated the city, whose occupation he had never approved, returning at once to his New York headquarters, only pausing to fight the battle of Monmouth on the way.

Clinton was now the last of the three imposing British major-generals who had arrived at Boston in the summer of '75 to show the colonists who was boss. The ship they came in was named the *Cerberus*, out of which another popular jingle was born.

> "Behold the *Cerberus* the Atlantic plow,
>   Her precious cargo, Burgoyne, Clinton, Howe,
>   Bow, wow, wow!"

Clinton was a different kind of man from the other two. With Cornwallis, who returned to America from his leave at home in England just as Howe departed from Philadelphia, Clinton went on to almost win the war. We shall find him again at Charleston.

From Whitemarsh in December Washington marched his ragged army to Valley Forge, where he spent the winter of 1777–78, while Howe was enjoying himself in Philadelphia. Lossing visited the Valley Forge Headquarters house, which was "a substantial stone dwelling situated at the mouth of the creek," and was then occupied by James Jones, a member of the Society of Friends, who was eighty-three years old. "He was quite feeble," Lossing relates, "but his wife, a cheerful lady of nearly the same age, was the reverse, and with vigorous step proceeded to show us the interior of the building. Washington's room was small indeed. In the deep east window, whence he could look out upon a large portion of his camp upon the neighboring slopes, are still preserved the cavity and little trap-door arranged by the Commander-in-chief as a private repository for his papers. It answered the purpose admirably; for even now the visitor would not suspect that the old blue sill upon which he was leaning to gaze upon the hallowed hills might be lifted and disclose a capacious closet. Mr. Jones and his wife were not residents at Valley Forge when the Americans encamped there, and hence they had no interesting traditions of their own experience.

"This view is from the Reading rail-head, looking east, and includes a portion of the range of hills in the rear whereon the Americans were encamped. The main building was erected in 1770; the wing is more modern and occupies the place of the log addition mentioned by Mrs. Washington in a letter to Mercy Warren, written in March, 1778; 'The general's apartment,' she wrote, 'is very small; he has had a log cabin built to dine in, which has made our quarters much more tolerable than they were at first.'

"Here, after an arduous campaign of four months, during which neither party had obtained an advantage other than good winter quarters at Philadelphia on the part of the enemy, the shattered

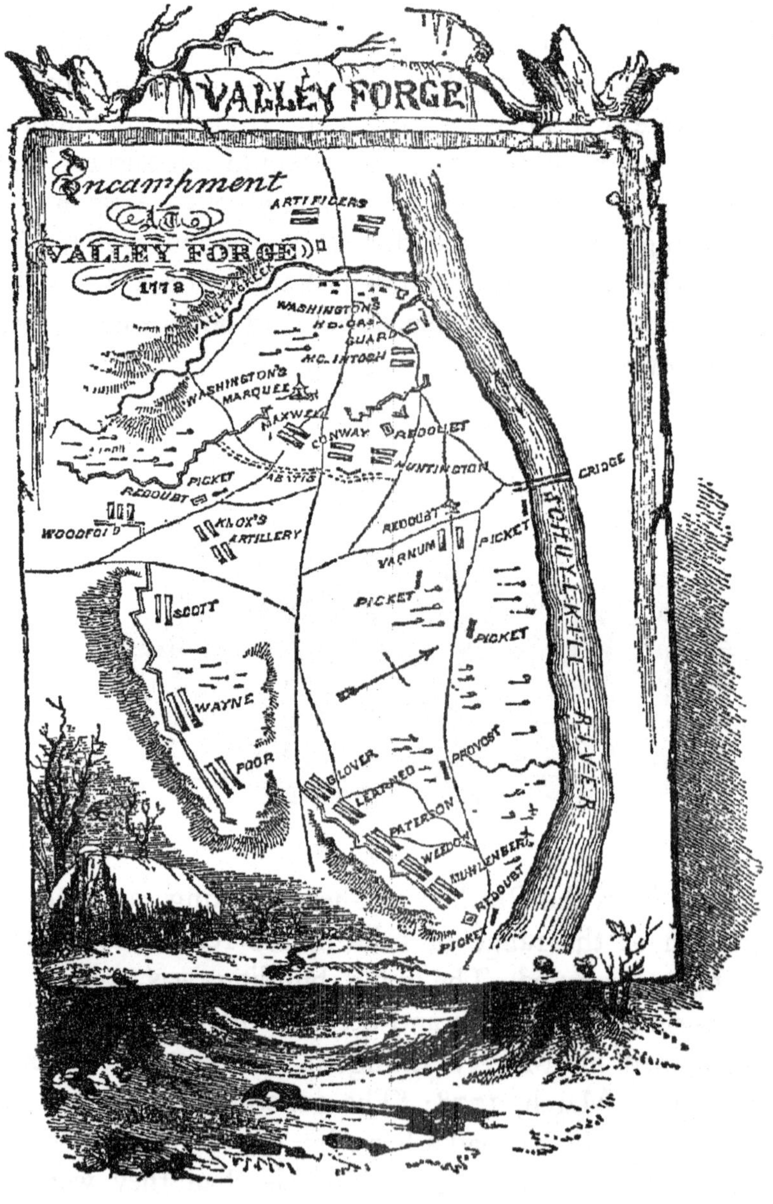
VALLEY FORGE
Encampment
AT
VALLEY FORGE
ARTIFICERS
WASHINGTON'S
GUARD
WASHINGTON'S
MARQUEE
MAXWELL
CONWAY
REDOUBT
HUNTINGTON
PICKET
REDOUBT
BRIDGE
WOODFORD
KNOX'S
ARTILLERY
REDOUBT
VARNUM
PICKET
PICKET
SCOTT
PICKET
WAYNE
POOR
GLOVER
LEARNED
PROVOST
PATERSON
WEEDON
REDOUBT
PICKET
SCHUYLKILL RIVER

remains of the American army vainly sought repose. In General Orders Washington directed the preparation of huts for the comfort of the soldiers, assuring them 'that he himself would share in the hardships and partake of every inconvenience.' All was activity among those who were sufficiently clad to allow them to work in the open air. Some cut down trees, others fashioned them, and in a few days the barracks, erected upon the plan of a regular city, was completed. Until his soldiers were thus comfortably lodged, Washington occupied his cheerless marquee, after which he made his quarters at the house of Mr. Potts.

"But few horses were in the camp; and such was the deficiency in this respect that the men cheerfully yoked themselves to vehicles of their own construction, for carrying wood and provisions when procured; while others performed the duty of pack-horses, and carried heavy burdens of fuel upon their backs. As the winter advanced, their sufferings increased. On the 16th of February ['78] Washington wrote to Governor Clinton [of New York]: 'For some days past there has been little less than a famine in the camp. A part of the army has been a week without any kind of flesh, and the rest three or four days. Naked and starving as they are, we cannot enough admire the incomparable patience and fidelity of the soldiery, that they have not been, ere this, excited by their sufferings to a general mutiny and desertion.'"

The marquee is now on exhibition at Valley Forge Museum in a realistic setting. It was made for Washington in Philadelphia during the first summer of the war, of heavy linen with a scalloped red-flannel edge to the domed roof, and it went with him all the way to Yorktown. Its ridge-pole was thirteen and a half feet, its circumference eighty feet. Its weight when wrapped around its poles was sufficient to bend the backs of two men to get it into a wagon, but there is a legend that Washington once heaved it in all by himself, "as though it were a pair of saddle-bags," with only an ordinary effort of his phenomenal strength. It was usually furnished with a couple of chairs borrowed from the nearest house, stump stools, a rough table for his lantern, ink-pot, quill-holder, and sand-box—and if he was lucky, a cot for his blankets.

As everyone knows, Valley Forge is now a national pilgrimage well worth the journey, laid out as a park, and containing a museum, reconstructions, and a modern memorial chapel. The original Headquarters house still stands pretty much as the Washingtons left it in the spring of '78, furnished again so that they could walk back into it today with no feeling of strangeness. It is a stout stone dwelling, with only two rooms and a kitchen wing on the ground floor. Narrow stairs dividing on a landing to serve four bedrooms lead up from the small entrance hall. From the front windows of these they would have looked out across a pretty stream to the slope, probably then denuded of trees, where DuPortail's engineers and artificers were encamped. But a remarkably good topographical model, illuminated by push-button lights, in the basement of the museum, makes it quite clear that from the east windows the Washingtons could have seen only the Lifeguard huts behind the house, beyond which the ground rose enough to cut off a view down the valley to the company streets and the parade ground, even though the trees which grow there today were then cut away—mercifully, when one considers the sights and sounds which must anyway have met Martha's eyes and ears when she left the house on her social calls or her errands of kindness and comfort to the sick.

Some of the huts have been reconstructed according to Washington's own specifications—"Fourteen feet by sixteen each; the sides, ends, and roofs made of logs; the roofs made tight with split slabs, or some other way; the sides made tight with clay; a fireplace made of wood, and secured with clay on the inside, eighteen inches thick; this fireplace to be in the rear of the hut; the door to be in the end next the street; the doors to be made of split oak slabs, unless boards can be procured; the side walls to be six feet and a half high. The officers' huts are to form a line in the rear of the troops, one hut to be allowed to each general officer; one to the staff of each brigade; one to the field officer of each regiment; one to the staff of each regiment; one to the commissioned officers of two companies; and one to every twelve non-commissioned officers and soldiers." *Twelve*. The space between the tiered bunks is hardly more than an aisle, and the bunks are too short for a man of any size at all.

General Varnum of Rhode Island was fortunate enough to have a headquarters house within the camp area, which has also been furnished as he must have known it. The rooms are small and dark, the windows narrow and few, but no doubt many distinguished guests were glad of a billet there in relative comfort. The headquarters of Lafayette lie on the far side of a covered bridge on a dirt road, a long ride in bad weather. The house is privately owned and occupied, as is that which sheltered Knox, on the same road nearer the camp.

Dreadful as the Valley Forge winter was in its every aspect, it was there during the following spring that the German drillmaster, General Steuben, fashioned an army out of the half-starved, half-naked derelicts who survived, taught them to march with their heads up, to step out to a cheerful drum-beat in unison, to wheel and maneuver on a parade ground, until when next under fire—at Monmouth—they handled themselves better than they had ever done before.

"The Baron," as he was affectionately known to everyone, had seen service in Europe with Frederick the Great, and was apparently sent by heaven to devise a book of rules for Washington's amateur army. He had almost no English at first, and his often apoplectic commands had to be filtered through a grinning bi-lingual aide before they reached the perspiring companies. Often the Baron seized a musket and marched along with his harried pupils, step by step, like a sergeant. When he swore at them, which was constantly, that too had to be translated before it could bite. But somehow they loved him, and obeyed him, and learned from him. And it was a proud day for them all when the news of the French Alliance came and the American army staged a celebration on a sunny day in May, '78, with maneuvers and bands and a cold collation laid outdoors, graced by the presence of the officers' wives, including Lady Washington herself, who had endured the winter hardships in camp, to see the hills garlanded with dogwood and the grass full of wild-flowers.

IV

Kennet Square to Annapolis

Travelling southward from Valley Forge with Elkton in Maryland as his next objective, Lossing spent the night of December 1st at Kennet Square beyond the Brandywine, lodging in the same tavern which had served Howe as headquarters, during the debarkation around Elkton in the summer of '77.

"I arose at daybreak," he resumes, "in anticipation of beholding a furious snowstorm, for the wind roared in the spacious chimneys and the neighboring shutters and signboards were beating a tattoo. But the wind had changed to the southeast, and although blowing with the fury of a December tempest, it was as warm as the breath of early spring. I breakfasted early, and departed for Elkton, twenty-four miles distant, with a prospect of receiving a drenching, for scuds, dark and billowy, came up from the ocean upon the wings of the gale like a flock of monster birds.

"I had just passed the *Hammer and Trowel* inn, a few miles from Kennet, when a thick mist came sweeping over the hills in the van of a tempest of wind and rain. For more than an hour it seemed as if the 'windows of heaven were opened' and that Aeolus and Jupiter Pluvius were joined in merry-making upon the earth. The huge leafless oaks in the forests swayed to and fro like the masts and spars of tempest-tossed navies; and a thousand turbid streamlets poured from the hillsides and made rivers of the gentle watercourses in the vales. Twice, while passing over a lofty hill, I felt my wagon lifted from the ground by the wind, its spacious cover acting like a parachute.

"The storm ceased as suddenly as it arose, and when I reached New London, a village of some twenty houses, about ten miles from Kennet Square, the clouds broke, and the winds were hushed. A brilliant, mild afternoon made the ride from London to Elkton a delightful one, and fully compensated for the suffering of the morning. The country is hilly, until within a few miles of the Head of Elk, when it becomes flat and marshy, and penetrated by deep estuaries of the bay and river.

"Elkton is an old town, situated at the junction of the two branches of the Elk River, the upper portion of Chesapeake Bay, and at the head of tide-water. The rail-way from Philadelphia to Baltimore passes within half a mile of the town, which may be considered the dividing point, in the military operations of the Revolution, between the North and South.

"My tarry at Elkton was brief. While Charley, my horse, was 'taking a bite' at an inn stable, I made inquiry of the post-master and other citizens, concerning vestiges of the Revolution, and ascertained that nothing was visible in the neighborhood of Elkton except the water, and the fields, and the hills, on which Howe encamped [before Brandywine] some two miles from the town. The place of the debarkation of the British was Turkey Point, a cape formed by the junction of the Elk River and the broad mouth of the Susquehanna, twelve miles below the village. Informed that the enemy cast up no entrenchments, and consequently left no tangible marks of their presence there, and assured that a fine view of the Point might be obtained from the steam-boat when going down the Chesapeake, I resolved to be satisfied with a distant observation.

"I accordingly rode to Frenchtown, three miles below Elkton, whence the boats connecting with the Delaware and Chesapeake rail-way depart for Baltimore; 'took tea' with a widow lady residing in a fine brick dwelling on the bank of the river, and just before sunset embarked. Charley was restive when walking the plank, but using all the philosophy he possessed, he soon decided that the hubbub in the steam-pipe was harmless, and his footing on deck secure. These problems settled, he seemed to enjoy the evening voyage quite as much as the bipeds around him.

"It was, indeed, a glorious evening. When the *George Washington* cast off her moorings the last gleams of the sun gilded the hills of Delaware, and while passing Turkey Point the scene was truly gorgeous. We arrived at Baltimore, sixty-eight miles from Elkton, at ten o'clock. I had travelled since dawn, by land and water, in rain and sunshine, full ninety miles; and it was a pleasant thought that tomorrow would be the Sabbath again—a day of rest.

"Sunday was as mild and bright in Baltimore as May, although it was the 3rd of December. That city has no old churches hallowed by the presence of the patriots of the Revolution. Annapolis was the only city in Maryland, except little St. Mary's on its western border, when the battles for independence were fought; and 'Baltimore towne,' though laid out as early as 1729, contained in 1776 less than one hundred houses. It is a city of the present; and yet, in extent, commerce, and population, it is the third city of the republic, numbering now about one hundred and sixty-five thousand inhabitants."

Small as it was, Baltimore was chosen as a handy refuge when the Congress first ducked out of Philadelphia in December of '76, after the British had chased Washington the length of New Jersey and nothing but his exhausted army and the ice-churned waters of the Delaware River lay between Cornwallis and the capital. Small as it was, Baltimore attempted to put on a social whirl for its unexpected and preoccupied guests, and must have met with scant enthusiasm. "This dirty, boggy hole beggars all description," grumbled a North Carolina delegate in a letter home. "We are obliged, except when the weather paves the streets, to go to Congress on horseback, the ways so miry that carriages almost stall on the sides of them."

They had felt a bit sheepish about lighting out like that, but General Putnam, who had been assigned to defend the capital, had advised it, obviously with Washington's consent. "Mere personal safety I suppose would not have induced many of them to fly," Robert Morris of Philadelphia wrote at the time, "but their security as a body was the object. Had any number of them fallen into the enemies' hands so as to break up the Congress, America might have been ruined before another choice of delegates could be had, and in such an event that would have been criminal and rash to the last degree."

Lossing found the brick building in which they met still standing at the corner of Baltimore, Sharpe, and Liberty Streets. Its first story was being used "for commercial purposes" but otherwise it looked the same.

Congress was in session here when on the last day of the year they received Washington's unemotional report on the victory at Trenton, which was read aloud to the delegates assembled. At the end of February, 1777, when it was plain that the British had had enough of New Jersey for a while, the Congress adjourned back to Philadelphia, where it remained in comparative safety and comfort until September of the same year. Then, after Washington's defeat at Brandywine, Philadelphia was abandoned to the British for nearly a year, and their winter in the backwoods at York—the same which Washington spent at Valley Forge—must have made the delegates homesick even for Baltimore.

"When Lafayette passed through Baltimore on his way to the fields of his conflicts in the South [in 1781] he was greeted with the greatest respect by the people," Lossing relates. "A ball was given in his honor, at which the Marquis appeared sad.

" 'Why so gloomy at a ball?' asked one of the gay belles.

" 'I cannot enjoy the gayety of the scene,' replied Lafayette, 'while so many of the poor soldiers are without shirts and other necessaries.'

" 'We will supply them,' was the noble reply of the ladies; and the gayety of the ballroom was exchanged for the sober but earnest service of the needle. They assembled the next day in great numbers to make up clothing for the soldiers, out of materials furnished by fathers and husbands. One gentleman, a Mr. Poe, out of his limited means gave Lafayette five hundred dollars to aid him in clothing his soldiers. His wife with her own hands cut out five hundred pairs of pantaloons, and superintended the making of them."

When Lafayette revisited Baltimore during his grand tour in 1824, Mrs. Poe was still living, an elderly widow, and the French stripling hero had become a stout old gentleman of sixty-eight. They met again, and one is left wondering again. George Washington Lafayette, then in his forties, accompanied his father on the tour. Mrs. Poe's grandson Edgar was a boy of fifteen, at school in Richmond.

The story of Lafayette in America is a great temptation to digression. He was still two months short of his twentieth birthday when he arrived in Philadelphia in June, '77, but he had already been three years married to a beautiful young heiress who bore their first child after he had left France on his voyage to America. He was a commissioned captain of artillery in the French army, and had seen some routine service in the garrison at Metz.

At first he seemed to the harassed Congress just one more in the swarm of foreign adventurers who had begun to besiege the American army for commissions—and pay—and troops to play about with, and he encountered a coolness amounting to rudeness. When he managed with his still limited English to convey to them that he only wanted to serve as a volunteer at his own expense, they recovered from their surprise with an offer of a major-general's commission—and the news soon got round that his family was influential in France, and his wealth formidable, while it was plain to see that he possessed youth, charm, and a sword.

There is a legend that at his first meeting with Washington at a dinner party in Philadelphia shortly before the battle of Brandywine, he singled out the Commander-in-chief from a group of unidentified officers with a clairvoyance similar to Joan of Arc's recognition of the unthroned Dauphin. In any case, before long he was regarded almost as a son in the General's military Family, and the two men maintained a correspondence after Lafayette returned to France in 1781, for as long as Washington lived. Lafayette never learned to spell English, even by eighteenth-century standards, but he soon spoke it fluently, always with a devastating accent, of course.

As a volunteer aide on Washington's staff, he was present at the battle of Brandywine, where he received a rifle-ball in the leg while unhorsed and trying to rally his men—"what I pompously call my wound," he wrote to his wife during his two months' convalescence in the care of the Moravians at Bethlehem. He recovered to distinguish himself again at Monmouth the following year. And when the traitor Arnold invaded Virginia with a British force early in 1781, it was Lafayette who led the avenging army southward through Baltimore to embark at the head of Elk, enchanting the ladies along his way. We shall meet him again before Yorktown.

Lossing left Baltimore for the thirty-mile drive to Annapolis on the afternoon of December 4th, and crossed the "long, rickety draw-bridge" over the Patapsco River at sunset.

"The sky was clear," he says, "and the moon being sufficiently advanced to promise a fair degree of light, I resolved to push forward as far as the 'half-way house' fifteen miles from Baltimore, before halting. Soon after leaving the bridge the road penetrated a forest of oaks and chestnuts, filled with those beautiful evergreens, the laurel and the holly. Passing several cultivated openings, where the country was rolling, I reached a level sandy region, and at dark entered a forest of pines, its deep shadows relieved occasionally by small openings recently made by the woodmen's ax.

"I had passed only two small houses in a journey of six miles, and without seeing the face of a living creature, when I met a Negro man and woman, and I inquired for the 'half-way house.' The woman assured me that it was two miles ahead, and in the plenitude of her kind feelings promised that I should find 'plenty o' liquor dar.'

"After driving at least four miles, I perceived that I had 'run off the track,' mistaking one of the numerous branches of the main road for the highway itself. After traversing the deep, sandy way in the gloom until almost eight o'clock, when traveller and horse were thoroughly wearied, I was cheered by the barking of a dog, and in a few minutes crossed a stream and came in sight of a spacious mansion, surrounded by many broad acres of cultivation. The merry voices of children who were playing in the lane were hushed as I halted at the gate and hailed. A servant swung it wide for my entrance, and when I asked for entertainment for the night, the kindest hospitality was extended.

"The proprietor of the plantation was the widow of a Methodist clergyman who was drowned in the Severn a few years ago. Her mother, residing with her now, had been in former years a parishioner of my own pastor, the Reverend H. Tyng, D.D. This fact was a sympathetic link; and a home feeling, with its gentle influence, came over me as the evening passed away in pleasant conversation. I left the mansion of Mrs. Robinson the next morning with real regret. I had had there a foretaste of that open hospitality which I experienced everywhere at the South, and must ever remember with gratitude.

"Under the guidance of a servant, I traversed a private road to the public one leading to Annapolis. The highway passes through a barren region until within two miles of the town, relieved occasionally by a few cultivated spots; and so sinuous was its course that I crossed the Baltimore and Annapolis rail-way seven times in a distance of thirteen miles. The deep sand made the journey toilsome, and extended its duration until almost an hour past meridian.

"Annapolis is really an old town. Many of its houses are of the hip-roofed style of an earlier generation, with the distinctive features of Southern houses, so odd in appearance to a Northern man —the chimneys projecting from the gable, from the ground to their tops. Like Baltimore, it was frequently the scene of military displays, but not of sanguinary conflicts."

V

Queen Anne to Occoquan

"Towards the decline of a brilliant afternoon," Lossing continues on the 5th of December, "I left Annapolis for Washington City. The air was as balmy as spring, when I crossed the long bridge over the South River, and quaffed a cup of cold water from a bubbling spring at the toll-house on the southern side. The low, sandy country was exchanged for a region more diversified, and my ride during the early evening, with a half moon and brilliant stars casting down their mild effulgence, would have been delightful but for the provoking obstructions which a lack of public spirit and private enterprise had left in the way.

"The highway was the 'county road,' yet it passed almost the whole distance from Annapolis to Washington through plantations, like a private wagon-path, without inclosure. Wherever the division of fields crossed the road, private interest had erected a barred gate to keep out intrusive cattle, and these the traveller was obliged to open. Being my own footman, I was exercised in limbs and patience to my heart's content, for during a drive of thirteen miles that evening I *opened* fifteen gates; who *closed* them I have never ascertained.

"I crossed the Patuxent at seven o'clock, and halted at Queen Anne, a small, antiquated-looking village, some of the houses of which, I doubt not, were erected during the reign of its godmother. There was no tavern in the place, but I procured a supper and comfortable lodgings at the post-office. We breakfasted by candlelight, and before 'sun-up' as the Southerners say, I was on my way towards the Federal city, twenty-three miles distant.

"I had hardly left the precincts of Queen Anne before a huge red gate confronted me! I thought it might be the ghost of one I had encountered the night before, but its substantiality as a veritable gate was made manifest by the sudden halt of Charley before its bars. I was preparing to alight when a colored boy came from behind a shock of corn and kindly opened the way.

" 'How far is it to the next gate?' I inquired.

" 'Don't know, massa,' said the lad. 'But I reckons dey is plenty t'ick, dey is, twixt here and Uncle Josh's.'

"Where Uncle Josh lived I do not know, but I found the gates more than 'plenty t'ick' all the way until within a short distance of Bladensburg. In the journey of thirty-six miles from Annapolis to Washington, I passed through fifty-three gates! Unlike the doors and windows of the people of the South, I found them all *shut*.

"From the brow of a hill eight miles from Washington, I had the first glimpse of the Capitol dome, and there I opened the last gate; each a pleasing reminiscence now. I passed to the left of Bladensburg, crossed the east branch of the Potomac, and entered Washington City, eastward of the Capitol, at one o'clock. For thirty minutes I had witnessed a rare phenomenon at that hour in the day. Dark clouds, like the gathering of a summer shower, were floating in the northeastern sky, and upon them refraction painted the segment of a quite brilliant rainbow. I once saw a lunar bow at midnight in June, but never before observed a solar one at midday in December.

"Washington City has no Revolutionary history of its own. Our national metropolis is a city of the present century; for before the year 1800, when the seat of the Federal government was permanently located there, it was a small hamlet composed of a few houses. The selection of a site for the Federal city was entrusted to the judgment of the first President, who chose the point of land on the eastern bank of the Potomac, at its confluence with the Anacostia, or east branch of that river. A territory around it, ten miles square, was ceded to the United States by Virginia and Maryland in 1788.

The owners of the land gave one half of it, after deducting streets and public squares, to the Federal government to defray the expenses to be incurred in the erection of public buildings.

"The city was surveyed under the chief direction of Andrew Ellicott, and was laid out in 1791. The Capitol was commenced in 1793, but was not yet completed on the original plan when in 1814 the British troops under General Ross burned it, together with the Library of Congress, the President's house, and all the public buildings except the Patent Office. The city then contained about nine hundred houses, scattered in groups over an area of three miles. The walls of the Capitol remained firm, though scarred and blackened. The present noble edifice was completed in 1827, more than a quarter of a century after the seat of government was located at Washington.

"The city was full of the life and activity incident to the assembling of Congress, and I passed four days there with pleasure and profit. My first evening was spent in the company of the venerable widow of Alexander Hamilton, a surviving daughter of General Philip Schuyler. Mrs. Hamilton was then ninety-two years of age, yet her mind seemed to have all the elasticity of a woman of sixty. A sunny cheerfulness, which has shed its blessed influence around her during a long life, still makes her society genial and attractive. Her memory, faithful to the impressions of a long and eventful experience, is ever ready, with its varied reminiscences, to give a charm to her conversation upon subjects connected with our history. With an affectionate daughter (Mrs. Holly) she lives in elegant retirement in the metropolis, beloved by her friends, honored by strangers, venerated by all. She is, I believe, the last of the belles of the Revolution—the last of those who with Lucy Knox and others graced the social gatherings honored by the presence of Washington and his lady during the struggle for independence, and gave brilliancy to the levees of the first President."

Elizabeth was the "plain" one of General Schuyler's several daughters. She made a romantic wartime marriage with Washington's dashing aide—the bride born of a rich and powerful New York family, the groom the illegitimate son of an obscure West Indies scandal. They had first met at her father's Albany mansion in the autumn of '77, when Hamilton arrived there on a delicate mission for Washington after the surrender of Burgoyne at Saratoga. The Schuyler hospitality was famous, and the aides were always treated like members of the family. Betsey was twenty then, and no longer overshadowed by her sparkling elder sister Angelica, who had eloped a few months before. Betsey had a more quiet charm—"a brunette with the most good-natured dark lovely eyes that I ever saw, which threw a beam of good temper and benevolence over her entire countenance," another smitten aide had written a year or so earlier. And again, "Who should bless my eyes again this evening, but good-natured, agreeable Betsey Schuyler, just returned from Saratoga."

On his way back from Albany to Washington at Valley Forge, Hamilton was laid up with a fever, and had time to think—he spent it composing a letter to Betsey. He was only a few months older than she was, with a slender, boyish build and graceful carriage, violet eyes, a complexion like a girl's, and an enormous sophistication. He stood very high in Washington's regard at that time, and had given up the guns he handled so expertly at Trenton for the post of military secretary and aide to the Commander-in-chief—which he was sometimes heard to regret.

Two years passed before Betsey and Colonel Hamilton met again, and a good many letters travelled to and fro. In the interim Hamilton again distinguished himself under fire and was painfully injured at Monmouth, where his horse was shot and rolled on him when it fell. As one of Washington's military Family, he was a charming deputy host to the visiting Congressmen and foreigners who came to Headquarters, and he had brought literary polish and system to the burden of his chief's massive correspondence.

The winter of 1779–80 was the second the army spent at Morristown, and it was the coldest ever known, in some ways surpassing in sheer miseries the one at Valley Forge two years before. The intervening winter at Middlebrook had been comparatively mild.

Lossing says: "It was the custom of General Washington during these winter encampments, where Mrs. Washington was with him, to cultivate a social spirit. To accomplish this he invited a certain number of officers every day excepting Sundays to dine at his table; also the wives of officers who might be in camp, and sometimes ladies and gentlemen of the neighborhood." So the heroic women were there at Morristown, some with small children who suffered and died, while other babies were born, and there were flirtations and engagements and brave little balls—dancing was a good way to keep warm. The younger officers and aides got up sleigh rides and amateur theatricals—Washington always loved a play. And there were concerts, when "everyone who could sing, sang." The local belles, from Governor Livingston's daughters down, usually managed to attend in spite of the weather, and Martha Washington, who said she always heard the first and last gun of every campaign, encouraged everything that would relieve the tedium and anxieties of the long winter months. Herself, she never was seen to dance, but sat serenely with her knitting while the general led out all the ladies in turn.

Always in poor health for campaigning in the field, General Schuyler had left the army for Congress. He and Washington had been warm friends ever since the days of the Second Congress, and he was valuable as a counsellor because he was not only an old Indian fighter himself, but also understood how to get along with them in council, where tribal protocol was important. Now he maintained a sort of private intelligence service at his residences in Albany and at Saratoga on the frontier, where the Six Nations still caused uneasiness, and the lake route from Canada was always an invitation to the British at Montreal. As the situation worsened in the Mohawk valley, Schuyler was called from Philadelphia to Morristown for consultation, and took lodging in a modest house near Headquarters, where his wife and daughter Betsey joined him. And there young Hamilton came calling, whenever his duties permitted—which may have been what Betsey had in mind.

Linked to his interview with Mrs. Hamilton at Washington was

Lossing's visit to Judge Ford at Morristown on a previous tour, for there again he had heard the authentic voice of the Revolution recalling its own first-hand memories, which included the courtship of Betsey Schuyler. Judge Ford still occupied the "fine mansion" where as a boy of fourteen he was living with his widowed mother when it was Washington's Headquarters during that bitter winter of 1779–80.

"His well-stored mind is still active," wrote Lossing, "notwithstanding he is eighty-four years old, and he clearly remembers even the most trifling incidents of that encampment which came under his observation. He entertained me until a late hour with anecdotes and facts of interest, and then kindly invited me to spend the night under his hospitable roof, remarking, 'You shall sleep in the room which General Washington and his lady occupied.' The carpet upon the floor, dark and of a rich pattern, is the same that was pressed by the feet of the chief nearly seventy years ago; and in an apartment below were a looking-glass, secretary, and book-case that formed a portion of the furniture of the house at that time. I have preserved drawings of them. Judge Ford expressed his surprise that the mirror was not demolished, for the room in which it hung was occupied at a later time by some of the subalterns of the Pennsylvania line—gentlemen by birth, but rowdies in practice. They injured the room very much by their nightly carousals, but the mirror escaped their rough treatment.

"Washington and his suite occupied the whole of the large building except two rooms on the east side of the main passage, which were reserved for Mrs. Ford and her family. He had two log additions made to the house, one for a kitchen and the other was used as the office and orderly room for his aides, among them Hamilton and Tilghman [he who had once written of Betsey's dark lovely eyes.] In the meadow a few rods southeast of the buildings, about fifty log huts were erected for the accommodation of the Lifeguard, which consisted of two hundred and fifty men under Captain Colfax.

"During the winter many false alarms occurred, which set the whole camp in motion. Sentinels were placed at intervals between the camp and Headquarters, and pickets were planted at distant points with intervening sentinels. Sometimes the alarm would begin by the firing of a gun at a remote point. This would be answered by discharges along the whole line of sentinels to the Headquarters. The Life-guard would immediately rush to the house of the General, barricade the doors, and throw up the windows. Five soldiers, with their muskets cocked and brought to a charge, were placed at each window, and there they would remain until the troops from the camp marched to Headquarters and the cause of the alarm was ascertained. It was frequently the case that some young suitor who had been *sparking* till a late hour, and attempted to pass a sentinel without giving the countersign, caused the discharge of a musket and the ensuing commotion in the camp. These occasions were very annoying to the ladies of the camp, for both Mrs. Washington and Mrs. Ford were obliged to lie in bed, sometimes for hours, with their rooms full of soldiers and the keen winter air from the open windows piercing their drawn curtains."

Although the Arnold Tavern, which housed Washington's household during the first Morristown winter, has disappeared, the Ford mansion remains today one of the most satisfying survivals of American history, second only to Mount Vernon itself. It has been most happily restored and furnished, with many pieces of unquestioned pedigree, and the new museum and library at the end of the lawn behind the house is a scholar's paradise. On the other side of the town at the end of a delightful woods road is the site of the army's encampment, now a park preserve, with markers and reconstructed huts. The distance between explains the frequent alarms and the necessity for the Life-guard post directly across the road from Headquarters, where a church now stands. It would have been very easy for an enterprising enemy to kidnap the American Commander-in-chief with a small sortie from Staten Island, the nearest British post. But the idea seems to have occurred much more forcibly to his own officers than to the British.

Courtship in the middle of an armed camp must certainly have had its hazards and humors, and Alexander Hamilton himself was once caught sparking in circumstances which provided Judge Ford with one of his best stories. Lossing set it down as it was told to him that night at Morristown, before he retired for the night in the General's bedroom. Being a favorite of Hamilton's, said Judge Ford, as a lad he was often given the countersign with Washington's permission, so that he might play at the village after the sentinels

were posted for the night. "On one occasion," Lossing's version runs, "young Ford was returning home about nine o'clock in the evening, and had passed the sentinel, when he recognized the voice of Hamilton in reply to the soldier's demand of 'Who comes there?' He stepped aside and waited for the Colonel to accompany him to the house. Hamilton came up to the point of the presented bayonet of the sentinel to give the countersign, but he had quite forgotten it. 'He had spent the evening with Miss Schuyler,' said Judge Ford, relating the incident to me, 'and thoughts of her undoubtedly expelled the countersign from his head.' The soldier lover was embarrassed, but the sentinel, who knew him well, was stern in the performance of his duty. Hamilton pressed his hand upon his forehead, and tried hard to summon the cabalistic words from their hiding-place, but like the faithful sentinel they were immovable. Just then he recognized young Ford in the gloom.

"'Ay, Master Ford, is that you?' he said in an undertone; and stepping aside, he called the lad to him and whispered, 'Give me the countersign.'

"He did so, and Hamilton, stepping in front of the sentinel again, delivered it. The sentinel, seeing the movement, and believing that his superior was testing his fidelity, kept his bayonet unmoved.

"'I have given you the countersign. Why do you not shoulder your musket?' asked Hamilton.

"'Will that do, Colonel?' asked the soldier in reply.

"'It will for this time,' said Hamilton. 'Let me pass.'

"The soldier reluctantly obeyed the illegal command, and Hamilton and his young companion reached Headquarters without further difficulty."

The boyish-seeming colonel was hard-headed enough in matters to do with his personal career, and even regarding the great man he served, but Betsey reduced him to writing lover's verse at least once. After her death a cherished scrap of yellowed paper was found, which had apparently passed between their lingering hands during that supercharged winter at Morristown, perhaps on the very evening when he turned up so absent-minded at the advanced hour of nine P.M.

ANSWER TO THE INQUIRY WHY I SIGHED

>Before no mortal ever knew
>A love like mine, so tender—true—
>Completely wretched—you away—
>And but half blessed e'en when you stay.
>
>. . . . .
>
>No joy unmixed my bosom warms
>But when my angel's in my arms.

Circumstances were unfavorable to secrets, and the whole camp soon knew that Hamilton was in love with the New York general's daughter. Schuyler approved, though the young man's early background was certainly as dubious as that of her sister Angelica's choice, which had so riled him when she eloped with John Carter, who later resumed his real name of Church. But Hamilton had the manners to approach Betsey's father first, with no backstairs fly-with-me nonsense, and Washington's colossal respectability covered his beloved aide like a cloak. To no one's surprise, the engagement was announced before Betsey left Morristown with her parents in June.

Throughout that gloomy summer of 1780, which witnessed Hamilton's discovery of Arnold's treason at West Point just in time to save Washington from being taken prisoner by riding into the trap, his letters arrived frequently at Albany to further enchant his angel. "I would not have you imagine, Miss, that I write to you so often to gratify your wishes or please your vanity," he announced characteristically in one of them, "but merely to indulge myself, and to comply with that restless propensity of my mind which will not be happy unless I am doing something in which you are concerned." In December, when Washington went into winter quarters at New Windsor, the colonel was given leave to ride to Albany and marry her.

Less than a year later, when the great Yorktown venture had been decided upon and Washington was about to move southward with Rochambeau on what proved to be the final decisive campaign of the war, Hamilton wrote to Betsey who was at Albany expecting their first child during the coming winter. He was a young man in love, but he wouldn't have missed the excitement in Virginia for anything in the world. His letter takes flight in dramatic contrast to the one which went to Mount Vernon from Philadelphia in '75: "I cannot announce the fatal necessity without feeling everything a fond husband can feel. I am unhappy; I am unhappy beyond expression. I am unhappy because I am to be so remote from you; because I am to hear from you less frequently than I am accustomed to do. I am miserable, because I know you will be so; I am wretched at the idea of flying so far from you, without a single hour's interview, to tell you all my pains and all my love... I must go without seeing you—I must go without embracing you—alas! I must go."

Cornwallis thoughtfully surrendered in time for Hamilton to arrive back home before the birth of his son in January, '82. In the spring, having left the army to start a law practice, he was writing to a brother officer who was still at Headquarters: "You cannot imagine how domestic I am growing. I lose all taste for the pursuits of ambition. I sigh for nothing but the company of my wife and baby. The ties of duty alone, or imagined duty, keep me from renouncing public life altogether." There follows a description of his firstborn which does much to illuminate Betsey's unswerving devotion to the man who was later to try her so sorely. "He is truly a very fine young gentleman," the twenty-four-year-old father reports, "the most agreeable in his conversation and manners of any one I ever saw, nor less remarkable for his intelligence and sweetness of temper. You are not to imagine by my beginning by his mental qualities that he is defective in personal. It is agreed on all hands that he is handsome; his features are good, his eye is not only sprightly and expressive but full of benignity. His attitude in sitting is by connoisseurs esteemed graceful, and he has a method of waving his hand that announces the future orator. He stands however rather awkwardly, and his legs have not all that delicate slimness of his father. It is feared that he may never excel in dancing, which is probably the only accomplishment in which he will not excel. If he has any faults in his manners, he laughs too much. He is now in his seventh month."

This is the man who within ten years was involved in what began as a stupid secret infidelity, ran on into blackmail, and then became a sordid scandal. Betsey's compassionate character stood fast, and she always considered that her husband had been betrayed by an unscrupulous woman, rather than that she herself as a wife had been publicly humiliated. And this was the son who at the age of nineteen died after a duel on the Weekawken meeting-ground —fought because of a youthful political quarrel which turned personal. Three years later, on the same spot, in a duel forced on him by an old political enemy, Hamilton himself fired into the air and simultaneously received Burr's bullet in a vital spot. He was forty-seven, and Betsey was fifty years his widow. Neither his foolish infidelities nor his tragic end destroyed the sunny disposition for which she was noted as a girl, and which as Lossing observed at the end of her long life had supported her through numerous trials.

After paying his respects to Hamilton's widow, Lossing next day visited the rooms of the National Institute which had been established ten years earlier in the Patent Office Building, and where were exhibited in a glass case some of the most precious relics of the Revolution. "Upon the floor," he says, "stands Washington's *camp chest*, an old-fashioned hair-trunk, twenty-one inches in length, fifteen in width, and ten in depth, filled with the table furniture used by the chief during the war. The compartments are so ingeniously arranged that they contain a gridiron; a coffee and tea-pot; three tin sauce-pans (one moveable handle being used for all); five glass flasks used for honey, salt, coffee, port wine and vinegar; three large tin meat dishes; sixteen plates; two knives and five forks; a candle-stick and tinder-box; tin boxes for tea and sugar, and five small bottles for pepper and other materials for making soup. Such composed the appointments for the table of the Commander-in-chief of the American armies, while battling for independence and laying the cornerstone of our republic."

This is probably the table service referred to in a letter of Washington's written at his West Point Headquarters in the summer of '78, which reveals a glimpse of his rarely recorded humor. He had apparently on a social impulse invited the wives of two of his officers to come to dinner with him and the Staff, when they had paid him a call on the previous day—and he then had time for second thoughts. Martha was at Mount Vernon. Addressing Dr. John Cochran, Surgeon-general of the Northern Department of the Continental Army, who was married to General Schuyler's sister, he wrote:

"Dear Doctor,—I have asked Mrs. Cochran and Mrs. Livingston to dine with me tomorrow; but am I not in honor bound to apprise them of their fare? As I hate deception, even where the imagination only is concerned, I will. It is needless to premise that my table is large enough to hold the ladies. Of this they had ocular proof yesterday. To say how it is usually covered is rather more essential; and this shall be the purport of my letter.

"Since our arrival at this happy spot, we have had a ham, sometimes a shoulder of bacon, to grace the head of the table; a piece of roast beef adorns the foot; and a dish of beans, or greens, almost imperceptible, decorates the center. When the cook has a mind to cut a figure, which I presume will be the case tomorrow, we have two beef-pies, or dishes of crabs, in addition, one on each side of the center dish, dividing the space and reducing the distance between dish and dish to about six feet. Of late he has had the surprising sagacity to discover that apples will make pies; and it is a question if, in the violence of his efforts, we do not get one of apples, instead of having both of beef-steaks. If the ladies can put up with such entertainment, and will submit to partake of it on plates *once tin but now iron* (not become so by any labor of scouring) I shall be happy to see them; and am, dear Doctor, yours, etc...."

Returning to Lossing's account of the National Institute Exhibit, we find: "Standing near the camp-chest is Washington's war sword, and with it Franklin's cane, bequeathed to the hero by the sage. Dr. Franklin, in the codicil to his will, wrote as follows: 'My fine crab-tree walking-stick, with a gold head curiously wrought in the form of a cap of liberty, I give to my friend, and the friend of mankind, General Washington. If it were a sceptre he has merited it, and would become it. It was a present to me from that excellent woman, Madame de Forbach, the Dowager Duchess of Deux-Ponts, connected with some verses which should go with it."

However, the verses which Lossing prints along with his account of the sword he attributes to Morris, doubtless George P., who was a contemporary journalist and author of poems and songs, including the more familiar "Woodman, Spare That Tree." It would do us no harm to contemplate for a moment the simple sentiments of an innocent age.

THE SWORD AND THE STAFF

The sword of the Hero!
　The staff of the Sage!
Whose valor and wisdom
　Are stamp'd on the age!
Time-hallowed mementoes
　Of those who have riven
The scepter from tyrants,
　The lightning from heaven!

This weapon, O Freedom!
　Was drawn by thy son,
And it never was sheath'd
　Till the battle was won!

No stain of dishonor
  Upon it we see.
'Twas never surrender'd—
  Except to the free!

While Fame claims the hero
  And patriot sage,
Their names to emblazon
  On History's page,
No holier relics
  Will Liberty hoard
Than Franklin's staff guarded
  By Washington's sword.

"The war sword of the chief is encased in a black leather sheath, with silver mountings. The handle is ivory, colored a pale green, and wound spirally with silver wire at wide intervals. It was manufactured by J. Bailey, Fishkill, N.Y., and has the maker's name engraved upon the hilt. The belt is white leather, with silver mountings, and was evidently made at an earlier period, for upon a silver plate is engraved '1757.'

"Upon the wall of the room is a full-length portrait of Washington, painted by Charles Wilson Peale, under interesting circumstances," Lossing continues. "Peale was a remarkable man. Possessed of great versatility of talent, he brought all his genius into play as circumstances demanded. He was a sturdy patriot, and entered the army at an early period of the contest. He commanded a volunteer company at the battle of Trenton, and also at Germantown; and he was with the army at Valley Forge. He employed his leisure hours incident to camp duty in painting, and it was at Valley Forge that he commenced the picture in question. When the army crossed the Delaware into New Jersey in pursuit of Sir Henry Clinton before the battle of Monmouth [June, 1778] Peale went with it, taking his unfinished picture and his materials with him; and at Brunswick, a day or two after the Monmouth conflict, he obtained the last sitting from the Commander-in-chief. The picture was finished at Princeton. A distant view of Nassau Hall, at that place, with a body of British prisoners marching, compose a portion of the background. The picture of the sword hanging upon the thigh of Washington is an evidence of the truthfulness of the costume, for it is an exact representation of the real weapon which stands in the case on the opposite side of the room.

"I passed the morning of the 8th in the library of Mr. Force, preparing from old maps a plan of my Southern route. At meridian I crossed the Potomac upon the mile-long bridge, and rode to Arlington House, the seat of George Washington Parke Custis, Esq. His mansion, wherein true Virginia hospitality prevails, is beautifully situated upon high ground overlooking the Potomac, half surrounded by a fine oak forest, and fronting broad lawns.

"Mr. Custis received me, though a stranger, with cordiality, and when the object of my visit was made known, the Washington treasures of Arlington House were opened for my inspection. As executor of the will, and the adopted son and member of the immediate family of Washington, Mr. Custis possesses many interesting mementoes of the great man. With books and pencil, in the bosom of an affectionate family, Mr. Custis is enjoying the blessings of a green old age. He has been present at the inauguration of every president of the United States, now numbering thirteen, and he has grasped the hand in friendly greeting of almost every distinguished personage who has visited our national metropolis during the last half century."

The son of Martha's son Jacky by her first husband, "little Washington" Custis was born in the spring of '81, not long before his father departed for the Yorktown campaign as Washington's volunteer aide. The following November, within a few days of the surrender, Jacky was dead at twenty-eight of camp-fever, leaving his wife and mother distracted with grief in the midst of the general rejoicing at what soon proved to be the decisive victory of the war. His mother soon married again, and young Custis and his sister Nelly grew up at Mount Vernon as his father had done—spoilt, secure, and charming. He was eighteen when Washington died in '99, and stayed on at Mount Vernon with his grandmother till her death three years later. Having inherited a considerable fortune from his father's estate, he built Arlington House near Alexandria, at ruinous cost, as a home for his bride, Mary Fitzhugh Lee, of Ravensworth, whom he married at the age of twenty-three. They had no sons. Their daughter Mary married Robert E. Lee. After Custis's death in 1857, it was Lossing who assisted Mrs. Lee to prepare her father's *Recollections* of George Washington for publication. The book remains a valuable source of material today.

Arlington House is furnished and open to visitors, a short drive from Washington, D.C., and its size and grace and unusual arrangement make it an interesting companion to the more conventional simplicity of nearby Mount Vernon.

Early the next morning Lossing was on the road to Alexandria, on the Virginia side of the Potomac. It had little Revolutionary history of its own, but Washington was often there in the happy days before the war began, and in its museum Lossing found one of the flags which the Hessians had surrendered at Trenton in '76. Before noon he was on the road again, bound for Mount Vernon, nine miles below Alexandria.

"It was a mild, clear day, almost as balmy as the Indian summer time," he says, always enchanted with the weather as he went. "After crossing an estuary of the Potomac the road was devious, passing through a rough, half-cultivated region, and almost impassable in places on account of gulleys scooped by recent rains. Suddenly upon ascending a small steep hill from the edge of a wild ravine, the mansion and its surroundings were before me, and through the leafless branches of the trees came the sheen of the sun from a distant bay of the Potomac.

"I was met at the gate by an intelligent colored lad, who ordered another to take charge of my horse, while he conducted me to the mansion. I bore a letter of introduction to the present proprietor of Mount Vernon, John Washington, a grand-nephew of the General; but himself and family were absent, and not a white person was on the premises. I felt a disappointment, for I desired to pass the time there in the company of a relative of the beloved one whose name and deeds hallow the spot.

"Silence pervaded the life-dwelling of Washington, and the echoes of every footfall as I moved at the back of the servant from room to room seemed almost like the voices of intruders. I entered the library which, with the breakfast room, is in the south wing of the building, and in the deep shadows of that quiet apartment sat down in the very chair often occupied by the patriot, and gazed and mused with feeling not to be uttered.

"This view is from the lawn in front, looking down the Potomac. The mansion is built of wood, cut so as to resemble stone, and is two stories in height. The central part was built by Lawrence Washington, a [half] brother of the chief. The wings were added by the General. Through the centre of the building is a spacious passage, level with the portico, and paved with tesselated Italian marble. This hall communicates with three large rooms, and with the main stairway leading to the second story. The piazza on the eastern or river front is of square paneled pilasters, extending the whole length of the edifice. There is an observatory and cupola in the center of the roof, from whence may be obtained an extensive view of the surrounding country."

John Washington, whom Lossing hoped to see at Mount Vernon, was descended from Washington's favorite brother Jack, and had inherited the house in a zigzag line from his uncle Bushrod. John had allowed the estate to run down, but not from negligence, as he had been pretty well impoverished by his enforced hospitality to the many visitors to what was now regarded as a shrine. Although Lossing does not mention any actual deterioration which came to his notice, only five years after his visit the property was described as almost in ruins, the paint peeling, the roof sagging, one of the columns gone, the lawn waist-high in weeds.

John had quite rightly refused a $300,000 offer by speculators who wanted to commercialize the place, and Congress had then refused to purchase it from him for $200,000. Discouraged and humiliated by his position, which had received some adverse publicity, John at first took no interest in the association of patriotic women, headed by Anne Pamela Cunningham of South Carolina, which in 1853 undertook to raise the purchase price and preserve the home of Washington for the nation.

This remarkable woman, who had been a semi-invalid since a hunting fall at the age of sixteen, set herself to rescue Mount Vernon. Beginning with an open letter to the Ladies of the South published in the Charleston *Mercury*, within five years she was in a position to offer a substantial down payment with annual installments to follow.

Making a personal visit to Mount Vernon in 1858, she had to use all the charm and persuasion at a Southern gentlewoman's command to induce John Washington to sign the contract of sale. By

1859 practically all the purchase money was paid, and John agreed to move out, as a nice touch, on February 22, 1860, when Miss Cunningham and a secretary named Sarah Tracy moved in, to superintend the work of restoration and repair which had already been begun. As the furniture belonged to the departing Washingtons, only the key to the Bastille, presented to the General by Lafayette, and the Houdon bust, and some kitchen utensils remained for the new tenants' use until necessities could be brought down from Washington City.

They had no sooner settled in than the War Between the States began to threaten. Miss Cunningham returned to South Carolina for what was intended as a temporary visit, and she was forced to remain there for six years. Miss Tracy sent for a Philadelphia friend to join her in the house, and the two women sat it out at Mount Vernon through the war, living a little epic of stark terror and military chivalry in a sort of No Man's Land between the Union and Confederate lines.

There hardly remains any necessity to say that a visit to Mount Vernon nowadays should be a required part of every American's education. The unchanging serenity of its location, above the broad, tranquil river—the simple good taste of its proportions and furnishings—and the intangible evidence which lingers there of the lofty yet humble and dedicated spirit who built and loved it, and dwelt there, are both chastening and uplifting to the beleaguered modern citizen. Here a truly great man, truly innocent of self-importance, breathed the mild Virginia air, established an orderly, affectionate family society, and sacrificed precious years of its peace and beauty to his country's demands. It is as close as we can come to the fountainhead of the things America was founded on, and wants to stand for now—freedom from political tyranny, and the right to private happiness. There is a sort of magic in the place, for those who stand still and wait.

The sun was setting when Lossing drove away from the west front of Mount Vernon, towards Occoquan about twelve miles distant, where he proposed to spend the Sabbath halt. The road was in wretched condition, passing through a series of small swamps and pine barrens, on the way to Pohick Church, where Washington worshiped, and where Weems, his first biographer, preached.

"It is about seven miles southwest of Mount Vernon, upon an elevation on the borders of a forest," he says, "surrounded by ancient oaks, chestnuts and pines. The twilight lingered long enough to allow me to make the annexed sketch from my wagon in the road, when I gave my horse a loose rein and hastened toward Occoquan as fast as the deep mud in the highway would permit.

"A thick vapor came up from the southwest and obscured the stars, and when I heard the distant murmurs of the falls of the Occoquan the heavens were overcast, and the night was intensely dark. As I approached the village I perceived that I was upon the margin of the waters lying deep below, for there came up the reflected lights from a few dwellings upon the opposite shore. I had more confidence in my horse's sight than in my own, and allowed him to make his way as he pleased along the invisible road to the bridge; how near to the precipice I knew not, until the next morning when I retraced my wagon-tracks in one place, within a few feet of the brow of a cliff scores of feet above the deep waters.

"Occoquan is a small manufacturing village in Prince William County, near the mouth of the creek of that name, and at the head of navigation up from the Potomac. After Lord Dunmore, the last Royal Governor of Virginia, with his motley force of whites and Negroes, was driven from Gwyn's Island in July, 1776, he sailed up the Potomac and with petty spite laid waste several fine plantations upon its banks. He proceeded as far as the mills at Occoquan Falls, where the village now is, and destroyed them. He was repulsed and driven on board his ships by a few of the Prince William County militia, and then descended the River. It is supposed that Dunmore intended to capture Lady Washington and destroy the estate at Mount Vernon. A heavy storm and the Prince William militia frustrated his design.

"To me, the remembrance of a night at Occoquan is the most unpleasant reminiscence of my journey. There was but one tavern in the place. It was kept by a kind-hearted woman who seemed desirous of contributing to my comfort, but her *bar-room*, where strong liquors appeared to be dealt out with an unsparing hand, was the source of all my discomfort. There I could hear the ribald voices of loungers growing more vociferous as the evening wore away. It was midnight before the revelry ceased, and then two or three Negroes with wretched voices, accompanied by a more wretched fiddle, commenced a serenade in the street. It was two hours past midnight before I slept, and when I awoke in the morning the dram-drinkers were there again, guzzling and talking profanely.

"Greatly annoyed, I determined to leave the place and contrary to my custom travel on towards Fredericksburg, rather than spend the Sabbath there. Informed that the roads between Occoquan and Fredericksburg were worse than those I had traversed the day before, I concluded to return to Alexandria and go down the Potomac to Aquia Creek on Monday."

Lord Dunmore was the arrogant, unpopular Royal Governor who resided in the Palace at Williamsburg from 1772 until June, '75, when he fled with his numerous family on board a British man-o'-war in the York River. He was "deficient in sound judgment and that common sense which is so essential in public life," says Lossing, "and possessed of an irritable temper and vindictive spirit. In manners and feelings he was the reverse of Botetourt [his predecessor] and before he was fairly seated in the official chair he had quarreled with some of the leading men of the colony."

Washington was one of those Virginians who maintained correct social relations with Dunmore as long as possible, dining at the Palace in powder and uniform even after the Governor's violent dismissal of the Williamsburg Assembly in 1774. But in December, '75, he wrote with rare severity from the camp at Cambridge: "I do not think that forcing his lordship on shipboard is sufficient. Nothing less than depriving him of life or liberty will secure peace to Virginia, as motives of resentment actuate his conduct to a degree equal to the total destruction of that colony." Dunmore's behavior in the coastal and river raids which followed justified this opinion.

On his return journey to Alexandria, Lossing again paused at Pohick Church, which he found in sad disrepair, with swallows nesting under the sounding-board and perching on the pulpit. Of Parson Weems, whom it has become the fashion to disparage as an historian, he says: "He was possessed of considerable talent, but was better adapted for a 'man of the world' than a clergyman. Wit and humor he used freely, and no man could easier be 'all things to all men' than Mr. Weems. His eccentricities and singular conduct finally lowered his dignity as a clergyman, and gave rise to many false rumors respecting his character. He was a man of great benevolence, a trait which he exercised to the extent of his means. A large and increasing family compelled him to abandon preaching for a livelihood, and he became a book-agent. In that business he was very successful, selling in one year over three thousand copies of a high-priced Bible. He always preached when invited, during his travels, and in his vocation he was instrumental in doing much good, for he circulated books of the highest moral character. Mr. Weems wrote an attractive *Life* of Washington which became so popular that it passed through some forty editions. He also wrote a *Life* of Francis Marion, which the contemporaries and fellow soldiers of that leader disliked. They charged the author with filling his narrative with fiction, when facts were wanting to give it interest."

And so the smug little legend of the hatchet and the cherry tree rests only on the questionable authority of Parson Weems.

VI

Aquia to Hanover Courthouse

Back at Alexandria, Lossing learned that he could not get on the Potomac steamer with his horse and wagon without retracing his journey to Washington City. He returned there through a thunderstorm, which in December was "a phenomenon so rare that I almost enjoyed the misery," he remarks with the cheerful philosophy of the born wayfarer.

"The steam-boat for Aquia Creek left Washington the following morning at two o'clock. I was upon her deck in time, but a careless servant having left a part of my luggage behind, I was obliged to remain in Washington yet another day. It proved a fine one for travelling, and the very reverse of the next day, when I was again upon the road. The dawn opened with sleet and rain, and a raw east wind. This was sufficiently unpleasant for a traveller; yet a more vexatious circumstance awaited my debarkation at Aquia Creek.

"From the landing to the plantation road leading to the Fredericksburg pike, almost two miles, there was no wagon-track, the rail-way being the only highway. I mounted my wagon upon a handcar, employed two stout Negroes as locomotives, and leading my horse along the rough-ribbed iron way, finally reached a plantation lane on the edge of a swamp. Where the rail-way traverses a broad marsh deep ditches cross it transversely. My horse, in attempting to leap one of these, fell between the iron bars, with a hinder leg over one of them, which prevented the use of his limbs in efforts to leap from the ditch. I momentarily expected to hear the thighbone snap, for almost the entire weight of his body rested on it.

"The salvation of the animal depended upon getting that leg free. I had no aid, for the Negroes had neither will nor judgment to assist. At the risk of being made a foot-ball, I placed my shoulder in the hollow of the hoof, and with strength increased by solicitude, I succeeded in pushing the limb over the rail, and the docile animal, who seemed to feel the necessity of being passive, stood erect in his prison of iron and soft earth.

"Within a rectangle of a few feet, and a bank, shoulder-high, he was still confined. He made several efforts to spring out, but his knees would strike the margin. At length, summoning all his energies, and appearing to shrink into smaller compass, he raised his fore-feet upon the bank, gave a spring, and to my great joy he stood safe and unhurt, though trembling in every limb, upon the road. With a light and thankful heart I travelled the sinuous pathway, through gates and bars, for five or six miles, to the high road, the storm increasing.

"The distance from Aquia Creek to Fredericksburg is fifteen miles. I crossed the Rappahannock upon a long toll-bridge, and entered Fredericksburg at noon. The city is old in fact, and antique in appearance—interesting chiefly from the fact that Washington passed his youthful days in its vicinity, and that near the city, beneath an unfinished monument, repose the remains of his beloved mother.

"The place of Washington's birth was about half a mile from the junction of Pope's Creek with the Potomac, in Westmoreland County, upon the Wakefield estate, now owned by John E. Wilson, Esq. The house in which he was born was destroyed before the Revolution. Upon its site, his foster-[grand] son, George Washington Parke Custis, placed a memorial stone, on which is the simple inscription: HERE, THE 11TH OF FEBRUARY (O.S.) 1732, GEORGE WASHINGTON WAS BORN.

"It was a beautiful June day in 1815 when Mr. Custis and three other gentlemen sailed from Alexandria in his own little vessel, with the memorial stone wrapped in an American flag, and landing at a convenient place, bore it to the destined spot. They gathered a few bricks from the ruins of one of the ancient chimneys and constructed a rude pedestal on which they laid the stone in a recumbent position. With a few words Mr. Custis commended this *first monument* to the memory of Washington to the care of the American people and the citizens of Westmoreland in particular.

"When I visited the spot (thirty-years later) it was a scene of desolation. There was a solitary chimney standing like a guardian of the place. The memorial stone was broken and almost concealed by tangled vines, briers, and rank weeds, and all around the hallowed spot were wild shrubs, the remains of some fig-trees, with here and there a stunted cedar sapling. The vault of the Washington family, at Bridge's Creek nearly a mile distant, was in an open field and so dilapidated that some of the remains were exposed to view, and near by were broken slabs with the names of some of the Washingtons inscribed upon them, which had been set up as mementoes of affection and respect. The vault could be distinguished only by the top of a brick arch, just rising above the ground. The old Pope's Creek Church in which the first three children of Mary Washington had been baptized had long since fallen into ruin.

"On the northwest corner of Charles and Lewis Streets in Fredericksburg is the house where the mother of Washington resided during the latter years of her life, and where she died. There that honored matron, and more honored son, had their last earthly interview, in the spring of 1789, after he was elected President of the United States. Just before his departure for New York to take the oath of office, Washington, actuated by that filial reverence and regard which always distinguished him, hastened to Fredericksburg to visit his mother, then fourscore and five years old. Their interview was deeply affecting."

Lossing's sentimentalities are understandable, but the evidence is that Washington's mother was always a bit of a tartar, and while his exquisite courtesy prevailed in public there were times when he was capable of putting his foot down. At Washington City during Lossing's visit to Betsey Hamilton she related to him a story which she probably had from her husband, who may have witnessed the incident as one of Washington's officers. On his return journey northward to Philadelphia after the surrender at Yorktown, Washington passed through Fredericksburg with an elated retinue including some of the resplendent French, and paused to call on his mother and attend a ball organized by the town in his honor. Remarking that her dancing days were over, the senior Mrs. Washington nevertheless consented to accompany him, made a formal entrance on his arm, and was made much of, especially by the attentive foreigners. "At nine o'clock in the evening," Lossing tells us, "the aged matron approached her son, placed her arm in his, and said, 'Come, George, it is time for us to be at home; late hours are injurious.' With the docility of a child, the General left the company with his mother. 'But,' said Mrs. Hamilton, *he came back again!*'"

There is no record of his mother ever having visited Mount Vernon after his marriage, but surviving letters indicate that she made repeated demands on him for money and for advice as to her small estate and her daily life, for both of which he made the most careful arrangements. She was comfortably established at the beginning of the war in a house a short walk from the home of her daughter Betty, whose husband, Fielding Lewis, was "proprietor of half the town of Fredericksburg" and certainly was able to see that she lacked for nothing. But the elder Mrs. Washington apparently had some sort of obsession about poverty and continued to complain and to borrow from neighbors until Washington was further distressed and humiliated by a well-meant proposal in the Virginia Assembly to grant her a pension, which with firm courtesy he squashed.

A letter to her, written from Mount Vernon in 1787, before his election to the Presidency, is almost embarrassing in its frankness and apologetic tone, and reveals the low state of his personal finances owing to his absence at the war and his determination "to shut my hand against every pecuniary recompense" for the years he had spent leading the army to victory. "In consideration of your communication to George [Augustine] Washington of your lack of money," he writes, "I take the [first safe] conveyance to send you 15 guineas, which believe me is all I have, and which indeed ought to have been paid many days ago to another.... I have now demands upon me for more than £500, three hundred and forty of which is due for the tax of 1786; and I know not where or when I shall receive one shilling with which to pay it. In the last two years I made no crops. In the first I was obliged to buy corn, and this year have none to sell, and my wheat is so bad, I cannot neither eat it myself nor sell it to others, and tobacco I make none. Those who owe me money cannot or will not pay it without suits, and to sue is to do nothing, whilst my expenses, not from any extravagance or an inclination on my part to live splendidly, but for the absolute support of my family and the visitors who are constantly here, are exceedingly high; higher indeed than I can support without selling part of my estate, which I am disposed to do, rather than run in debt, or continue to be so; but this I cannot do, without taking much less than the lands I have offered for sale are worth. This is really and truly my situation...."

Further along in the letter, he again puts his foot down, though the worry still shows through.

"... My sincere and pressing advice to you is, to break up housekeeping, hire out all the rest of your servants except a man and a maid, and live with one of your children.... On this subject I have been full with my brother John, and it was determined that he should endeavor to get you to live with him. He, alas, is no more, and three only of us remain. My house is at your service, and I would press you most sincerely and most devoutly to accept it, but I am sure, and candor requires me to say, it will never answer your purposes in any shape whatsoever. For in truth it may be compared to a well resorted tavern, as scarcely any strangers who are going from north to south, or from south to north, do not spend a day or two at it. This would, were you to be an inhabitant of it, oblige you to do one of 3 things: 1st, to be always dressing to appear in company; 2d, to come into the room in dishabille, or 3d, to be as it were a prisoner in your own chamber. The first you'd not like; ... the second, I should not like.... and the 3d, would not be pleasing to either of us...."

Obviously her daughter Betty's home at nearby Kenmore was the solution, and apparently she was never satisfied to accept it.

As he was assured that nothing of interest remained of the old Washington farm, Lossing contented himself with a distant view of its rolling acres on his way out of Fredericksburg, having paused in a sleet storm to sketch the grave of Washington's mother, with "the half-finished and neglected monument which was erected over it a few years ago. It stands near a ledge of rocks," he says, "where she often resorted in fine weather for private meditation and devotion. The monument is of white marble, and even in its unfinished state has an imposing appearance. The corner-stone was laid by Andrew Jackson, then President of the United States, in 1833, in the presence of a great concourse of people. Almost twenty years have passed away since then, and yet the monument is unfinished."

The house of Wakefield where he was born became the residence of Washington's older half-brother Augustine, and seems to have burned down when Augustine's son William Augustine [not William the soldier] was having a Christmas house-party there. It has been handsomely reconstructed, with gardens and furnishings, by a memorial association, with the assistance of John D. Rockefeller, Jr., as a part of a national park and picnic ground, completed in 1931. And since Lossing's visit to the area, Kenmore, the home of Washington's sister, Mrs. Fielding Lewis, is also shown in all its original beauty. Lewis had not the health to take the field with his brother-in-law, but expended his strength at home to a fatal degree in the effort to provide arms and ammunition from his nearby foundry. He died in '81, leaving his wife and family in such straitened circumstances that she could not afford to go on living in the home he had built for her in their early days together.

The monument of Washington's mother was still incomplete and derelict at the time of the War Between the States, when it suffered considerable damage by gunfire as the town changed hands seven times during the conflict. In 1894 it was replaced by a granite obelisk dedicated by Grover Cleveland.

Lossing left Fredericksburg early in the afternoon, with the intention of lodging at Bowling Green, twenty-two miles away. "The post road is one of the finest I have ever travelled," he says, "broad and in good condition. It passes through a gently rolling, fertile country, and apparently well cultivated. When within about twelve miles of my destination, I passed a farm-house from which two men with a span of horses were just departing for Richmond, whither I was making my way. They too intended to lodge at Bowling Green, and offered to pilot me.

"Their fresh horses tried Charley's speed and bottom to the utmost. We crossed the Mattapony River at twilight, over two high bridges. Night came on with a sudden and intense darkness; so dark that I could not see my pilots. At a fork I 'lost my reckonings;' they taking one branch and I the other. Charley neighed and tried to follow them. I was 'wise in my own conceit' and reined him into the other fork. I rode on for nearly an hour without passing a habitation, and entirely unconscious of the nature or direction of the road I was travelling. A heavy mist shrouded the country. At length the rays of a candle came feebly from a window at the roadside. I hailed, and asked for and obtained lodgings for the night. It was the hospitable mansion of Mr. Burke, a planter, some seven miles from Bowling Green. I had wandered four miles from the direct road to that village, but was not far from the nearest highway to Hanover Court House, my next point of destination.

"I resumed my journey at daybreak, leaving Bowling Green on the left; breakfasted at a small tavern after a ride of six miles, and soon overtook my pilots, who in attempting to reach a point beyond Bowling Green the night before had broken an axle while crossing a swamp. We journeyed on together to Hanover Court House, within nine miles of Richmond. The appearance of the country changed materially after crossing the Mattapony. It became more hilly, sandy, and sterile, producing dwarf pines in abundance. We crossed the Pamunkey a little below the confluence of its branches and reached Hanover Court House in time for a late dinner.

"When the [Virginia] House of Burgesses were deliberating upon the subject of removing the Capital from Williamsburg [in 1779] they came within a few votes of deciding upon Hanover instead of Richmond. The village now consists of the ancient courthouse and tavern, one brick house, several Negro huts, and a jail. The latter was in process of reconstruction when I was there, having been burned a few months previously. Here was a flourishing town before Richmond, now containing thirty thousand inhabitants, was an incorporated village. The Pamunkey was then navigable for sloops and schooners; now the channel is filled with sand. Hanover was a place of considerable business. Sixteen hundred hogsheads of tobacco were annually exported from it, and it was regarded as an eligible site for the state capital. Where the populous village once stood I saw traces of a recent corn crop, but not a vestige of former habitations.

"The old tavern where I lodged, and the courthouse, are objects of much interest, from the circumstance that in the former

Patrick Henry was a temporary *bar-tender*, and in the latter he made those first efforts at oratory which burst like meteors from the gloom of his obscurity. He had passed his youthful days in apparent idleness, and lacking business tact and energy, he failed to succeed in mercantile pursuits, in which he was engaged. He became bankrupt, and no one was willing to aid him. He had married at eighteen, and yet in the twenty-fourth year of his age he had done little toward supporting a wife. They lived most of the time with his father-in-law who kept the tavern at Hanover, and when the proprietor was absent young Henry took his place behind the bar.

"As a last resort, he studied law. He applied himself diligently for six weeks, when he obtained a license, but for nearly three years he was briefless, indeed, he hardly knew how to draw a brief correctly. At the age of twenty-seven [in 1763] he was employed in the celebrated *Parson's Cause*; and in Hanover Court House on that occasion his genius was first developed. The case was a controversy between the clergy and the Legislature of the State, relating to the stipend claimed by the former. A decision of the court in favor of the clergy left nothing undetermined but the amount of damages in the cause which was pending. Young Henry took part against the clergy, and in his plea his wonderful oratory beamed out for the first time, in great splendor....

"The people, who had with difficulty kept their hands off their champion from the moment of closing his harangue, no sooner saw the fate of the cause finally sealed, than they seized him at the bar, and in spite of his own exertions and the continued cry of 'Order!' from the sheriffs and the court, they bore him out of the courthouse and, raising him on their shoulders, carried him about the yard in a kind of electioneering triumph...."

It was all of twelve years later, at the Convention held in the Church at Richmond, which is just ahead of us, that Patrick Henry electrified his fellow members by voicing that immortal rallying cry, "Give me liberty or give me death!"

The Marquis de Chastellux in his account of his travels in

America at the end of the Revolution mentioned the tavern at Hanover as a "tolerably handsome inn, with a very large saloon and a covered portico, and destined to receive the company who assemble every three months at the courthouse, either on private or public affairs. Mr. Tilghman, our landlord, though he lamented his misfortune in having lodged and boarded Cornwallis and his retinue, without his lordship having made the least recompense, could not help laughing at the fright which the unexpected arrival of Tarleton's cavalry spread among a considerable number of gentlemen who came to hear the news and were assembled in the courthouse. A Negro on horseback came full gallop to let them know that Tarleton was not above three miles off. The resolution of retreating was soon taken; but the alarm was so sudden and the confusion so great that everyone mounted the first horse he could find, so that few of these curious gentlemen returned upon their own horses."

Banastre Tarleton, whom we shall meet again in the Carolinas, was one of the real villains of the Revolution. He commanded a mixed troop of prize cut-throats, British regulars augmented by the worst type of Tory volunteer, mounted on horses commandeered in the American countryside, for their own cavalry horses had mostly perished during the voyage southward. The conditions under which fine horses were transported by the army, even as late as the Crimean War, are unthinkable, a cruel and needless waste. The distinctive green uniforms of Tarleton's troop, and their lawless behavior, spread terror through any district in which they operated, and "Tarleton's quarter" stood for wholesale butchery of a helpless enemy.

Lossing slept in the large saloon mentioned by de Chastellux and under the shelter of the portico sketched the courthouse, which was of imported brick with an arcade in front, erected in 1740. It is still there today, and in the courtroom there is a portrait of Patrick Henry. The tavern too remains, somewhat enlarged, with a long veranda.

Rain was still falling when Lossing started for Richmond after an early breakfast. "The roads through this desolate region are wretched," he says, "abounding in those causeways of logs known as *corduroy roads*. Within ten miles of Richmond the scenery becomes diversified, and the vicinage of a large town is denoted by the numerous vehicles upon the broad road, consisting chiefly of uncouth market-wagons drawn by mules, frequently six or eight in a team, as pictured in the sketch below. The Negro driver is usually seated upon one of the wheel mules, and without guiding lines conducts them by the vocal direction of *haw* and *gee*. To the eye of a Northern man looking upon these caravans for the first time, they appear quite picturesque.

"I reached Richmond at meridian [December 14, 1848] where I tarried with esteemed friends for several days."

VII

Richmond to Jamestown

LOSSING comes into the Southern campaign backwards in time, as he arrived at Richmond, Jamestown, and Yorktown, where the 1781 fighting occurred, before he reached the Carolinas, where in 1780 an American army from the North first encountered Cornwallis's victorious army coming up from Charleston after the American surrender there. It is difficult to compress into a few lines two years of mortal combat in the field, but there follows a stripped-down outline of events in sequence, which will be enlarged upon daily as we follow the dearborn wagon southward.

In the summer of 1776, while Washington was still in New York with the disastrous Jersey retreat still to come, the British had made their first attempt to take Charleston, which was the most important port south of Philadelphia. Admiral Sir Peter Parker's fleet, bearing a land force to augment a force commanded by General Clinton which had sailed from Boston, was beaten off in an epic stand by the Americans in the island forts around Charleston harbor, with Marion, Moultrie, and Charles Lee taking part in the defence. Clinton returned to New York, where with Howe and Cornwallis he fought the campaign which, in spite of Washington's victory at Trenton, ended in the capture of Philadelphia, in September, '77, and while those battles were being fought in the North Charleston was left alone.

But the British inability to cope with Washington sufficiently to end the war led to a second attempt on the South by Clinton after he evacuated Philadelphia in the summer of '78 and disengaged his punished forces from the battle of Monmouth, on his way back to New York.

Clinton was a soldier, first and last, hard, aggressive, without Howe's social stature or Cornwallis's aristocratic charm. Short and stout, with a beaky nose and a blunt manner, Clinton did not get along with people. He had objected to practically every move Howe made, and after the war he conducted a bitter controversy with Cornwallis in print. Howe had sent him off to Charleston from Boston in 1776, but he failed there and returned in time to join the New York campaign. Howe then sent him to take Newport, as a useful sea base, which was accomplished, and Clinton was back in New York in time to protest the Philadelphia venture, and was left behind as a sort of garrison officer while Howe and Cornwallis took possession of the capital. When Howe sailed for England in June, '78, Clinton became Commander-in-chief, and in December he dispatched Sir Archibald Campbell by sea to take Savannah, as the first move in a plan to come at Charleston again, from both sides, overland from Georgia as well as from the sea.

Campbell was successful at Savannah early in '79, defeating a North Carolina general named Robert Howe, and General Lincoln of the Continental Army was appointed to the Southern command over Howe, who had escaped capture when Savannah fell. After heavy skirmishing in Georgia, which was finally lost to the British, Lincoln sat down in Charleston to wait out the hot weather and collect an army and the wherewithal to run it. There was more unproductive fighting in Georgia in the autumn, and in February, 1780, Clinton himself again arrived off Charleston, with a fleet commanded by Admiral Arbuthnot, which carried an army including Tarleton's Dragoons, and Cornwallis as second in command. This time they cut off Charleston at the Neck and laid siege, and on the 12th of May Lincoln surrendered after a gallant but hopeless stand of more than a month.

Confident that he had at last delivered a knockout blow to the American cause, Clinton returned to New York in June, leaving Cornwallis to establish and consolidate the British position in the

South. But the Carolinas had only begun to fight. It was now that Marion and Sumter, and the Hugers, the Horrys, the Pinckneys and the Hamptons were heard from. And some of the most spectacular actions of the war took place during the long campaign between Cornwallis and the second army Congress dispatched southward, which was led first by DeKalb and Gates, and was later joined by Greene, Steuben, Lafayette, and Wayne.

As early as April, 1780, DeKalb, who like Steuben was a professional European soldier fighting in the American army, had started South with a small force to join Lincoln at Charleston. Before he had gone beyond Virginia, Charleston fell to the British, and Lincoln was taken prisoner. General Gates was then sent after DeKalb, outranking him, and together they lost a desperately fought battle at Camden in South Carolina on August 16th. DeKalb was killed in action, and Gates hastily left the scene before the battle was over. He was replaced by General Greene, who took over the Southern command in December, 1780.

Greene wintered at Cheraw, on the border between North and South Carolina, recouping his army after the march and co-operating with Marion and Sumter, who were carrying on a constant guerrilla warfare against the British outposts. In the spring of '81 a long running fight began between Greene, Morgan, and the partisans on one side, and Cornwallis, Rawdon, and Leslie on the other. It ranged from the up-country fort of 96 in South Carolina to the Dan River in Virginia, with an American victory at the Cowpens and a sort of draw at Guilford Courthouse, where both sides retired from the field. At Eutaw Springs in September, '81, Greene fought a battle with General Alexander Stewart, and both sides claimed the victory, though the British held the field, briefly.

Cornwallis was by then at Yorktown, having marched all the way from Wilmington in North Carolina to the James River to join General Phillips and Benedict Arnold there in May. All that summer of '81, it had been Virginia's turn to witness the same kind of cat-and-mouse campaign which Greene and Cornwallis had waged in the Carolinas. This time Lafayette, who had come South with a detachment of Washington's army in pursuit of Arnold, was the opponent, and this time Cornwallis was caught in the mouse-trap. His army laid down its arms at Yorktown in October, 1781, after a siege by the combined forces of Washington, Lafayette, and the French General Rochambeau.

To end this exceedingly dull recital of bare facts devised to provide the guide-posts of the rest of Lossing's journey, it may be as well to table the more important dates which lie ahead of him, but in the order in which they occurred historically:

> First British attack on Charleston failed, June, 1776
> Savannah taken by the British, January, 1779
> Lincoln surrendered Charleston, May, 1780
> Gates and DeKalb defeated at Camden, August, 1780
> Ferguson defeated at King's Mountain, October, 1780
> Arnold arrived in James River, January, 1781
> Morgan defeated Tarleton at the Cowpens, January, 1781
> Greene and Cornwallis at Guilford Courthouse, March, 1781
> Greene and Stewart at Eutaw Springs, September, 1781
> Cornwallis surrendered at Yorktown, October, 1781

The main Revolutionary interest at Richmond is St. John's Church, the simple white-painted frame building where at the Virginia Convention in March, '75, Patrick Henry demanded liberty or death. This meeting fell between the adjournment of the first Continental Congress at Philadelphia and the shooting at Lexington and Concord. They met at Richmond because Governor Dunmore had interfered with them at Williamsburg, and they were in the church because it was the largest room Richmond had to offer. There were a hundred and twenty delegates crowded into the high-backed pews—the cream of Virginia, assembled there on a spring morning, one of their duties being to name the delegates for the Second Continental Congress at Philadelphia, which more than a year later would approve the Declaration of Independence. Jefferson was at Richmond that day, almost as silent as the tall, attentive man from Mount Vernon. Jefferson wrote, instead of speaking. Patrick Henry was there, and though he spoke like an angel, he scarcely wrote at all Washington did neither. He watched and listened.

They were droning on about another address to the King. Then there was an amendment or resolution by Patrick Henry, about the need of militia *now*—"Resolved, therefore, that this colony be put into a posture of defence...." It was opposed, and defended. Voices sharpened, spines stiffened. Then Patrick Henry rose—tall, lean, stooping, but better dressed than usual, with his wig on straight. His voice was quiet, almost confidential, as he began: "No man, Mr. President, thinks more highly than I do of the patriotism, as well as the abilities of the very honorable gentlemen who have just addressed the House," he announced in silky tones, and then proceeded to demolish the gentlemen and all their utterances in a speech of such fervor and fire that whole sentences burned themselves into the memories of his hearers for the remainder of their lifetimes.

He never wrote out his speeches, they flowed from him spontaneously, without even notes. No one took down what he said that day, except possibly in hurried jottings interrupted by surprise and excitement, and some later attempts to recapture a few of the incandescent phrases. And yet there is a text, which has been widely quoted. Assuming that this is largely the work of his worshipful biographer Wirt, who later interviewed several of the men who had been present, there isn't much doubt that even after many years some of it was genuinely unforgettable.

Henry would have been a great actor. He dramatized slavery and doom and shackles as he spoke. His ungraceful figure straightened, the cords of his thin neck showed taut, his eyes blazed, his magnificent voice rolled and thundered. His audience was stunned as much by his theatrical delivery as by his heretical words. He was transfigured and ablaze. And whoever assembled the speech as it has come down to us, Patrick Henry has no cause to be ashamed of it, and it is just as good nowadays as it was a hundred and eighty-four years ago.

"... They tell us, Sir, that we are weak—unable to cope with so formidable an adversary. But when shall we be stronger? Will it be the next week, or the next year? Will it be when we are totally disarmed, and when a British guard shall be stationed in every house? Shall we gather strength by irresolution and inaction? Shall we acquire the means of effectual resistance by lying supinely on our backs, and hugging the delusive phantom of Hope, until our enemies shall have bound us hand and foot? ...

"... Gentlemen may cry Peace, but there is no peace! The war has actually begun. The next gale that sweeps from the north will bring to our ears the clash of resounding arms. Our brethren are already in the field. Why stand we here idle? Is life so dear, or peace so sweet, as to be purchased at the price of chains and slavery? Forbid it, Almighty God! I know not what course others may take, but as for me, *give me liberty, or give me death!*"

When he finished there was silence, while he stood spent, burnt out. Then he looked round at them, with a kind of radiance, and resumed his seat. Even then there was no applause.

"After the trance of the moment," says the faithful Wirt, "several members started from their seats. The cry *To arms!* seemed to quiver on every lip, and gleam from every eye. Richard Henry Lee arose and supported Mr. Henry with his usual spirit and eloquence, but his melody was lost amid the agitation of that ocean which the master spirit of the storm had lifted on high. That supernatural voice still sounded in their ears, and shivered along their arteries. They heard, in every pause, the cry of Liberty or Death! They became impatient of speech—their souls were on fire for action."

Well, anyway, they passed the resolutions by a large majority. They put both Henry and Washington on the committee for raising and training the necessary men, and named them both to represent Virginia again at the Second Continental Congress in Philadelphia.

Lossing visited and sketched Old St. John's Church at Richmond. "The burial ground which surrounded it is embowered in trees and shrubbery," he says, "and from its southern slope there is a noble view of the city and surrounding country. The main portion of the building is the same as it was in the Revolution, the tower alone being modern."

The little white church still stands in its little green lawn in the middle of Richmond—its beams still echoing, no doubt, to the "supernatural voice" whose spell was so soon to burn itself out and leave Patrick Henry a querulous, aging invalid, while most of his colleagues went on and on—into the Continental Congresses, into the first and second administrations. After serving three terms as governor, Patrick Henry was somehow left behind, the earthbound stick of the rocket, except for a brief flare-up in 1788, in wrong-headed opposition to the new Constitution.

Richmond's only peril during the Revolution was a raid led by Benedict Arnold in January of '81 and another side-swipe by Tarleton in May when they nearly caught Thomas Jefferson at home at Monticello. After Arnold's plot to betray West Point to the British failed in the previous autumn, he had escaped to a British warship while his accomplice, Major André, was caught and hanged. Arnold's reward for the attempt was something like $50,000 and the rank of brigadier-general in the British army—and the open contempt of his associates in that army.

They gave him a small force which included Simcoe's Rangers, a well-trained Tory cavalry troop led by a tough commander, and sent him South by water to rally the Tories in Virginia and destroy the military stores which Steuben was collecting at Richmond and Petersburg for Greene, who was then at Cheraw recouping the army Gates had deserted at Camden. After a stormy passage from Sandy Hook, Arnold had arrived in the James River on January 3d, '81, and anchored near Jamestown.

Since a British sea raid on Norfolk in May, '79, the capital of Virginia had been moved to Richmond from Williamsburg, which was considered too exposed. There was a general alarm on Williamsburg Neck when Arnold appeared in the River, but the old town was not molested. He passed it by and sailed on up the James to Westover plantation about twenty-five miles below Richmond, where he disembarked his force and marched unopposed towards the new capital, with panic running before him.

"Arnold, advised of the weakness of the place, had sent Colonel Simcoe with the Rangers to drive the militia from their positions upon Richmond Hill, near St. John's Church, on the South side of the Shockoe Creek," Lossing explains. "Arnold marched up the hill in small detachments, when the militia, after firing a few shots, fled to the woods in the rear. Along the base of the hill, leading into the portion of the town lying in the valley, Simcoe sent his cavalry to surprise the militia there. The latter escaped across the creek to Shockoe Hill, followed by the whole body of Rangers, and made a stand near the site of the Capitol. A large number of spectators were also there, and as the Rangers ascended the hill they fled to the country, hotly pursued by the enemy's cavalry.

"After taking possession of Richmond, Arnold ordered Simcoe to proceed to Westham and destroy the cannon-foundry and the magazine there. The trunnions of most of the cannon were broken off; the powder in the magazine which they could not carry away was thrown into the river, and before night, the foundry was a desolation. The Rangers returned to Richmond and the whole hostile force quartered in the town during the night. Arnold and Simcoe made their quarters at the Old City Tavern, yet standing on Main Street, but partly in ruins when I visited Richmond. Many houses were entered and plundered by the invaders. They obtained a considerable quantity of rum, and a large portion of them spent the night in drunken revelry.

"The public records had been saved through the vigilance of Jefferson; and Arnold, finding no more plunder or objects on which to pour out his wrath—the ire of a vindictive heart toward those whom he had foully wronged—withdrew to Westover, and reembarked to commit other depredations upon the river shores and the coasts of the Virginia bays. On the same day Jefferson returned to Richmond, and quiet was restored. . . .

"Before leaving Richmond I endeavored to ascertain the exact location of Westover, the famous estate of Colonel Byrd, and memorable as the landing place of Arnold's troops. I could not learn its relative position in distance from the direct road to Charles City Courthouse, the goal of my next day's journey, and I thought I should pass it by unvisited. After leaving Richmond a few miles, the hilly country disappeared, and there spread out a level or gently rolling region, bearing extensive pine forests, which inclose quite large plantations. I dined in my wagon upon cold turkey and biscuit, furnished by my kind friend Mrs. G. of Richmond, after giving Charley a lunch of meal and water, by the side of a small stream on the way.

"The day was very warm [December 18]—too warm to ride comfortably with an overcoat. Not suspecting that I might diverge into a wrong road by one of the numerous forks which characterize the highway, I allowed Charley to jog on leisurely, and with a loose rein, while I gave myself up to contemplation, which was occasionally interrupted by a passing regret that I was obliged to forego the pleasure of visiting Westover.

"Suddenly, on emerging from a pine forest into an open cultivated region, the bright waters of a broad river, dotted with occasional sail, were before me. On the bank of the river was a spacious brick mansion, approached from the country by a broad lane in which a large number of servants, men and women, were engaged in shucking or husking corn. The gleaming water was the James River, the mansion was that of John A. Seldon, Esq., once the residence of Colonel Byrd. I was at Westover, scarcely conscious how I had reached it; for I supposed myself to be upon the direct road to Charles City Courthouse, and probably a dozen miles from the spot I desired to see. I was between two and three miles from the main road, led thither by a deceptive byway, and was obliged to retrace the journey, after passing half an hour in viewing the location.

"The family of the proprietor was absent, and not a white person was upon the plantation. It must have been a delightful place in summer, and when it was occupied by the accomplished family of the widow of Colonel Byrd, doubtless justified the Marquis de Chastellux in giving his glowing account of the beauty of its location and the charms of society there. Mrs. Byrd was a cousin of Benedict Arnold, and this relationship, and the fact that Westover was made the place of landing for the British troops three times under Arnold and Cornwallis, so excited the suspicions of the vigilant Whigs that the government once took possession of her papers. She was wrongfully suspected, and the landings of the enemy were great misfortunes to her in various ways.

"I made a sketch of the fine old mansion before leaving Westover, but lost it that very evening."

The relationship of Arnold to Mrs. Byrd was rather far-fetched, as she was cousin to his second wife, Peggy Shippen of Philadelphia, whom he married during the time he reigned there as commandant after the British evacuation in '78. Still limping from his Saratoga wound, and very much a hero from that victory, Arnold had almost outdone the departed British gallants in extravagant display and entertainment. He at once took possession of Howe's recently vacated headquarters in the handsome Penn House on Market Street—which was later to serve Washington as a presidential mansion—put his servants in livery, kept a handsome carriage, and got about picturesquely leaning heavily on a cane. His hospitality was lavish and indiscriminating, and he had no objection to ladies of notoriously Tory sympathies if they were pretty enough. He was always in pain, irritable, ambitious, resentful of other men's promotions which he considered passed him by, reckless of his own reputation, which was soon clouded by charges of graft and peculation.

Peggy Shippen had been quite openly in love with Major André during the British occupation, and it was apparently through her acquaintance with him that the fatal connection between him and Arnold was made, and the West Point plot was hatched. She was a young beauty of eighteen, spoilt and desirable, daughter of a well-to-do Philadelphia lawyer of Tory sentiments. Arnold was a swaggering adventurer twice her age, several years a widower, with three unruly sons who were being brought up in his household by his devoted sister. But Peggy married him, while he still required the support of a soldier's arm in order to stand upright during the ceremony, and without much doubt she influenced him in the course of action which ruined him, and they both paid very dearly in the end.

Mary Willing Byrd, the mistress of Westover in 1781, was a Philadelphia girl, whose grandmother was a Shippen, and after she married William Byrd III as his second wife they divided their time between a mansion in the city and his ancestral home at Westover on the James. Byrd began the war as a Tory, but was so much incensed at Governor Dunmore's behavior that he turned patriot and tried to get a commission in the American army. For some reason it was refused. Overcome by this final humiliation on top of his gambling losses, which had told on the estate, and by his private anxieties, he committed suicide in Philadelphia early in '77, at the age of forty-eight. His wife's subsequent patriotism is still debatable.

The observant Marquis de Chastellux, who was one of Rochambeau's aides, and whom Washington loved next to Lafayette among the French, made his tour of Virginia in the spring of 1782, while Rochambeau's headquarters were still at Williamsburg, where he had remained after the Yorktown surrender. It was at Westover that de Chastellux first encountered humming-birds, and renewed his acquaintance with Mrs. Byrd's two elder daughters, who had passed the previous winter at Williamsburg, "greatly complimented by M. de Rochambeau and the whole [French] army," he records. "I had also received them in the best manner I could, and received the thanks of Mrs. Byrd, with a pressing invitation to come and see her; I found myself, in consequence, quite at home."

He guessed the widow's age as "about two and forty"—he himself was forty-seven—"with an agreeable countenance and great sense. Four of her eight children are daughters, two of whom are near twenty, and they are all amiable and well educated. Her care and activity have in some measure repaired the effects of her husband's dissipation, and her house is still the most celebrated and the most agreeable of the neighborhood.... She takes great care of her Negroes, makes them as happy as their situation will admit, and serves them herself as a doctor in time of sickness. She has even made some interesting discoveries on the disorders incident to them, and discovered a very salutary method of treating a sort of putrid fever which carries them off commonly in a few days, and against which the physicians of the country have exerted themselves without success...

"As for the humming-birds," de Chastellux goes on, "I saw them for the first time and was never tired of beholding them. The walls of the garden and the house were covered with honeysuckles, which afforded an ample harvest for these charming little animals. I saw them perpetually flying over the flowers, on which they feed without ever alighting, for it is by supporting themselves on their wings that they insinuate their beaks into the calix of the flowers.

Sometimes they perch, but it is only for a moment; it is then only that one has an opportunity of admiring the beauty of their plumage, especially when opposite to the sun, and when in moving their heads they display the brilliant enamel of their red necks, which almost rival the splendor of the ruby or the diamond. It is not true that they are naturally passionate, and that they tear to pieces the flowers in which they find no honey. I have never observed any such circumstances myself, either at Westover or since at Williamsburg; and the inhabitants of the country assured me that they had never made any such observation. These birds appear only with the flowers, with which likewise they disappear, and no person can tell what becomes of them. Some are of the opinion that they hide themselves and remain torpid the remainder of the year. In fact, it is difficult to conceive how their wings, which are so slight and slender as to be imperceptible if not in motion, could possibly resist the winds, and transport them to distant climates. They are not intractable, for I have seen one of them which was taken a few days before in no wise frightened at the persons who looked at it, but flew about the room as in a garden, and sucked the flowers which they presented to it; but it did not live above a week. These birds are so fond of motion that it is impossible for them to live without the most unrestrained liberty. It is difficult even to catch them, unless they happen, as was the case I am speaking of, to fly into the chamber or be driven there by the wind."

The inquisitive French Marquis would have been entranced to learn that the ruby-throated humming-bird is capable of migrating as far as Mexico and the West Indies. Westover is still one of the most beautiful of the James River mansions, and remains now very much as he saw it, through almost continuous occupation and care. For a fee, one can enter the grounds and cross the broad lawn which runs to the river bank under great tulip trees, to the garden, where William Byrd II is buried under an impressive epitaph composed by himself.

Lossing found his way from Westover back to the highway, which ran through beautiful level country, "garnished with fertile plantations and handsome mansions" to Charles City Courthouse six miles away. "It was just at sunset," he says, "and there I passed the night with Mr. Christian, who was the clerk of the county, the jailer, and inn-keeper. His house of entertainment, the old courthouse and jail, and a few outhouses and servants' quarters, compose the village. The county is the smallest in Virginia, yet bears the honor of having given birth to two presidents of the United States [William Henry Harrison and John Tyler] and of being the place of marriage of a third [Thomas Jefferson].

"Mr. Christian allowed me to pass the evening searching among the dusty records in the old courthouse. I found nothing there relating to Revolutionary events; but in a bundle of papers wrapped up and laid away probably for more than half a century, I discovered the marriage licence-bond of Thomas Jefferson, in his own handwriting...

"Mr. Jefferson was married to Martha Skelton of Charles City County, in January, 1772. She was the widow of Bathurst Skelton, and daughter of John Wayles, an eminent lawyer of Virginia. She brought her second husband a considerable fortune, and was only twenty-three years of age when she was married to Mr. Jefferson. Through the stormy period of the Revolution she shared his joys and sorrows, and died in 1782, leaving two surviving daughters."

Jefferson's widowed Martha had a very different idea of "sharing" than Washington's indomitable lady, whose unfailing devotion took her back to his side at each winter headquarters for eight comfortless years of war, and kept her there through two strenuous terms of the presidency. Washington's lofty destiny would have been even bleaker and lonelier than it was, if he had not had a warm-hearted wife with a genius for home-making wherever his duty lay.

But Martha Jefferson seldom left the conveniences of Monticello, being always in delicate health, and although his daughter wrote that Jefferson was prostrate with grief at the death of his wife, he might have had no career or usefulness beyond the Virginia Legislature if she had lived. He had already refused two appointments because of a promise to her that he would accept no public office which involved their separation, and she committed the ultimate selfishness of exacting from him on her deathbed a promise that he would never marry again. He was then free to perform the great service to his country which began with his appointment as Minister to France in 1784. In Paris there occurred that wistful romance with the beautiful Maria Cosway, wife of the elderly foppish miniature painter who was said to resemble a monkey in the face.

Though she accompanied her husband to England more than once while Jefferson was at Paris, he and Maria corresponded by letters privately conveyed by the young painter John Trumbull, who was Jefferson's protégé and friend. "Kneel to Mrs. Cosway for me, and lay my soul in her lap," he wrote to Trumbull during one of Maria's absences in England. She was an accomplished musician and had a pretty talent of her own for painting, jealously suppressed by her husband whom she always despised. But she remained with him, at least nominally his wife, until his death in 1821. As the difference between her age and Jefferson's was no less than between hers and Cosway's, he was in his seventies by the time she was a widow. Maria ended her days in nunlike seclusion in Italy, where she conducted a girls' school.

"It was another glorious morning when I left Charles City Courthouse," Lossing relates. "Traversing a rough road for nearly four miles, I crossed a rapid stream at a mill, and ascending to a plain about half a mile beyond, I reined up at the entrance gate to Sherwood Forest, the estate of ex-President Tyler. His mansion is very spacious, and stands upon the brow of a gentle slope, half a mile back from the highway. It is sheltered in the rear by a thick forest of oaks, pines, and chestnuts, while from the front the eye overlooks almost the whole of his plantation of fourteen hundred acres, with occasional glimpses of the James River.

"The distinguished proprietor was at home, and received me with that courteous hospitality so common in the South, which makes the traveller feel at ease, as if at the house of a friend. Mr.

Tyler is tall and slender in person, his locks are long, thin, and slightly grizzled, and he was dressed in the plain garb of a Virginia planter."

(As Sherwood Forest was built by President Tyler after he left the White House with his young second wife, it had no Revolutionary history.)

"After giving warm expressions of interest in my enterprise, and an invitation to remain longer at Sherwood Forest, the ex-President sketched a map of my route to Jamestown, as a guide among the diverging ways. Time was precious and I passed only an hour at the hospitable mansion, and then departed for the Chickahominy.

"Soon after leaving Sherwood Forest, I entered a low, wet region covered with pines, called the *slashes*. The word is applied to tracts of wet clay soil, covered with pine woods, and always wet. The clay is almost impervious to water, and as evaporation goes on slowly in the shadow of the pines, the ground is seldom dry. Here, where once broad fields were smiling with culture-blessings, and this road, now almost a quagmire, but fifty years ago was one of the finest highways in Virginia, wild deer and turkeys abound, as if the land was a primeval forest.

"It was at meridian when I emerged from the slashes and halted upon the high sand-bank of the Chickahominy, a few miles above its confluence with the James River. Above, all appeared bright and beautiful; below all was gloomy and desolate. Silence reigned where once the busy ferryman had plied his oars from morning until night. No voice was to be heard. No human habitation was to be seen. The broad and turbid river moved sluggishly on without a ripple, and on the beach a scow, half filled with water, told only of desolation.

"There appeared no way for me to cross the stream. If denied that privilege, I must make a circuit of thirty miles' travel to a public crossing above! I looked for the smoke of a dwelling, but saw none. I shouted; there was no response but that of echo. Remembering that, just before reaching the clearing on the Chickahominy River, I saw a road, covered with leaves, diverging towards the James, I returned, reined into it, and followed it with hope. Presently I saw a log hut upon the shore, and heard the voices of men. They were Negroes, busily preparing a canoe for a fishing excursion. I enquired for a ferryman, and was informed that nobody crossed now and that the scow would not float. Two of the men speedily changed their opinion when I offered a bright half dollar to each if they would bail out the craft and pole me across.

"They worked faithfully, and within half an hour I was embarked upon the stream, with my horse and vehicle, in a shell just long enough and broad enough to contain us. To keep Charley quiet, so as to 'trim the boat,' I allowed him to dine upon some oats which I had procured at Charles City Courthouse. The Chickahominy is here about a quarter of a mile wide. The current was quite strong, and so deep that the poles, by which the bateau was impelled, were sometimes too short for use.

"We drifted some distance down the stream, and at one time I anticipated an evening voyage upon the James River, but by the great exertions of the motive power we reached the landing-place in safety, after rather a dangerous voyage of nearly three quarters of an hour. The bateau was again almost half filled with water, and the ferrymen were obliged to empty it before returning. I was too much occupied while crossing with apprehensions of an involuntary bath to reflect upon the perils which Captain John Smith encountered upon this very stream, before the empire of white men had commenced; but when safely seated in my wagon upon the Jamestown side of the river, I looked with intense interest upon the wooded shores of those waters up which that adventurer had paddled. More than sixty miles above the place where I crossed he was captured by Opechancanough, the king of Pamunkee, and carried in triumph to Powhattan, at Werowocomoco, where he was saved from death by the gentle Pocahontas.

"I was now eight miles from old Jamestown, the goal of my day's journey. Hungry and thirsty, I was about entering another dreary region of slashes, five miles in extent, when I saw a log hut on the verge of the woods. I hailed, but no person appeared, except a little child of six years, black as ebony, and having nothing on but its birthday-suit and a tattered shirt. It brought me a draught of cool water in a gourd from a spring near by. Dropping half a dime into the emptied shell, I pursued my way.

"Emerging from the slashes again, I passed through a portion of the celebrated Green Spring plantation, its mansion appearing among the trees on my left, half a mile distant. This was the residence of Sir William Berkeley, one of the early Royal Governors of Virginia, and afterward belonged to Philip Ludwell, one of the King's Council. It is now in possession of two brothers named Ward, formerly of New Jersey, who for many years as skippers upon the James River, bartered for products of this plantation until they were able to purchase it. Green Spring was the theater of an interesting episode in our Revolutionary history, for there the American army, under Lafayette, Wayne, and Steuben, were encamped for a few days in the summer of 1781, while watching the movements and foiling the designs of Cornwallis in Virginia."

The fight at Green Spring took place on a hot July day, during Cornwallis's withdrawal from Williamsburg to Yorktown, which had for him such fatal consequences. By concealing the main body of his troops in the pine woods beside the Williamsburg road, he deceived Lafayette into thinking all but his rear guard had crossed on to Jamestown Island, and Lafayette ventured to attack. At the crucial moment three crack Royal regiments were led out against the American militia, which fell back in disorder on Wayne's Pennsylvania veterans, who were drawn up in the field in front of Mr. Coke's mansion.

"Wayne's presence of mind never forsook him," says Lossing, "and in moments of greatest danger, his judgment seemed the most acute and faithful. He now instantly conceived a bold movement, but one full of peril. He ordered the trumpeters to sound a charge, and with a full-voiced shout his whole force, cavalry, riflemen, and infantry, dashed forward in the face of a terrible storm of lead and iron, and smote the British line with ball, bayonet and cutlass so fiercely that it recoiled in amazement.

"Lafayette, who had personally reconnoitered the British camp from a tongue of land near the present Jamestown Landing, perceived the peril of Wayne and immediately drew up a line of Continentals half a mile in the rear of the scene of conflict, to cover a retreat if Wayne should attempt it. When the latter saw this, and perceived the flanking parties of the enemy halting or retrograding, he sounded a retreat, and in good order his brave band fell back upon Lafayette's line. Never was a desperate maneuver better planned or more successfully executed. Upon that single cast of the die depended the safety of his corps. It was a winning one for the moment, and the night shadows coming on, the advantage gained was made secure.

"Cornwallis was astonished and perplexed by the charge and retreat. The lateness of the hour and the whole movement made him view the maneuver as a lure to draw him into an ambuscade; and instead of pursuing the Republicans, he called in his detachments, crossed over to Jamestown Island during the evening, and three days afterwards crossed the James River with his troops and proceeded by easy marches to Portsmouth. The Americans, under Lafayette, remained in the vicinity of Williamsburg until the arrival of the combined armies, nearly two months afterward, on their way to besiege Cornwallis at Yorktown."

Very early in the exploration of General Wayne's record, the reader is ready to scream if he encounters the "Mad Anthony" thing in quotes once more, and he always does. Seldom has a man been so obliterated by a catch-penny label, and the desire to see behind it compels research, especially as Washington's word for him was "prudent." He was a fine fighting man, it's true, for once the war began he considered that his business. He was also called Dandy Wayne, and always carried a company barber in his immediate suite, and insisted that his men should keep themselves shaved and clean though their clothing might be in tatters. He served from the beginning of the war in the North to long past Yorktown in the tedious Carolina skirmishes which went on until the evacuation of Charleston in December of '82.

By the death of his father Wayne was left at an early age the head of a household of eccentric women at the family estate at Waynesborough outside Philadelphia, and he added to it by marrying a young friend of his sister's in '66. His wartime portrait by Peale shows a dark, handsome, virile man who would not go unnoticed in female society anywhere, but although his wife was continuously jealous of his rumored interest in this woman or that, she was not one of the heroic camp wives who followed the drum to winter headquarters. On a plea of ill health she never once joined him in the field, though he was several times stationed a convenient distance from home. She waited for him to come to her, and then wept about his affairs. While he was at Valley Forge, eight miles from Waynesborough, she went to Maryland for the air. Somehow his mother too became estranged and unfriendly, and one sister was an outright mental case. Except for his two small children, his infrequent visits at home were dreary intervals in the bustle and camaraderie of the army life which suited his temperament very well. But Anthony was sane.

Arriving at Albany early in the war on his way to the Canadian campaign, he cast an appreciative eye on General Schuyler's pretty daughters, including that Betsey who was to marry Alexander Hamilton several years later. "... accomplished, fine sweet girls, and very handsome," he called them, and added with a sigh, "Had I been single, perhaps I might have made some impression...." They made him a cockade for his tricorne hat, and saw him on his way. During Arnold's command in Philadelphia after the British evacuation, Wayne joined in the rather feverish festivities there, when he became the Dandy. ("Mad Anthony" was not coined till '81.) He distrusted Arnold even then, and never called him friend. He was later one of several lonely, impressionable officers who were attracted to Quaker Greene's pretty wife Kitty, and after the General's death soon after the war ended they were for a while neighbors on adjoining estates in Georgia. But when Kitty married again, it was some one else.

At Green Spring a bullet clipped the plume from his hat, but his most troublesome wound came shortly before Yorktown—a discharge of buckshot in the leg from one of his own sentries to whose challenge he somehow failed to respond in time. During the siege he was in the lines, hobbling about with a cane, when he immortalized a joke by grim old Steuben. They both threw themselves into a ditch one day as a cannon ball came over, Wayne landing on top, and Steuben thanked him for covering his general's rear.

Being present at the re-occupation of Charleston by the American army, he lived for a while in the South, with an occasional visit home, and then went to the Ohio country to fight the Indians, where he died at fifty-one. Spectacular, aggressive, vain, and challenging—theatrically brave and reckless—but not a bit mad.

We left Lossing at Jamestown, where Wayne was shot in the hat.

"It was almost sunset when I passed the morass in front of Green Spring, over which the Americans crossed to the attack of Cornwallis at Jamestown Ford. I crossed the plantation of John Coke, Esq., and halted upon the shore of an estuary of the James River, at the cottage of Mr. Bacon, opposite Jamestown Island. It was too late to visit the consecrated spot that evening. I sketched this distant view of the portion of the island whereon the ancient city stood, and then returned to the mansion of Mr. Coke, to pass the night under his roof, where I experienced the true Virginia hospitality.

"This view is from the north side of what was once a marsh, but now a deep bay, four hundred yards wide. On the left is seen the remains of a bridge, destroyed by a gale and high tide a few years ago; and beyond is the James River. Near the point of the island, toward the end of the bridge, are the remains of an ancient church. Mr. Coke resided upon the island when the tempest occurred which destroyed the bridge. The island was submerged, and for three days himself and family were prisoners. It was in winter, and he was obliged to cut the branches of ornamental trees that were close to his house, for fuel.

"I was gravely informed by the man on the beach, while making the sketch, that Pocahontas crossed at that very spot 'in her skiff' when she went to warn the Jamestown settlers of threatened danger. The dear child had no need of a skiff, had such a thing existed in America, for I was told by Mr. Coke that his father-in-law well remembered when a marsh, so narrow and firm that a person might cross it upon a fence rail, was where the deep water at the ruined bridge now is.

"Every year the current of the James River is changing its margins in this region, and within a few years Jamestown Island, made so only by a marsh on the land side, will have a navigable channel around it. Already a large portion of it, whereon the ancient town was erected, has been washed away. I was informed that a cypress tree, now many yards from the shore, stood at the end of a carriage-way to the wharf, sixty yards from the water's edge, only sixteen years ago. The destructive flood is gradually approaching the old church tower, and if the hand of man shall not arrest its sure progress, that too will be swept away, and not a vestige of Jamestown will remain. Virginians, look to it, and let a wall of masonry along the river margin attest your reverence for the most interesting historical relic within your borders! Some remains of the old fort may be seen at low water, several yards from the shore.

"Mr. Coke, my host for the night, was for many years sheriff of the county, is an influential man, and an excellent practical agriculturist. He owns a plantation of nineteen hundred acres, nearly one thousand of which is under cultivation. Unlike too many agriculturists of the South, he is his own general overseer, and his family of seventy persons, only eleven of whom are white, receive his daily personal care. He owns all the soil that is left unsubmerged on which the English built their first town in America. His house has many bullet-marks, made there during the battle at Jamestown Ford, on the 6th of July, 1781; and in the broad level field in front of his mansion the French army was encamped on its way to Yorktown later the same year. Mr. Coke's plantation is truly classic ground, for upon it occurred events connected with those widely separated events, the opening and the closing of the heroic age of America. Over it the lordly Powhattan once walked, and the feet of his gentle daughter pressed its soil when speeding on her mission of mercy to the doomed settlement of Jamestown. Over it the Royal and Republican armies marched, and there fought desperately for victory."

It was not until 1901 that Lossing's warning on the erosion by the river at Jamestown Island was heeded, and a stone sea-wall was constructed to preserve what remained of the site. The stump of the cypress tree he saw still stands in the water, some distance from the shore.

Lossing is not often caught in error, but the house he saw at Green Spring was not the one built by bad old Governor Berkeley, which had thirty bedrooms and gave asylum to Cavalier refugees from England, and which witnessed some hangings after the Bacon Rebellion in 1676. That house passed by the marriage of Berkeley's widow to the Ludwells, and thence by the complicated interrelationships of the Tidewater families to the Stratford Lees. It fell into disrepair during the Revolution when the family was abroad and the armies both made free with it, and around 1790 William Ludwell Lee had it taken down to make room for a new mansion designed and built by Latrobe. This one too has now disappeared except for its foundations, the entrance drive, and the spring, which lie opposite Jamestown Island.

VIII

Jamestown to Williamsburg

I was at Mr. Bacon's cottage on the shore soon after an early breakfast, and before nine o'clock crossed the estuary in a punt and sat within the shadow of the old church tower, which stands like a sentinel watching the city of the dead at its feet. This crumbling pile, surrounded by shrubbery, brambles, and tangled vines; and the old churchyard wall, of English brick, inclosing a few broken monuments half buried in earth or covered with a pall of ivy and long grass, are all the tangible records that remain of the first planting of an English colony in America.

"I sat upon the hollow trunk of a half-reclining old sycamore, and sketched the broken tower. This view is from the old churchyard, looking towards the James River, a glimpse of which may be seen through the arches. The stream is here about three miles wide. Although it was late in December the sun was shining almost as warm as at the close of May. While finishing my sketch I was glad to take shelter from its beams in the shadow of the sycamore. Here, upon this curiously wrought slab, clasped by the roots of the forest *anak*, let us sit a while and ponder the early chronicles of Virginia."

The slab he describes as a blue stone about four inches thick, bearing the date of 1608, the remainder of the inscription so broken and defaced that he could not decipher the name—which must be that of some unlucky settler who died within a few months of the first landing. The roots of the sycamore were so firmly entwined around it that no graveyard vandal could move it, though almost every monument had had a fragment broken from it. Lossing himself carried away a small piece with some letters on it, which he found lying on the grass, "not, however, without a sense of being an accessory after the fact in an act of sacrilege."

Buried in the old churchyard is the spirited Sarah Harrison, who married Dr. James Blair in 1687, two months after signing a written promise to marry a man called Roscow. One is inclined to blame her father, and not Mr. Roscow, for trying to make the engagement binding, in view of his fury at her change of mind. He swore to separate Sarah from Blair, and though he did not succeed during their lifetime an ancient sycamore tree still thrusts up between their tombs, tilting the stones apart and fulfilling her father's curse. There seems to be no valid reason for his objections to Dr. Blair, who was admittedly a contentious man and ran afoul of Royal Governors, but was tireless in his devoted efforts to raise an endowment and found a college, which was William and Mary, chartered in 1693, with Blair as its first president. Anxious as

Sarah was to be his wife, she three times refused the word "obey" in the marriage service, until the parson proceeded without it. She was then seventeen, Dr. Blair was thirty-one.

Another strong-minded woman now at rest at Jamestown was Lady Berkeley, widow of the Governor and heiress to Green Spring, who although she later married Philip Ludwell I, insisted upon retaining her title the rest of her life, and had it engraved on her tombstone.

Nowadays, as there must have been for generations, a little ferry crosses the broad river from a wooden pier at Jamestown, to Scotland Wharf on the other side where there is nothing much, it is true, but the round trip is only a dollar and you see the Virginia shore from approximately where those first sea-weary exiles saw it, when they decided to land there in 1608.

Lossing drove straight on to Williamsburg, arriving at noon, "and proceeded immediately to search out the interesting localities of that ancient and earliest incorporated town in Virginia. They are chiefly upon the main street, a broad avenue pleasantly shaded, and almost as quiet as a rural lane. I first took a stroll upon the spacious green lawn in front of William and Mary College, the oldest literary institution in America except Harvard University. The entrance to the green is flanked by stately live oaks, cheering the visitor in winter with their evergreen foliage. In the center of the lawn stands the mutilated statue of Lord Botetourt, the best beloved of the colonial governors. I did not make a sketch of it because a student at the college promised to hand me one made by his own pencil before I left the place. He neglected to do so, and therefore I can give nothing pictorially of 'the good Governor Botetourt,' the predecessor of Dunmore.

"I next visited the remains of the palace of Lord Dunmore, the last Royal Governor of Virginia. It is situated at the head of a broad and beautiful court extending northward from the main street, in front of the City Hotel. The palace was constructed of brick. The center building was accidentally destroyed by fire while occupied by the French troops immediately after the surrender of Cornwallis at Yorktown. Attached to the palace were three hundred and sixty acres of land, beautifully laid out in gardens, parks, carriage-ways, and a bowling-green. Dunmore imported some fine linden-trees from Scotland, one of which, still in existence, is one of the finest specimens of that tree I have ever seen. All that remains of the spacious edifice are the two wings seen in the engraving; the one on the right was the office, the one on the left was the guard-house.

"A little eastward of Palace Street or Court, is the public square, on which area are two relics of the olden time, Bruton Church, a cruciform structure with a steeple, and the old Magazine, an octagon building erected during the administration of Governor Spotswood. (1716.) Surrounding it, also in octagonal form, is a massive brick wall, which was constructed when the building was erected. This wall is somewhat dilapidated, as seen in the engraving. The building was occupied as a Baptist meeting-house when I visited Williamsburg, and I trust it may never fall before the hand of improvement, for it has an historical value in the minds of all Americans."

The first guns of the Revolution might well have gone off at Williamsburg on April 20, '75, instead of at Concord on the 19th. Almost simultaneously with the Massachusetts fracas, Dunmore arranged to have the powder at the Williamsburg Magazine removed secretly at night by some British marines, who conveyed it on board an armed schooner in the James. When the theft was discovered the town was in an uproar, and as the news spread the militia began to assemble as far away as Fredericksburg. Frightened and furious, Dunmore barricaded himself in the Palace behind a couple of cannon, and swore "by the living God" that if any of his defenders were attacked he would raise the Royal standard, free and arm the slaves, and lay the town in ashes.

Patrick Henry, on the point of leaving Hanover Courthouse for the Second Congress at Philadelphia, paused to raise a company of armed volunteers for a march on Williamsburg to demand the powder back or compensation for its value. Before he could arrive there, word of the fight at Concord was published in a broadside by the Virginia *Gazette*, which ended on an ominous note: "The sword is now drawn, and God knows when it will be sheathed."

Considering that money was more harmless than gunpowder in the hands of the inflamed patriots, Dunmore paid £330 into the treasury and kept the powder. Perhaps in some surprise, if not in relief, Henry disbanded his little force and proceeded on his way to Philadelphia, where he was in time to witness with approval the appointment of Washington as Commander-in-chief.

But in Virginia the militia was all astir, and the action of Patrick Henry in defying the Governor was much applauded, while committees of safety and vigilance met, rumors flew, and when some gunpowder was found under the floor of the Magazine there was an outcry that Dunmore had planned to blow it up. On June 8th he fled with his family on board a British man-o'-war in the York River—the first Royal Governor to abdicate before the alarming tide of independence.

Henry returned from Philadelphia to attend another Convention in Richmond, where he found himself elected—lacking Washington—to command the Virginia forces now being raised; not without some murmurs, which arose in his case from a conservative feeling that—unlike Washington—he was not quite a gentleman. Also unlike Washington, he delayed for several weeks at home, where his wife was ailing, and by the time he reached Williamsburg Dunmore was ravaging around Norfolk and there was already a feeling that Henry had committed a tardiness, at best.

He was not in any sense a soldier, and for a few months he watched abler, more experienced men assume the authority and responsibilities in Virginia which he believed were rightfully his. Then to the regret of only a few, he resigned his commission and went home to his dying wife, while Washington spent the winter outside Boston. In May of '76, a widower, Henry was in his seat in the Capitol when the Convention met at Williamsburg. In an elegant atmosphere of velvets and powder, he was still obstinately clothed like a parson. It was from this assembly that Richard Henry Lee at Philadelphia received the instructions which triggered the Declaration of Independence. And this was the assembly which after exhaustive debate framed the constitution of Virginia. And finally in a vote of sixty to forty-five, it elected Patrick Henry as the first Governor of Virginia, over the ranking aristocrat, Thomas Nelson.

Henry has been called the Dick Whittington of America—the shabby backwoods lawyer, speaking with what was suspected to be a deliberately maintained up-country accent, now residing in the handsome Palace of the Royal Governors, with a coach and horses at his disposal. He rose somewhat to the occasion. He went to a good tailor, he bought a new wig. And at the age of forty, plagued by recurrent ailments and fevers, father of six children, he married a new wife—young Dorothea Dandridge, twenty-one, whom he had known since her childhood when he first visited her father's house with his friend Thomas Jefferson when Jefferson was a student at William and Mary College—granddaughter of a Royal Governor herself, and cousin to Martha Washington. With a long list of eligible young men at her disposal, including one called John Paul Jones, Dolly Dandridge chose to become the second wife of the simple, kindly man who would make her the Governor's lady. It was a true marriage, for she considered him the best husband in the world, nursed him devotedly in his increasing debilities, bore him nine children, and survived him to marry again.

From the Magazine, Lossing made his way to the Raleigh Tavern, where in the supper room the Burgesses used to gather to form their committees and pass their resolutions and hold their debates after the Governor had dissolved the Assembly in the State House at the end of the street. He was just in time, for the inevitable alterations and destruction were at work.

"When I visited Williamsburg in December, 1848," he records, "the front part of the old Raleigh Tavern had been torn down and a building in modern style was erected in its place. The old tavern was in the form of an L, one portion fronting the street, the other extending at right angles, in the rear. Both parts were precisely alike in external appearance, and as the rear building was yet standing and unaltered, I am able to give a restored view of the Raleigh as it appeared during the Revolution. The leaden bust of Sir Walter Raleigh, which graced the front of the old inn, now ornaments the new building.

"The room used for public meetings is in the rear building of the tavern, and up to the day of my visit it had remained unaltered. Carpenters were then at work remodeling its style, for the purpose of making it a ball-room; and now, I suppose that apartment, hallowed by so many associations connected with our war for independence, has scarcely an original feature left. Had my visit been deferred a day longer, the style of the room could never have been portrayed. Neat wainscoting of Virginia pine ornamented the sides below and partly between the windows, and over the fireplace, which was spacious.

"This view is from the entrance door from the front portion of the building. On the left were two large windows; on the right were two windows and a door; and on each side of the fire-place was a door opening into small passage ways, from the exterior. Through the door on the left is seen a flight of stairs leading to the dormitory. The walls were whitewashed, and the woodwork painted a lead color. In this room the leading patriots of Virginia, including Washington, held many secret caucuses, and planned many schemes for the overthrow of Royal rule in the colonies. The sound of the hammer and saw engaged in the work of change seemed to me like actual desecration; for the Raleigh Tavern, and the Apollo room, are to Virginia relatively what Faneuil Hall is to Massachusetts."

The story of the Restoration of Williamsburg by the Rockefellers is not new, but is always stupendous. Each year thousands of people arrive there by every form of modern transportation, to wander bemused and delighted through its magic re-creation of a vanished world. Some eighty million dollars have now gone into this noble project, and while it is always possible to deplore commercialism and to wish that this or that were different, it is graceless and unimaginative to find fault with the over-all achievement.

Infinite research, care, and expense have made possible the refabrication of the lost buildings and the rehabilitation of those that remained when the project was undertaken in 1928, so that the Palace, the Capitol, the Raleigh, and several private houses, stand today as once they stood under George Washington's cool blue eyes. The furnishings of the interiors are designed to seem as though the rightful inhabitants had only just stepped out of the rooms—a pair of spectacles on an open book, an unfinished game on a small table, flowers in all the vases—the illusion is well sustained. Hostesses, gardeners, and maid-servants wear the clothes of the period. A handsome Negro lad in knee-breeches, snowy shirt, and three-cornered hat is clipping a hedge in the Palace garden, a costumed Negro coachman drives an open carriage containing three ladies in hooped skirts to their duties as guides. And on the candlelight nights at the Palace and the Capitol there is real enchantment.

Contrary to his habit, Lossing seems not to have made friends at Williamsburg and enjoyed the local hospitality. His narrative here wanders away into the Indian wars and the Assembly's quarrels with the Royal Governors, and then he is off to Yorktown. But Williamsburg was and still is full of associations with the Yorktown campaign, which he apparently did not discover.

The town had suffered cruelly under occupation by Cornwallis's army before he made the fatal move to Yorktown, with a plague of flies and small-pox which followed the British. Then Lafayette arrived, and fell ill of an ague at his quarters in the St. George Tucker house, though having just passed his twenty-fourth birthday he would have it that he was dying of old age. He was sufficiently recovered from his chills and fevers to ride out, somewhat pale and shaky, to greet Washington and Rochambeau when they arrived at the Jamestown camp the middle of September. Richard Butler, who was one of Lafayette's officers, kept a journal:

"September 14.—The Marquis LaFayette still continues ill of the ague. Yesterday the Marquis de St. Simon and a number of his officers paid a visit to our line, and the Baron Steuben and our good friend General Wayne, whose wound and gout continue still. About 3 o'clock an express arrived, announcing the approach of our great and good Commander-in-chief, and the Count de Rochambeau, the commander of the allied armies of France, now joining. At 4, the guns fired a royal salute as the General approached the camp, on which the two armies turned out their battalion parades; —his Excellency and the Count de Rochambeau, with their suites, attended by the Marquis de LaFayette, Major-General and commander of the American, and Major-General Marquis de St. Simon, commander of the allied army (lately arrived) and all their suites, visited the allied army first, and then the American army, and were saluted according to custom; these ceremonies finished, the whole of the officers of the French army attended at the Marquis de St. Simon's quarters and were introduced to the *Illustrious Hero*. The field officers of the American army all attended to bid him and the other Generals welcome. These ceremonies over, an elegant supper was served up.... To add to the happiness of the event and evening, an elegant band of music played an introductive part of a French Opera, signifying the happiness of the family when blessed with the presence of their father, and their great dependence upon him. About ten o'clock the company rose up, and after mutual congratulations and the greatest expressions of joy, they separated."

Rations were short around Williamsburg, as usual, and there must have been more polite toasts and good will and French opera than substantial fare at supper. Lafayette's behavior at this time glows with a gallantry and unselfishness which must have touched the hearts of older men seasoned to the jealousy of rank and glory common among military heroes. It was within his power, after De Grasse had landed his quota of land troops under St. Simon at Jamestown while Washington was still in Pennsylvania, to move in on Cornwallis and himself secure the first credit for the inevitable capture of Yorktown. Such a course was indeed urged upon him by his countrymen, for De Grasse was anxious to return to the West Indies. But with a loyalty and purity of motive which had distinguished his conduct from the day of his first interview with the Commander-in-chief in 1777, Lafayette resisted what must have been a very real temptation to an impulsive young man, and refused to jeopardize the ultimate victory or to diminish Washington's stature by rushing into action with his own force. His decision also ensured that the final engagement at Yorktown would be a decorous siege operation conducted by an adequate assaulting force, rather than a bloody storming of the British lines which would certainly have cost many more lives on both sides.

Washington's headquarters in Williamsburg were established at the house of his old friend George Wythe on the Palace Green, where he must sometimes have dined with Martha during his Burgessing days in the 60's. It was for him in a way a homecoming, as he had been attending the Assembly at Williamsburg for fifteen consecutive years before the Philadelphia Congress sent him on to Boston to take command, in the summer of 1775. Martha waited out the Yorktown campaign at Mount Vernon, with Lucy Knox as her guest, and on his way southward the Commander-in-chief had had the rare pleasure of entertaining in his beloved home the chief officers of the allied armies, during a two-day halt on the Potomac. When they rode on towards Yorktown, Jacky Custis, Martha's son by her first marriage and her only surviving child, rode with them as a volunteer aide on Washington's Staff, leaving his young wife and four small children in his mother's care.

At Williamsburg before the siege began, Rochambeau was quartered at what is now called the Randolph-Peachy house, on the Duke of Gloucester Street, as the guest of Peyton Randolph's widow. The Governor's Palace, which was by rights the residence of Thomas Nelson, Jr., was being readied as a hospital for the American sick and wounded, for Governor Nelson was a fighting man, out with his troops in the field. His family doubtless were housed somewhere in Williamsburg, as their own home was in British-occupied Yorktown. The French made use of the College buildings as hospital and officers' quarters.

The smell of victory was already in the air at Williamsburg, so soon after the tension and the dread and the flies and the sickness which had accompanied the British there. The little town was suddenly gayer than it had been since the old Assembly times under the Royal Governors, and there were balls and dinner parties to entertain the fascinating French, whose white uniforms with colored facings and buttons and sashes quite dazzled the Virginia belles, whose natural bright complexions and forthright ways were a novelty to the men of the Old World.

Day by day the troops came in, forming a vast encampment around the town—till they numbered 12,000. Early on the 28th of September Washington emerged from Mr. Wythe's broad front door with its polished brass eagle knocker—followed by his clanking aides in their sword-belts and spurs and gold-laced hats, with the diagonal green Staff ribbon across their waistcoats—and they all mounted their groomed and rested horses and rode out, reflecting the sun, to Yorktown and the siege. Soon the guns began, only four miles away, and the wounded came back to the hospitals at the Palace and the College....

And finally, some six weeks later, the British were there again, as the guests—and the prisoners—of the American officers, whose hospitality left little room for hard feelings.

IX

Yorktown

"EVENING was approaching when I left Williamsburg for Yorktown, twelve miles distant," Lossing continues. "It was an exceedingly pleasant afternoon, so mild that wild flowers peeped cautiously from the hedges, and a wasp and a grasshopper alighted on the splash-board of my wagon, while stopping on the margin of a clear stream. Soon after leaving Williamsburg the road entered a pine forest; and all the way to Yorktown these solitudes form the principal feature in the landscape. The country is quite level, and the cultivated clearings are more frequent and extensive than further up the Chickahominy. The green foliage of the lofty pines, of the modest holly, and the spreading laurel, made the forest journey less gloomy than it would otherwise have been; for the verdure, the balmy air, and the occasional note of a bird, made me forget that the Christmas holidays were at hand, and that the mountains of New England were probably white with snow.

"I arrived at Yorktown at twilight, and passed the night at the only inn in the place, which is owned by William Nelson, Esq., grandson of Governor Thomas Nelson, one of the Signers of the Declaration of Independence. To the kindness and intelligence of that gentleman I am indebted for much of the pleasure and profit of my visit there. We supped together upon far-famed York River oysters just brought from their oozy bed, and it was near midnight before we parted company. Mr. Nelson resides in the fine old mansion which belonged to his grandfather, and which yet bears marks of the iron hail poured upon it during the siege of Yorktown.

"Early the next morning I strolled over the village. It is situated upon a high bluff of concrete or stone marl, covered with a sandy soil, on the south side of the York River, about eleven miles from its mouth. The peninsula on which the town stands is level, and is embraced upon each side by deep ravines, which almost meet in the rear. The ground is the highest upon either the York or James Rivers, below Richmond. Being the shire town of the county, it contains the public buildings. These, with about forty dwellings, some of them decaying, compose the village, which formerly was one of the most flourishing towns on the peninsula. It contained about sixty houses at the time of the siege in 1781.

"A fire which occurred in 1814 destroyed much property there and from that blow the village seems never to have recovered. At that time its old church, built a century and a half before, was destroyed; nothing but its stone marl walls were left standing. In this picturesque condition it remained for thirty years, when it was repaired, and is now used as a place of worship. In the old burial ground adjoining it are the tombs and monuments of the Nelson family, situated a few yards from the banks of the York. The nearer one in the engraving, which stands over the grave of the first emigrant of the family, who was called "Scotch Tom," although mutilated is yet highly ornamental. In a vault at the end of the fragment of brick wall seen beyond the monuments rest the remains of Governor Nelson, the Signer of the Declaration. There is no monument above it, and nothing marks the spot but a rough stone lying among the rank grass. Around these are strewn fragments of the stone marl of the old church wall, beautifully crystallized and indurated by exposure. The view from this point is very charming, looking out upon the York stretching away toward the Chesapeake and skirted by woodlands and cultivated fields."

The grandfather of Lossing's host was one of the great figures of the Revolution who have been somewhat overlooked. He was

Thomas Nelson III, called Jr. to distinguish him from his uncle, Thomas II, Secretary of the Council under the Royal Governors, from whom Patrick Henry won the election in '75. Thomas III's father was William, President of the Council, who built the fine mansion and made it famous for its hospitality, its fox-hunts, and its horse-flesh, and died just before the Revolution began. A big, lively man of great spirit and integrity, Thomas III had been chosen to carry the instructions from the Convention at Williamsburg to Richard Henry Lee in Philadelphia in June, '76, which brought about his speech leading to the Declaration of Independence. Thomas remained to sign it, and after a bout of illness compelled him to resign his seat in Congress, he recovered at home to raise militia, lead troops in action, and exert himself in every possible way for the cause.

He advanced money to pay Virginia militia who would not march without receiving their arrears, and on his personal security raised an enormous loan for the French fleet, none of which was ever refunded to him. In 1781, having succeeded Thomas Jefferson as Governor of Virginia, he was present with his militia at the siege of Yorktown, while his house was being used as headquarters by Cornwallis.

Like several other patriots, including Washington, who sacrificed large fortunes in the service of the new republic, he suffered shamefully from ingratitude and neglect when the war was over. He died ruined but uncomplaining at fifty-one, of asthma at

Offley in Hanover County, leaving eleven children. His widow lived to be nearly eighty, blind and in actual want. Even his tomb was left to crumble away unhonored by the government he had helped to found and preserve. His grandson was apparently able to make a modest living as an inn-keeper, in the same town where his family had once dispensed the free-est hospitality in Virginia.

"After breakfast," says Lossing, "accompanied by Mr. Nelson in his carriage, I visited the several localities which make Yorktown historically famous. We first descended the river bank and visited the excavation in the marl bluff known as Cornwallis's Cave. It is square, twelve by eighteen feet in size, with a narrow passage leading to a smaller circular excavation on one side. It is almost directly beneath the termination of the trench and breastworks of the British fortifications, which are yet very prominent upon the bank above.

"Popular tradition says that this excavation was made by the order of Cornwallis, and used by him for the purpose of holding councils with his officers in a place of safety during the siege. Taking advantage of this tradition, cupidity has placed a door at the entrance, secured it by lock and key, and demands a Virginia ninepence (12½ cents) entrance fee from the curious. I paid the penalty of curiosity, knowing that I was submitting to imposition, for I was assured on the authority of an old lady who resided at Yorktown at the time of the siege that this excavation was made by some people wherein to hide their valuables. A house stood directly in front of it, the foundation of which is yet there. The building made the spot still more secluded. A quarter of a mile below, Lord Cornwallis did have an excavation in the bank, which was lined with green baize, and used by the General for secret conferences during the siege. No traces of his council chamber are left.

"We next visited the lines of entrenchments cast up by the British on the south and easterly sides of the town. They extend in irregular lines from the river bank to the sloping grounds in the rear of the village in the form of a figure five. The mounds vary in height from six to twelve and fifteen feet, and being covered by a hard sward may remain so half a century longer. The places of redoubts, the lines of the parallels, and other things connected with the siege are yet visible."

Nowadays Yorktown is part of a National Park and has been preserved and restored with taste and care. The Swan Tavern was reconstructed in 1934, the Nelson house is cherished and frequently occupied by its present owners, who allow it to be shown when they are not in residence. A cannon ball which during the siege lodged in the thickness of the brick wall is still there, and Lossing saw what he calls a huge unexploded bomb-shell in the yard.

A curving modern parkway now runs from Williamsburg to Yorktown, passing along the bluff close to the river. It leads through the little town and out to the reconstructed earthworks and redoubts of the British defences and the American lines, which are furnished with replicas of the guns and the log fraises done in concrete. The road becomes a charming country lane which circles through the encampment area of the American and French armies, a park in a forest, with even a shallow ford. The headquarters site of each corps, and the spot where Washington's famous domed marquee was set, are unobtrusively marked in the glades and thickets—an exquisite half hour's stretch for the modern imagination.

It is in a way unfortunate that Lossing's route entails consideration of the great surrender before he comes to the stirring battles which led up to it. But unlike the marshmallow-minded lady who objected to being robbed of suspense by hearing about Napoleon's divorce before she came to it in the book, no one doubts that the American Revolution ended happily for the colonists who had borne hunger, cold, privation, and despair for seven long years, and it doesn't spoil the story to tell it backwards.

The real drama of Yorktown began at Washington's headquarters on the Hudson in summer of 1781, when he was on the point of beginning a joint campaign with the French against the British army which was in possession of New York City. Then came that sudden change of plans which set the two armies rolling southward instead. There has been some controversy as to whether it was a spur-of-the-moment inspiration on his part, or a piece of carefully planned military strategy, or whether he was simply jockeyed into it by the French and contrived to fall on his feet.

Apparently there was a little of each. It was not a new idea to him, certainly, to leave New York behind and march into Virginia, which was his home state and which had already appealed to him for relief from the depredations of Cornwallis. He had discussed with Rochambeau at their earlier conferences a Southern campaign by their combined armies, but so much depended on the French Navy, which was not well-coordinated with their land army, and communications were so difficult, that after frustration and delays he had almost given up hope of such a thing. The message from the French Admiral De Grasse that he was at last ready to co-operate from the Chesapeake did come as a surprise to Washington, in that he had been disappointed before. But when it came, he was not caught without a plan of action for the South. It had occurred to him. He was ready. And although the New York campaign was already in motion, he made his decision swiftly and firmly, as he had done at Trenton, and this time with what inner exaltation can be imagined, for the road to Yorktown led past Mount Vernon, and even the most conscientious man could reasonably spend a night at home on the way.

"I wish to the Lord the French would not raise our expectations of a co-operation, or fulfill them," he had once exclaimed during one of the rare breaks in his habitual composure And even now he was not really sure of the French, as he led the march to Philadelphia, which was illuminated in his honor, and rode on past the city, brooding and rather grim, but always polite and correct to his well-wishers along the way—on to Head of Elk and the Chesapeake, where De Grasse was due with the French Fleet. The last time he took that road it had led to Brandywine and defeat. If the French failed him now it could be much worse than Brandywine.

Early on the afternoon of September 5th a dusty horseman from Baltimore came galloping towards him—an express rider with a message. Washington read it without leaving the saddle. Such good news must have been hard to believe at first. De Grasse was there. De Grasse was in the Chesapeake, where he had promised to be, with twenty-eight sail and three thousand French troops.

Washington's calm, almost impervious to disaster, was not proof against this sudden joy. He was radiant, transformed. He turned and galloped back to Chester, where Rochambeau was soon to disembark from a tour of inspection of the river defences. He was waiting on the wharf, waving his hat in one hand and his handkerchief in the other, when the boat pulled in. Rochambeau stepped ashore into an embrace which was probably more like a bear-hug. The French officers who followed him were touched and impressed by the show of emotion from a general they had thought cold and severe. "A child, whose wishes had been satisfied, could not have experienced a more lively sense of pleasure, and I think I am honoring the feelings of this rare man in seeking to describe them in all their vivacity," wrote the Comte de Deux Ponts.

After that, no one could keep the pace Washington set, and the French gave it up. He arrived at Mount Vernon with a single aide and the faithful black Billy, his body-servant, late at night on the

9th of September, rousing a startled household to unexpected delight, for they had had no word that he was so near. Rochambeau and the rest of them caught up with him the next day, and were duly impressed with the Virginia hospitality which gave him such pride. From Mount Vernon he wrote to Lafayette, who mounted guard at Williamsburg over Cornwallis at Yorktown:

"We are thus far, my dear Marquis, on our way to you.... Should there be any danger as we approach you, I shall be obliged if you will send a party of horse towards New Kent Courthouse to meet us. With great personal regard and affection, I am, my dear Marquis, your most obedient servant,
GEO. WASHINGTON

"P.S. I hope you will keep Lord Cornwallis safe, without provisions or forage, until we arrive. Adieu."

The stirring details of the siege of Yorktown and the solemn pageant of the British surrender, which left many of the burly red-coated men in actual tears of humiliation, can be found in any history book. Two or three small episodes supply those human sidelights which bring the whole drama into focus.

The first American casualty was Colonel Scammell of Massachusetts, who was reconnoitering near the redoubt known as the Fusiliers' on the second day, when he encountered several Hessian horsemen. Outnumbered and surprised, he very sensibly threw up his empty right hand and said, "Gentlemen, I am your prisoner." One of the Hessians, who may have misunderstood, fired point-blank, and they conveyed their wounded prisoner into Yorktown, where conditions of sanitation and supply were already lethal. The wound was recognized to be a serious one, and in this gentlemen's war Cornwallis promptly granted Washington's request that Scammell might be taken to the American surgeons at Williamsburg, where after several days of agony he died. The American army mourned him bitterly, for he was a gallant and popular officer, gay in spirit, and famous for his stories, which were said to have made even the grave Commander-in-chief laugh out loud. Lossing visited the site of the redoubt and was informed that Colonel Scammell was shot near the stream which crosses the river road from Williamsburg to Yorktown.

Cornwallis's position in his Yorktown fortifications was hopeless from the start, and on the 17th day of October a drummer boy climbed the parapet and beat the "parley." His drum could not be heard above the gunfire, and it was not until a large sergeant with a white flag was sent up beside him that an expectant silence fell over the field, and negotiations could begin.

Then there is the story of the sword. Cornwallis was so ill of chagrin that he was unable to appear at the appointed time for the ceremony of surrender. With the Allied armies drawn up in a double line half a mile long, the French troops facing the Americans with a wide lane between, Washington and his Staff opposite Rochambeau and his, it fell to General Charles O'Hara of the Guards to ride out at the head of the defeated British army, which advanced with a measured step, its colors cased, its bands and pipers playing unmilitary airs. According to the French diarists, who witnessed the scene from a different viewpoint from those on the American side, O'Hara bore Cornwallis's sword to present to the victor, and was escorted from Yorktown by the French Adjutant-General Damas, who was sent to show him the way. As they approached the group of mounted officers, O'Hara is said to have left

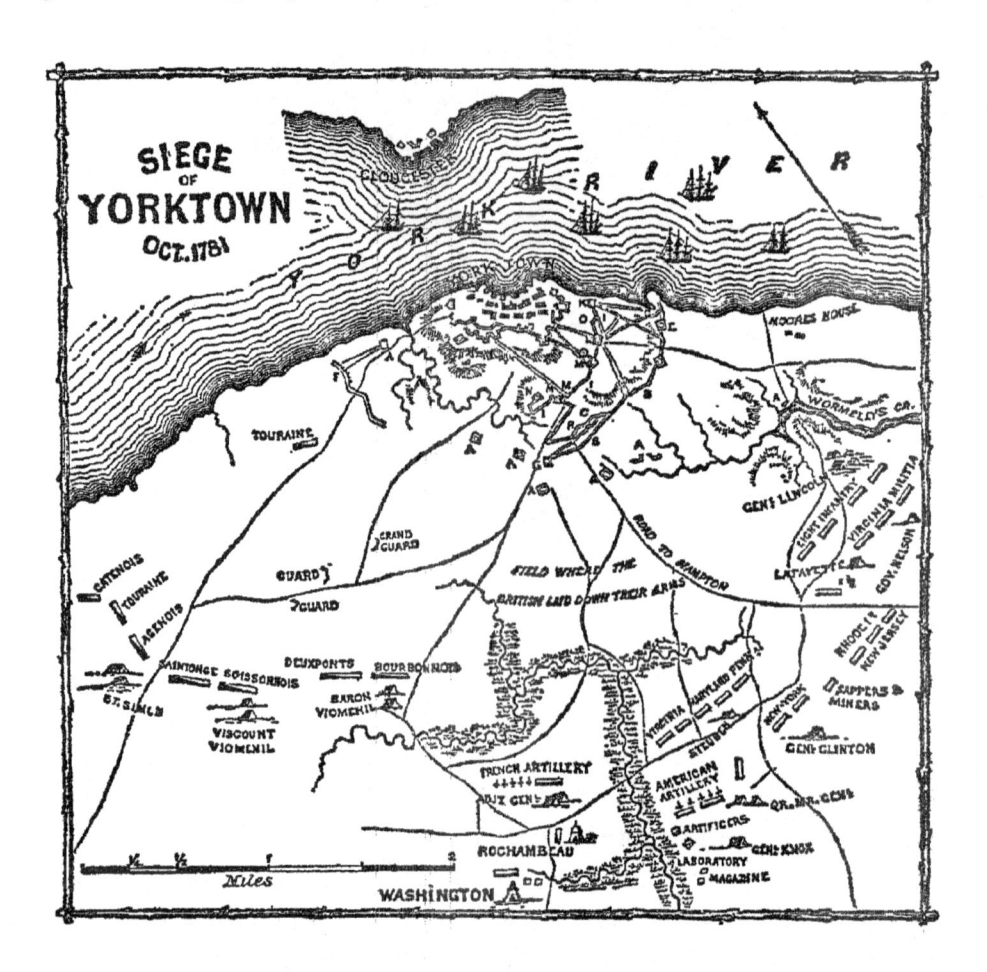

the escort and deliberately turned towards General Rochambeau, with the apparent intention of saving a little face by ignoring the American Commander-in-chief and acknowledging the French nobleman as the victor. Rochambeau bowed slightly in the saddle and indicated Washington as the proper recipient of the sword, and the mortified O'Hara was conducted by his escort to where Washington waited on the big sorrel horse which was never to do another day's work once his master retired to Mount Vernon at the end of the war, and was never ridden by anyone else. Having taken in with a glance that Cornwallis had sent a deputy, the Commander-in-chief with a courteous gesture referred O'Hara to General Lincoln, his own second in command, to whom O'Hara finally succeeded in handing over the unsheathed sword, hilt foremost, although it was promptly returned to him in a gracious gesture by the man who less than two years before had surrendered Charleston to General Clinton.

It has been objected that the American accounts do not mention the sword, and that the Articles of Capitulation allowed the British officers to retain their sidearms. But George Washington Parke Custis, who was Mrs. Washington's grandson and grew up in the family traditions, says in his *Memoirs* that Cornwallis sent out his sword, and it is probable, as he himself failed to accompany it.

Washington's entry in the diary which he had recently resumed after a gap of several years was characteristic of his usual maddening restraint. There had been "procrastination" by the British with regard to the Articles of Capitulation on the 18th, and on the following day Washington wrote: "October 19. In the morning early I had them [the Articles] copied and sent word to Lord Cornwallis that I expected to have them signed at 11 o'clock, and that the garrison would march out at 2 o'clock, both of which were accordingly done." That's all. His own inner elation and thankfulness to the Providence he had never doubted shows no more on the page of his private journal than it had done on his impassive face as the long red line marched past him to stack its arms in the dust.

By his express orders, everyone present remembered their manners, even the townspeople who were permitted to cluster behind the soldiery to watch the ceremony. Lighthorse Harry Lee, who was present, says in his *Memoirs*, that "universal silence was observed amidst the vast concourse, and the utmost decency prevailed; exhibiting in demeanor an awful sense of the vicissitudes of human fortune, mingled with commiseration for the unhappy."

Congress had sweated out the Yorktown campaign in Philadelphia, and Washington chose Tench Tilghman, a Maryland man who had served as a volunteer aide since the summer of '76, as his messenger to carry the news of the surrender. Colonel Tilghman made an epic journey against wind, weather, and the incredulity of those from whom he tried to hire boats and horses, and arrived at the Philadelphia lodgings in High Street of President McKean after midnight on the 23rd. Unable to rouse the house, he stood beating on the door and crying, "News, great news! Cornwallis is taken!" till night watchmen converged upon him for riotous and drunken behavior. The President put a nightcapped head out of an upper window in time to save him from being removed to gaol, and soon all the bells in Philadelphia were pealing.

Washington's straight-faced absence of excitement or exhilaration was maintained in his report to Congress as delivered by Colonel Tilghman: "I have the honor to inform Congress that a reduction of the British army under the command of Lord Cornwallis is most happily effected," he wrote, though the penmanship is that of his aide David Humphreys, who doubtless took it in dictation. "The unremitting ardor which actuated every officer and soldier in the combined army in this occasion has principally led to this important event, at an earlier period than my most sanguine hope had induced me to expect."

Dr. Thatcher, a surgeon in the American army who kept a copious journal of his experiences, described the scene at Yorktown after the British left it: "I have this day visited the town of York, to witness the destructive effects of the siege. It contains about sixty houses; some of them are elegant, many of them are greatly damaged, and some totally ruined, being shot through in a thousand places, and honeycombed, ready to crumble to pieces. Rich furniture and books were scattered over the ground, and the carcasses of men and horses, half covered with earth, exhibited a scene of ruin and horror beyond description. The earth in many places is thrown up into mounds by the force of our shells, and it is difficult to point to a spot where a man could have resorted for safety."

Once the ordeal at the surrender field was over, the British officers relaxed to enjoy the hospitality which etiquette required of the victors to the vanquished. O'Hara came to Rochambeau's headquarters on the field to dinner the same night, and behaved with as much charm and cordiality, it was remarked, as though he had been the host. Turning forty now, Charles O'Hara had seen service with the Coldstreams in Portugal and Senegal before he came of age, and was twice wounded at Guilford Courthouse. He lived to be an able Governor of Gibraltar until the turn of the century, where he was known as the Old Cock of the Rock.

Once Cornwallis brought himself to consent to a meeting with Washington, their natural good breeding and soldierly bearing established something almost like friendship between the two men, who after all had a good deal in common. Since they had last encountered each other in the field at Monmouth, Cornwallis had made another voyage to England and back, arriving in February, '79, at the bedside of his wife just before she died, whether or not of a broken heart at his continued absence, as she had threatened to do. He returned to America in August of the same year in time to join Clinton's second expedition to Charleston, and to fight the campaign following Charleston's surrender which brought him finally to Yorktown. He was now to go home to England to a distinguished career in colonial affairs in the Far East, from where he wrote back letters to his only son which were full of a touching wisdom and humor.

"At the grand dinner given at Headquarters to the officers of the three armies," General Washington's foster-grandson related in his *Memoirs*, "Washington filled his glass and, after his invariable toast whether in peace or war, of '*All our friends,*' gave '*The British Army,*' with some complimentary remarks upon its chief, his proud career in arms, and his gallant defence of Yorktown. When it came to Cornwallis's turn, he prefaced his toast by saying that the war was virtually at an end, and the contending parties would soon embrace as friends; there might be affairs of posts, but nothing on a more enlarged scale, as it was scarcely to be expected that the Ministry would send another army to America."

Cornwallis was right in his prediction that there would be no more full-scale battles, but it was another two years before the peace negotiations were concluded and the treaty was signed which released Washington and his bored, mutinous army in time to go home for Christmas, 1783.

He had resumed his brief daily jottings which can hardly be called a diary, in the spring of '81, with a laconic regret that he had allowed it to lapse so long. The entry for November 5th was made while he was still at his Williamsburg Headquarters after the surrender, arranging for the accommodation of prisoners, and the division of his own army, some of which was to return to the Hudson area where Clinton still held fast to New York City, and some to march south under St. Clair and Wayne to join Greene in South Carolina where Stewart still occupied Charleston. Reading as follows, it breaks off dramatically in the middle of a sentence:

"Nov. 5th. The detachment for the southward, consisting ... of Wayne's and Gist's brigades ... began their march and were to be joined by all the cavalry that could be equipped of the 1st, 3d, and 4th Regiments at—"

Perhaps at that very moment the breathless messenger arrived from Eltham, the nearby home of Martha's brother-in-law Burwell Bassett, where Jacky Custis lay ill of the camp-fever which had stricken him during the siege. The message was sufficiently urgent that Washington rode to Eltham the same day, accompanied by a single aide, perhaps rising from that unfinished page to do so. Jacky's wife and mother had already been summoned from Mount Vernon, and Washington arrived at Eltham in time to be present at Jacky's death, as he had been at that of Martha's only other child at Mount Vernon ten years before. He did not return to Williamsburg, but after Jacky was buried accompanied the two grieving women to Mount Vernon, the celebrations of his hard-won triumph shadowed by family sorrow.

No one realized then how completely the war had been won at Yorktown, and after a short interval at home, Martha dried her tears and set out with him for Philadelphia, where he spent the winter in the unceasing, familiar effort to persuade Congress to provide food and clothing and ammunition for the army which was still in the field.

X

Hampton to the Cowpens

FROM Yorktown Lossing drove to Hampton and Norfolk, both of which had been terrorized by Governor Dunmore after he fled from Williamsburg in the autumn of '75. He visited Great Bridge, on the edge of Dismal Swamp, where a handful of Virginians under Colonel Woodford won a sharp skirmish with Dunmore's crew of cut-throats in December, '75.

"Extensive marshes, filled and drained alternately with the flow of the tide, spread out on each side of the river, making the whole breadth of morass and stream, at this point, about half a mile wide," he notes. "The Great Bridge extends across the main stream from two islands of firm earth, which are covered with trees and shrubbery. Each of these islands is connected with the main stream by a causeway and smaller bridges. On the western side of the river is the small scattered village of Great Bridge, not much larger now than it was at the period of the Revolution. On the island at the western end of the bridge are two or three houses and a tide-mill, and upon the one at the Norfolk side, where Dunmore cast up entrenchments, is a wind-mill, constructed several years ago by a man whose acumen was certainly not remarkable. Placed in the middle of a morass and surrounded by trees, its sails never revolved, and it remains a monument of folly. The marsh is covered with osiers and tall coarse grass; and the whole scene, though picturesque, is rather dreary in aspect."

Dunmore, who had stayed safe on shipboard during the fight at Great Bridge, gathered up his beaten forces and some Loyalist

Norfolk families, in his ships in the harbor, where the refugees endured acute crowding and discomfort and actual hunger. Shore parties on foraging trips were cut off or driven away, and the ships were sniped at from the town. On December 31st Dunmore served notice that unless he was at once supplied with provisions and left unmolested he would bombard the town. He received a rude answer back, and on January 1st, '76, he opened fire, causing a night of terror, great damage by fire, but little loss of life.

He finally sailed away up the Chesapeake, and Norfolk rebuilt itself in peace until May of '79, when a British fleet appeared. The small American garrison abandoned the fortifications, and the British landed and took possession of the stores and ammunition which had been left behind, but did not occupy the town for long. At this point, on Governor Thomas Jefferson's advice, the capital was removed from Williamsburg inland to Richmond, and the Assembly set up there in temporary quarters.

At twilight on the 23d of December (1848) Lossing returned from Great Bridge to Norfolk at the opening of the Christmas holidays, meeting numbers of Negroes on their way to visit their friends on the plantations of their masters. "They all appeared to be happy and musical as larks, and made the forest ring with their joyous laugh and melodious songs. All carried a bundle, or a basket filled with presents for their friends. Some had new hats, and others garments; others were carrying various knicknacks and fire-crackers, and a few of the men were toting a little too much fire-water. From the youngest to the oldest, who rode in mule-carts, all faces beamed with the joy of the hour.

"I awoke [in Norfolk] at four o'clock on Christmas morning, and my first waking thought was of the dawn of 4th of July in a Northern city. Guns, pistols, and squibs were already heralding the holiday; indeed the revelry commenced at dark the previous evening, notwithstanding it was the night of the Sabbath."

At six A.M. he embarked with Charley and the wagon on a steamboat for City Point on the James River, where Benedict Arnold and the British General Phillips had landed during their operations against Steuben in '81, at which time Simcoe's Loyalist cavalry invaded Williamsburg itself, though he made no attempt to try to hold the town. There were skirmishes at Blandford and Petersburg, and minor damage to stores and shipping was accomplished by the British before Lafayette came down to Richmond and drove them off.

The death of General Phillips of a fever at his headquarters near Petersburg in May gave the command to Arnold, until Cornwallis hurried up from the Carolinas with the ruthless green-coated cavalry of Colonel Tarleton, which circled out towards Charlottesville, where the Legislature had adjourned when Richmond was threatened. Thomas Jefferson was no more a military man than Patrick Henry, and had declined re-election as Governor in favor of General Nelson of Yorktown. Jefferson then retired to Monticello, his home several miles outside Charlottesville, with some members of the Legislature as his guests. The household was unaware of the approach of Tarleton's detachment until the horsemen in green were seen coming up the long winding road to the house. There was barely time to hurry off his wife and family in a carriage to a neighbor's house six miles away, and make his own escape on horseback with his colleagues, to a nervous rendezvous at Staunton, which was for a time the home of the fugitive Virginia Assembly. Arriving to find the place deserted, the British did very little damage except to the wine-cellar.

In Lossing's time Jefferson's home was "somewhat dilapidated and deprived of its former beauty by neglect. The furniture of its distinguished owner is nearly all gone, except a few pictures and mirrors, otherwise the interior of the house is the same as when Jefferson died. It is upon an eminence, with many aspen trees around it, and commands a view of the Blue Ridge for one hundred and fifty miles on one side and on the other one of the most beautiful and extensive landscapes in the world.... Monticello was a point of great attraction to the learned of all lands, when travelling in this country, while Jefferson lived. His writings made him favorably known as a scholar, and his public position made him honored by the nations.... The remains of Mr. Jefferson lie in a small family cemetery by the side of the winding road leading to Monticello. Over them is a granite obelisk eight feet high, and on a tablet of marble inserted in its southern face is the following inscription, which was found among Mr. Jefferson's papers after his death: *Here lies buried THOMAS JEFFERSON, Author of the Declaration of Independence; of the Statute of Virginia for Religious Freedom; and Father of the University of Virginia.*" It is somehow very like Thomas Jefferson, to have made sure that his tombstone said exactly what he wanted it to, and to have died on the fiftieth anniversary, exactly, of his Declaration.

Like Washington, Jefferson had been impoverished by his own hospitality, and after his death the house was sold for his only surviving daughter, Martha, who had married Thomas Mann Randolph, to discharge his debts. Passing through several ownerships and suffering from gradual ruin, it was bought in 1923 by the Thomas Jefferson Memorial Foundation, which has restored and preserved it, so that it can now be seen pretty much as he knew it.

From Petersburg, after receiving minute directions for his route for the next hundred miles, Lossing took up the reins and set out southward towards the Roanoke, on roads where the horse Charley sank to his knees in soft earth which was almost as adhesive as tar. His destination was Hillsborough in North Carolina, which was the seat of the state Government at the time of General Gates's disastrous defeat at Camden in August of 1780, after which he made his headlong flight from the battlefield to Charlotte, a distance of seventy miles, and later attempted to rally the remains of his scattered army at a camp near Hillsborough.

Lossing crossed the Nottaway River at Jones Bridge in a storm of rain, snow, and hail, accompanied by a strong northwest wind, "but happily for me," remarks this incurable optimist, "I was riding with the wind, and kept dry beneath my spacious wagon-top." His luck deserted him, if his spirits never did. He took the wrong road, and had to turn about and face the storm until he was thoroughly drenched, when he reached the house of Dr Gregory, "who entertains strangers," at Gee's Bridge on the Meherrin River. There he passed a comfortable night after a wearisome day, and in the morning the storm was over, and the air was bracing, from the north.

"Ice skimmed the surface of the pools by the roadside, and all over the red earth the exhalations were congealed into the most beautiful creations of frost-work I ever beheld. There were tiny columns an inch in height, with gorgeous capitals like tree-tops, their branches closely intertwined. These gave the surface the appearance of a crust of snow. Art, in its most delicate operations, never wrought anything half so wonderful as that little forest, created within the space of an hour, and covering tens of thousands of acres. The road was wretched, and it was almost two hours past meridian when I reached St. Tammany on the Roanoke, a small post in Mecklenburg County about eighty miles from Petersburg. The Roanoke is here almost four hundred yards wide, with an average depth of about thirteen feet, and a strong current. I crossed upon a bateau, propelled by means of a pole worked by a single stout Negro. When the stream is much swollen, three or four men are necessary to manage the craft, and even then there is danger. After ascending the southern bank, the road passes over a marsh of nearly half a mile, and then traverses among gentle hills....

"Towards evening I arrived at Nut Bush Post Office in Warren County [where] the post-master owned a store and an extensive tobacco plantation. Under his roof I passed the night, in the enjoyment of the most cordial hospitality, and was warmly pressed to spend several days with him and join in the seasonable sports of turkey and deer-hunting in the neighboring forests. But eager to complete my journey, I declined, and the next morning, notwithstanding another strong northeast gale was driving a chilling sleet over the land, I left Nut Bush and pushed on towards Oxford....

"The morning of the thirtieth was clear and warm, after a night of heavy rain. I left Oxford early, resolved to reach Hillsborough, thirty-six miles distant, at evening. But the red clay roads, made doubly bad by the rain, impeded my progress and I was obliged to stop at the house of a Yankee planter, four miles short of Hillsborough. In the course of the day, I forded several considerable streams, all of them much swollen and difficult of passage for a stranger.... and when at three o'clock I crossed the Flat River I came very near being swamped. A bridge spans the stream, but the ground on either side is so flat that during floods the river overflows its banks and expands into a lake. I reached the bridge without difficulty, but when leaving it found the way much impeded by driftwood and other substances that came flowing over the banks. Charley was not at all pleased with these frequent fordings, and the masses of driftwood alarmed him. While my wagon-hubs were under water, and he was picking his way carefully over the submerged stones, a dark mass of weeds and bushes came floating towards him. He sheered suddenly, and for a moment the wagon was poised upon two wheels. I was saved from a cold bath by springing to the opposite side, where my weight prevented its overturning, and we were soon safe upon firm land. This was the last contest with the waters for the day, for the next stream, the Little River, was crossed by a bridge a good distance above the less rapid current."

Having spent the night in "the small, neat, and comfortable loghouse" of the planter, Lossing rode into Hillsborough the next morning in time for breakfast and comfortable quarters at the Union Hotel, and as it was the Sabbath took his ease all day before a wood fire. On Monday, which was New Year's Day, he called on a clergyman to whom he had a letter of introduction, and in his company visited the local sights, which included the house which had served as headquarters to Generals Gates, Greene, and Cornwallis successively. At sunset he was crossing the turbulent Haw River, into the worst roads he had yet experienced, and eventually reached Greensborough after dark; an active, thriving town five miles from the site of old Guilford Courthouse, where Nathaniel Greene, having gathered up the remnants of Gates's Camden defeat, was to encounter Cornwallis in his turn.

"A cloudy sky, a biting north wind, and the dropping of a few snowflakes when I left Greensborough (at nine the next morning) betokened an unpleasant day for my researches. It was ten o'clock when I reached Martinsville, once a pleasant hamlet, now a desolation. There are only a few dilapidated and deserted dwellings left; and nothing remains of the old Guilford Courthouse but the ruins of a chimney. Only one house was inhabited, and that by the tiller of the soil around it. Descending into a narrow, broken valley from Martinsville, and ascending the opposite slope to still higher ground on the road to Salem, I passed among the fields consecrated by the events of the battle at Guilford in March, 1781, to the house of Mr. Hotchkiss, a Quaker, who I was informed could point out every locality of interest in his neighborhood.

"Mr. Hotchkiss was absent, and I was obliged to wait more than an hour for his return. The time passed pleasantly in conversation with his daughter, an intelligent young lady, who kindly ordered my horse to be fed, and regaled me with some fine apples, the first fruit of the kind I had seen since leaving the James River. While tarrying there, the snow began to fall thickly, and when about noon I rambled over the most interesting portion of the battle-ground, the whole country was covered with a white mantle.

"The snow was falling very fast when I made this sketch and distant objects were seen with great difficulty. Our point of view, at the old log-house, is the extreme westerly boundary of the field."

Again we approach the battle from the rear of the situation, instead of leading into it from Charlotte, where General Greene had taken over from Gates the army which had met defeat at Camden. Charlotte lay still ahead of Lossing and Charley on that snowy day when he paused to contemplate the battle of Guilford Courthouse. Having wintered the army at Cheraw near the South Carolina border, Greene took the field in the spring of 1781 to fight the long campaign opposite Cornwallis which came to a showdown on March 15th, four months after he assumed command.

Greene himself chose the ground and made his stand. Cornwallis was at that time encamped near New Garden Meeting-house, and had no choice but to accept the challenge. He was low on supplies, and must either win a decisive battle soon or retreat to the sea-coast and refurbish. He chose to fight, and sent off his baggage, sick, and wounded to a camp on the Deep River. Early on the 15th he moved out towards Greene, with Tarleton's cavalry in the van.

Except for a few outstanding savage incidents, it was by modern standards a very polite war, but Colonel Banastre Tarleton and his Green Dragoons were notoriously without mercy. Although he had arrived in America with Cornwallis in '76, at the time of the first unsuccessful attack on Charleston, and then accompanied the British army northward to join Howe in the Jerseys, Tarleton's ugly reputation really began after the fall of Charleston in 1780, when he butchered a detachment under Colonel Buford on Waxhaw Creek by ordering a charge while the flags were still passing for a parley. Tarleton always maintained that Buford had refused to surrender and the attack was therefore in order—but his own preparations had been made secretly so that the charge came while Buford's men were still dismounted and unprepared for combat.

In Greene's van at Guilford Courthouse was the mettlesome Lighthorse Harry Lee's Legion, and a clash between these two famous cavalry commanders as they met in the road while Lee was reconnoitering towards the British camp touched off the battle. Lossing's description of that first skirmish can hardly be bettered:

"The vigilant Lee, with his Legion, was near New Garden Meeting-house when the van of the British army, consisting of cavalry, some light infantry, and yagers, under Lieutenant-colonel Tarleton, approached. Desirous of drawing them as far from the Royal army and as near Greene's as possible, Lee ordered a change of front, and a slow retreat. Hoping to produce a rout, Tarleton and his cavalry pressed forward upon Armstrong, who was now in the rear, but with little effect. They made a second charge, and emptied their pistols, when Lee wheeled suddenly and in a close column advanced upon Tarleton. The minute Tarleton saw the whole cavalry of the Legion upon him he sounded a retreat, for he well knew the superiority of the horses of the Americans. The reason for the inferiority of the British cavalry horses was owing to the fact that they had been taken chiefly from the plantations in South Carolina, and could not be compared in size and strength with those of Pennsylvania and Virginia, whence came those of Lee. The momentum of the latter, when meeting, was much greater than that of Tarleton's, and of course in a charge they had a greater advantage.

"Only one front section of the British cavalry met the shock, and these were all dismounted, and most of the horses were prostrated. Some of the dragoons were killed, and others made prisoners. The Americans lost neither man nor horse. Tarleton, with the remainder of his corps, withdrew in great haste and sought to regain the main army. Lee did not pursue, but endeavored to cut off Tarleton's retreat. While pushing forward with eager hope, he met the British vanguard in the midst of the lofty oaks at the Meetinghouse. They instantly displayed, and gave his cavalry a terrible volley. Lee ordered a retreat, when his infantry came running up, and delivered a well-directed fire. This was followed by a volley from Campbell's riflemen, who had taken post on the left of the infantry, and a general action ensued. It had been continued but a few minutes when Lee, perceiving that the main body of the British was approaching, ordered a general retreat, his cavalry falling in the rear to protect the infantry and riflemen. During this skirmish, Greene prepared for battle."

Lighthorse Harry Lee is a name like a banner, and the man who bore it has left a rather stodgy book of *Memoirs* and a rather round-faced, placid-looking portrait, both of which must fall far short of the exciting personality behind them. He was born at Leesylvania, near Mount Vernon, cousin to the Stratford Lees, son of Lucy Grymes, who was one of the Williamsburg belles during George Washington's coltish youth. Lee had arrived at the Morristown Headquarters in '77 as a captain in a Virginia cavalry troop, and before long had so distinguished himself for dash and enterprise that Washington gave him an irregular force of his own and assigned him to special missions. Early in 1780 he was sent to reinforce Greene at Cheraw, and at once joined in the partisan warfare which suited him almost as well as it did Marion and Sumter, who invented it. He was a bachelor, easy, lucky, and popular, with an apparently charmed life. At the end of the war he went home a hero, and married his cousin Matilda of Stratford, who, he discovered, had blossomed in his absence—and lived happily almost ever after, though grievous misfortunes dogged him towards the end. By his second wife, Anne Carter of Shirley, he became the father of Robert E. Lee.

The main engagement of Guilford Courthouse took place at noon on a bright March day—"The atmosphere calm, and illumined with a cloudless sun; the season rather cold than cool; the body braced, and the mind high toned by the state of the weather," Lee wrote in his *Memoirs*. It was a matter of deliberate, cold-blooded courage on the part of all concerned, from the green North Carolina militia who awaited the first British volley from behind a rail-fence at the edge of the forest to the scarlet-clad British Guards defiling at the double in drilled precision from the Salisbury road into the open fields, forming their line in full view of the waiting Americans, and advancing in solid column under a cannonade.

Even though the Carolinians broke before a bayonet charge accompanied by the spine-chilling British huzzah, and fled to the rear through the second-line Virginians, who opened to let them pass and closed behind them and tried to hold, only to crumple in their turn and fall back on the Continentals, there was nothing like a panic. General Greene, unlike Gates, rode up and down the lines among his men, and for a while entertained great hopes of a real victory.

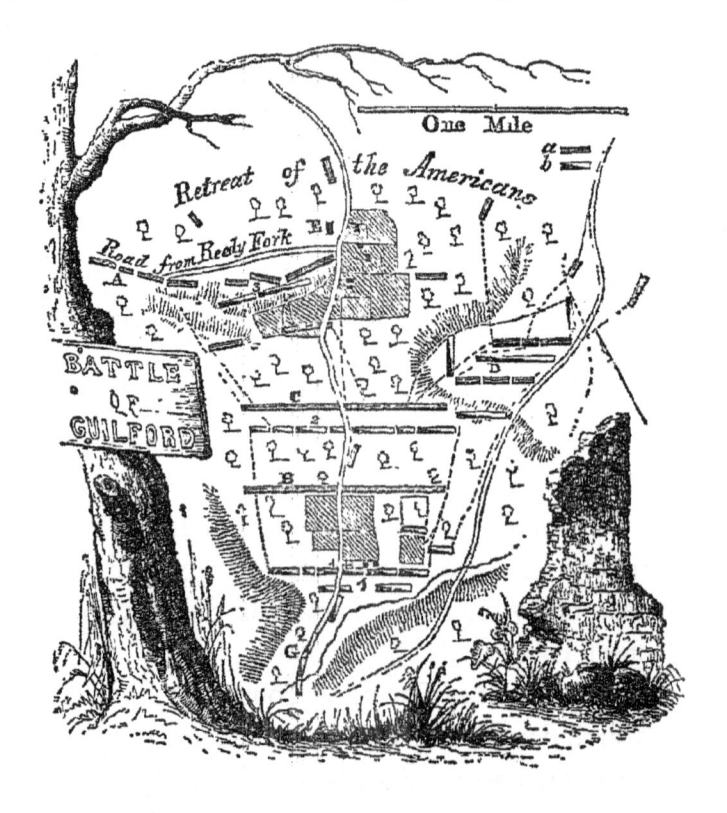

"*Explanation of the Plan:* The shaded parallelograms, A, B, and C, and others not lettered, represent American troops; the half-shaded ones the British troops. G, the British columns advancing along the road from the direction of the New Garden Meeting-house. 1. Their first position, in battle order. B. the first American line, consisting of North Carolina militia, posted at the head of a ravine, in the edge of a wood. C. the second American line, of Virginia militia. A, the American right wing, extending along the road to Reedy Fork, to its junction with the main road, near the court-house. E, the Maryland and Virginia Continentals, under Huger and Williams. 2. The second position of the British, after the retreat of the Carolinians. 3. The third position of the British, endeavoring to gain Greene's right. D. Severe conflict between Leslie with the Hessians and the Americans. E. Guilford Courthouse. The broken chimney in the corner of the map represents all that is left of the old courthouse."

It is not as complicated as it looks, to understand a battle plan if taken a step at a time, and it is well worth the effort. This is the day when Cornwallis could stop the Americans only by firing into his own troops in the melée—and he ordered his artillery to do so from the road, though his casualties were already tragic. Two of his best officers, the younger Stuart and Webster, were mortally wounded. Charles O'Hara, who was to recover and deputize for Cornwallis at the Yorktown surrender, though his brother died here, was disabled by two wounds and lay beside the guns entreating his commanding officer to spare his men, while the grapeshot and cannisters fell on Guards and Marylanders alike. The hot fire did force the Americans to withdraw, and in spite of their heavy losses the British doggedly re-formed for another charge. In the end they held the field, but at a terrible cost of more than a quarter of their comrades. They had started the day at a disadvantage, as Lee pointed out in his *Memoirs*, but their discipline never wavered.

"The disproportion in losses on this day is readily to be accounted for," says Lee. "We had every advantage in the ground, and were sheltered in various points until the enemy approached very near; while he was uncovered, and exposed from his first step to his last. We had spent the previous day in ease, and the night in rest; he had been preparing during the day, and marching part of the night. We were acquainted with wood and tree fighting; he ignorant of both. And lastly, we were trained to take aim and fire low; he was not so trained, and from this cause, or from the composition of his cartridge (too much powder for the lead) he always overshot."

Although the Americans fell back in good order to a former camp on Troublesome Creek, it was for the British a barren, bitter victory. The search for the wounded went on all night in a pitch-black storm of cold rain, conducted by the exhausted, hungry survivors. The nearest British base was two hundred miles away at Wilmington, and their rations were by now reduced to starvation level, their forage parties bottled up, their transport paralyzed by feeble, useless horses. Greene sent back American army surgeons under a white flag to tend his own wounded, and they worked beside the British search parties, but many helpless men died of exposure and neglect before they were found. Cornwallis left his wounded in the care of the Americans at New Garden Meeting-house, when he began his retreat towards the coast. He had lost the campaign and he had lost valuable officers and he had lost face. His army reached Wilmington on April 7th, in pitiable condition. In the South, as at Trenton in '76, the tide had turned.

At Philadelphia on April 7th a broadside was published by direction of Charles Thomson who was Secretary to the Congress, consisting of an extract from a letter written by General Greene to the Commander-in-chief from his camp on Buffalo Creek a few days after the battle, beneath a headline which exclaimed: CORNWALLIS RETREATING!

"On the 16th Instant I wrote your Excellency, giving an account of an action which happened at Guilford Courthouse the day before. I was then persuaded that notwithstanding we were obliged to give up the ground, we had reaped the advantage of the action. Circumstances since confirm me in opinion that the enemy were too much gauled to improve their success. We lay at the Iron-works three days, preparing ourselves for another action, and expecting the enemy to advance; but of a sudden they took their departure, leaving behind them evident marks of distress. All our wounded at Guilford, which had fallen into their hands, and 70 of their own, too bad to move, were left at New Garden. Most of their officers suffered—Lord Cornwallis had his horse shot under him—Colonel Stuart of the Guards was killed, General O'Hara and Colonels Tarleton and Webster wounded. Only three Field-officers escaped, if reports, which seem to be authentic, can be relied on.

"Our army are in good spirits, notwithstanding our sufferings, and are advancing towards the enemy; they are retreating to Cross creek.

"In South Carolina, Generals Sumpter and Marian have gained several little advantages. In one the enemy lost 60 men, who had under their care a large quantity of stores, which were taken, but by an unfortunate mistake were afterwards re-taken."

The magic names of Sumter and Marion are out of order here. Their deeds lie still ahead of us, in the rocky up-country and the Pedee swamps.

Nat Greene, the Rhode Island Quaker general, was already at Cambridge when Washington arrived there as Commander-in-chief in the summer of 1775, and he was still in the field outside Charleston long after the Yorktown surrender. He was a lovable, long-headed man, with a frivolous wife, Kitty, whom he and half the army adored. Kitty was one of the winter headquarters heroines—her second son, little Nat, was born at camp in January of the hard Morristown winter of 1780—and she was always indulged and welcomed by Martha Washington. When the Quartermaster Department went to pieces in '78, it was Greene who accepted—under protest—the thankless task of reorganizing it. When Gates lost an army at Camden, it was Greene who was sent South to repair the damage.

On March 18th, from the camp on Troublesome Creek, he wrote to his Kitty: "We have had a very severe general action with Lord Cornwallis, in which we were obliged to give up the ground. The action was long, bloody, and severe. Many fell, but none of your particular friends. Colonel Williams is Adjutant-General of the army, and was very active, and greatly exposed. I had not the honor of being wounded, but I was very near being taken, having rode in the heat of the action full tilt into the midst of the enemy; but by Colonel Morris calling to me, and advertising me of my situation, I had just time to retire. Our army, though obliged to give up the ground, retired in good order, and the enemy suffered so severely in the action that they dare not move towards us since. This day he has retired towards the Yadkin. He has great pride and great obstinacy, and nothing but sound beating will induce him to quit this state, which I am in hopes of effecting before long. The evening after the action I received your letter, which was some consolation after the misfortunes of the day. Thus the incidents of human life mix and mingle together; sometimes good, and sometimes bad.

"I see by your letter you are determined to come to the southward. I fear you will be disappointed in your expectations. Nothing but blood and slaughter prevail here, and the operations are in a country little short of a wilderness, where a delicate woman is scarcely known or seen. While the war rages in the manner it does, you will have little opportunity of seeing me.... Our fatigue has been excessive. I have not had my clothes off for upwards of six weeks; but am generally in pretty good health. Poor Major Burnet is sick, and is in a situation you would not think tolerable for one of your Negroes. Indeed the whole Family is almost worn out.... I should be extremely happy if the war had an honorable end, and I on a farm with my little family about me...." Gay, adventuresome Kitty was not permitted to make the journey South until the spring of 1782, but she was in time for the ball which celebrated the evacuation of Charleston by the British.

The original Park at Guilford Courthouse was the result of the enthusiasm of Judge Schenck of Greensborough, who in 1887 turned his personal hobby into a corporation for the preservation of some thirty acres, and the erection of a museum and monuments. In 1917 it passed into the care of the nation, and is now a part of the National Park System, with a modern museum containing relics, portraits, electric maps and diaramas, attended by Ranger-historians who know and can discuss every foot of the ground and every marker and monument. There are few more fully documented days in American history than March 15, 1781, and it is an unforgettable experience to visit this almost perfect example of Park service. Lossing would have been enchanted to see it as it is today, the embodiment of all his dreams of animating the great story he labored to tell.

Leaving Guilford in a snowfall, he came to the New Garden Meeting-house, which had served as a hospital to both sides after the battle, and which still stood in the midst of a stately oak forest, a plain frame building with a brick foundation.

He was just in time to witness a Quaker wedding between a young man of Randolph County, thirty miles away, and a young woman of Guilford. "They had just risen before the elders and people when I glided into a seat near the door," he relates, "and with a trembling voice the bridegroom had begun the expression of the marriage vow. His weather-bronzed features betokened the man of toil in the fields, and strongly contrasted with the blonde and delicate face and slender form of her who, with the downcast eyes of modesty, heard his pledge of love and protection, and was summoning all her energy to make her kindred response. I had often observed the simple marriage ceremony of the Quakers, but never before did the beauty of that ritual appear so marked with the sublimity of pure simplicity. . . .

"The storm yet continued, but anxious to complete my journey I rode on to Jamestown [N.C.], an old village situated upon the high southwestern bank of the Deep River, thirteen miles above Bell's Mills, where Cornwallis had his encampment before the Guilford battle. The country through which I passed from Guilford was very broken, and I did not reach Jamestown till sunset. It is inhabited chiefly by Quakers, the most of them originally from Nantucket and vicinity; and as they do not own slaves, nor employ slave labor, except when a servant is working to purchase his freedom, the land and dwellings presented an aspect of thrift not visible in most of the agricultural districts in the upper country of the Carolinas.

"I passed the night at Jamestown, and early in the morning

departed for the Yadkin. Snow was yet falling gently, and it laid three inches deep upon the ground; a greater quantity than had fallen at one time in that section for five years. Towards noon the clouds broke, and before I reached Lexington at half past two in the afternoon not a flake of snow remained. Charley and I had already lunched by the margin of a little stream, so I drove through the village without halting, hoping to reach Salisbury, sixteen miles distant, by twilight. I was disappointed, for the red clay roads prevailed, and I only reached the house of a small planter, within a mile of the east bank of the Yadkin, just as the twilight gave place to the splendours of a full moon and myriads of stars in a cloudless sky.

"From the proprietor I learned that the Trading Ford, where Greene and Morgan crossed when pursued by Cornwallis [during the great retreat in February, 1781, before Greene turned at Guilford for the battle], was only a mile distant. As I could not pass it on my way to Salisbury in the morning, I rose at four o'clock, gave Charley his breakfast, and at earliest dawn stood upon the eastern shore of the Yadkin and made the sketch.

"The air was frosty, the pools were bridged with ice, and before the sketch was finished my benumbed fingers were disposed to drop the pencil. I remained at the ford till all the east was aglow with the radiance of the rising sun, when I walked back, partook of some corn-bread, muddy coffee, and spare-ribs, and at eight o'clock crossed the Yadkin at the great bridge on the Salisbury road. The river is there about three hundred yards wide, and was considerably swollen from the melting of the recent snows. Its volume of turbid waters came rolling down in a swift current, and gave me a full appreciation of the barrier which Providence had there placed between the Republicans and the Royal army when engaged in the great race."

There was little evidence of Salisbury's lively part in the war, when it witnessed the gathering of local militia, and the passage of both armies during Greene's retreat to Virginia, and Lossing kept on to Charlotte, where he arrived on a Saturday (January 6) eager for his Sabbath rest, for "Charley too was jaded, and needed repose." Here at Charlotte, still travelling backwards in time through the autumn and winter of 1780–81, we come to Gates after his trouncing at Camden the previous August. It was here that he arrived in his seventy-mile panic, alone except for Richard Caswell of North Carolina, who seems to have joined his commanding officer's flight when he abandoned and outstripped his broken army. From here Gates continued without loss of time to Hillsborough, a still safer distance from the British, who followed as far as Charlotte and there rested briefly, while Gates's men straggled after him, only to retrace their steps to Charlotte where he intended to make his winter encampment after the British retired to their own winter camp at Winnsboro.

Gates had actually begun to build huts and shelters for his winter quarters at Charlotte when General Greene arrived there in December, 1780, to relieve him of the command. It was an embarrassing moment all around, and Colonel Otho Williams, who was Gates's Adjutant and later Greene's, has preserved in his *Memoirs* an account of the meeting as he witnessed it: "A manly resignation marked the conduct of General Gates on the arrival of his successor, whom he received at Headquarters with that liberal and gentlemanly air which was habitual to him. General Greene preserved a plain, candid, and respectful manner, neither betraying compassion nor the want of it; nothing like the pride of official consequence even *seemed*. In short, the officers who were present had an elegant lesson of propriety exhibited on a most delicate and interesting occasion."

Otho Williams was a Maryland boy, orphaned at twelve and raised by a devoted married sister, and put to work in the county clerk's office at Frederick while still in his teens, from where he went to the same employment at Baltimore, copying out deeds and mortgages in his beautiful handwriting. In 1775, when he was twenty-seven, he joined a rifle corps which was marching to the Cambridge camp. He was captured at Fort Washington during the Jersey retreat in the autumn of '76, and spent more than a year in the dreadful provost gaol in New York, which permanently damaged his health. When exchanged he returned to the main army in time for the battle at Monmouth, and was then assigned to the Southern expedition as colonel of the Sixth Maryland regiment. A tall, handsome bachelor, of strict moral principles and firm military discipline, he was generally beloved, and proved a strong right arm to Greene, who knew better than Gates how to make use of Williams's abilities.

Several other capable officers who had experienced the Camden campaign and remained at Gates's headquarters must have welcomed the new commanding officer with relief. Colonel John Eager Howard and big Dan Morgan we will meet again at the Cowpens. Isaac Huger, one of five brothers who were wealthy Santee planters, had been fortunately absent from Charleston on duty when the city surrendered. And Colonel William Washington, the young cousin of the Commander-in-chief, had also escaped capture at Charleston by swimming the Santee after a losing skirmish outside the town. Both had found their way to the American camp at Charlotte before Greene's arrival there.

Gates set out northward at once, to face a Congressional inquiry on his conduct at Camden. He was acquitted of cowardice, and following a suitable interval of obscurity, was back on Washington's hands during the long wait in the Hudson encampment for the peace terms to be completed, after the surrender at Yorktown. But Washington was sorry for him. At the same time that he was superseded by Greene, he had received the shattering news of the death of his only son at home.

It was now up to Greene to make what he could of the havoc Gates had created in the Carolinas. The countryside roundabout Charlotte had been exhausted of supplies by the disorganized troops which had been encamped there under Gates, and this determined Greene to winter his main army farther south, near the border between the Carolinas. Detaching Morgan with a small force to watch and harry Cornwallis at his Winnsboro base, Greene left Charlotte for Cheraw with his pitiful remnants on the 16th of December, 1780.

Lossing's perverse chronology, necessarily governed by his route, instead of following either Greene or Morgan now takes him towards the Catawba and the battleground on King's Mountain, which was fought in October, 1780, a few weeks after Camden, and which robbed the British of any lasting advantage arising from the victory over Gates. He crossed the Catawba at Tuckesegee Ford, piloted by a lad on horseback.

"The distance from shore to shore, in the direction of the ford, is more than half a mile, the water varying in depth from ten inches to three feet, and running in quite a rapid current. In the passage, which is diagonal, two islands, covered with shrubbery and trees, are traversed. This was Charley's first experience in fording a very considerable stream, and he seemed to participate with me in the satisfaction experienced in setting foot upon the solid ground of the western shore. I allowed him to rest while I made the sketch, and then we pushed on towards the South Fork of the Catawba, almost seven miles farther.

"I was told that the ford there was marked by a row of rocks, occurring at short intervals across the stream; but when I reached the bank, few of them could be seen above the surface of the swift and swollen current. The distance across is about two hundred and fifty yards, and the whole stream flows in a single channel. The passage appeared (as it really was) very dangerous, and I had no guide. As the day was fast waning away, a storm seemed to be gathering, and there was not an inhabitant within a mile, I resolved to venture alone, relying upon the few rocks visible for indications of the safest place for a passage. Taking my port-folio of drawings from my trunk, and placing it beside me on the seat, and then folding my wagon-top, I was prepared to swim if necessary, and save my sketches if possible. Charley seemed loth to enter the flood, but once in, he breasted the stream like a philosopher. Twice the wheels ran upon rocks, and the wagon was almost overturned, the water being in the meanwhile far over the hubs; and when within a few yards of the southern shore we crossed a narrow channel so deep that my horse kept his feet with difficulty, and the wagon, having a tight body, floated for a moment. The next instant we struck firm ground. I breathed freer as we ascended the bank, and with a thankful heart rode on towards Falls's house of entertainment, away among the hills near the South Carolina line, twenty-six miles from Charlotte....

"Mr. Falls was the postmaster, and an intelligent man, apparently about sixty years of age. I was entertained with the frank hospitality so common in the Carolinas, and at my request breakfast was ready at early dawn. A more gloomy morning cannot well be conceived. Snow had fallen to the depth of two inches during the night, and when I departed a chilling east wind, freighted with sleet, was sweeping over the barren country. King's Mountain battle-ground was fourteen miles distant, and I desired to reach there in time to make my notes and sketches before sunset.

"The roads, except near the water-courses, were sandy and quite level, but the snow made the travelling heavy. Six miles from Falls's I forded Crowder's Creek, a stream about ten yards wide, deep and sluggish, which falls into the Catawba. A little beyond it,

I passed a venerable post-oak, which was shivered but not destroyed by lightning the previous summer. It there marks the dividing-line between North and South Carolina. At noon the storm ceased; the clouds broke, and at three o'clock when I reached the plantation of Mr. Leslie, whose residence is the nearest one to the battle-ground, the sun was shining warm and bright, and the snow had disappeared in the open fields.

"When my errand was made known, Mr. Leslie brought two horses from his stable, and within twenty minutes after my arrival we were in the saddle and traversing a winding way towards Clarke's Ford of King's Creek. From that stream, to the group of hills among which the battle was fought, the ascent is almost imperceptible. The whole range in that vicinity is composed of a series of great undulations, from whose sides burst innumerable springs, making every ravine sparkle with running water. The hills are gravelly, containing a few small boulders. They are covered with oaks, chestnuts, pines, beeches, gums, and tulip poplars, and an undergrowth of post-oaks, laurel and sour-wood. The large trees stand far apart, and the smaller ones not very thick, so that the march of an army over these gentle elevations was comparatively easy. Yet it was a strange place for an encampment or a battle; and to one acquainted with that region, it is difficult to understand why Ferguson and his band were there at all."

The battleground was red-haired Patrick Ferguson's own free choice, however. He was a remarkable man, a soldier since boyhood, and was said at Minden in 1760 to have turned his horse in the face of an enemy charge to retrieve a pistol which had been jolted out of its holster in the action. He was then sixteen. A bout of illness interrupted his army career, during which at his home in Scotland he studied military tactics and invented the breech-loading Ferguson rifle, which used a pointed bullet and could be fired as much as five or six times a minute. He arrived in America in '77, and at Brandywine received a wound in the right arm which left it permanently disabled. "The length of our lives is not at our command," he wrote to his anxious mother at this time, "however much the manner of them may be."

Coming South for the siege of Charleston as a major in the 71st Regiment, he was sent by Cornwallis in June, 1780, to the back country around 96 to recruit Loyalists and fugitives to the British standard, and soon collected a raffish crew of outlaws who were second only to Tarleton's for terrorizing the countryside he plundered. The men from the mountain settlements rose against him and formed a little army of their own, as rugged as Ferguson's, to drive him out. The mountain men had no commissary, no baggage, no tents, and lived on pumpkins, roasted corn, and what meat their rifles could bring down.

Although Harry Lee was not present at that engagement on October 7th, 1780, having not yet left the North, he later set down a soldier's competent report of what happened there: "Ferguson took post on the summit of King's Mountain, a position thickly set with trees, and more assailable by the rifle than defensible with the bayonet. Here he was overtaken by our mountaineers, who quickly dismounted and arrayed themselves for battle. Our brave countrymen were formed into three divisions, under their respective leaders, and coolly ascended the mountain in different directions. Colonel Cleveland first reached the enemy, and opened a destructive fire from behind the trees. Ferguson resorted to the bayonet, and Cleveland necessarily gave way. At that instant, from another quarter Colonel Shelby poured in his fire; alike sheltered and alike effectual. Upon him Ferguson furiously turned, and advanced with the bayonet; gaining the only, though immaterial, advantage in his power, of forcing Shelby to recede. This was scarcely effected before Colonel Campbell had gained the summit of the mountain; when he too commenced a deadly fire. The British bayonet was again applied; and produced its former effect. All the divisions now returned in co-operation, and resistance became temerity. Nevertheless, Ferguson, confiding in the bayonet, sustained the attack with undismayed gallantry. The battle raged for fifty minutes, when the

British commander received a ball and fell dead. Deprived of their leader, the fire of the enemy slackened, and the second in command wisely beat a parley, which was followed by his surrender."

The battle was all the more bitterly fought as is was settling the score between Tory and patriot, and the Tories had a bad record and bad consciences, and dared not ask for quarter. Their losses in killed and wounded were over three hundred, as against twenty killed on the American side. On the day after the battle a court martial was held in the American camp, and ten of the Tory prisoners were hanged from a giant tulip tree for past crimes and cruelties in the neighborhood of the men who now confronted them.

"We tied our horses near the grave of Ferguson and his fellow-sleepers," Lossing records, "and ascended to the summit of the hill whereon the British troops were encamped and fought. The battle-ground is about a mile and a half south of the North Carolina line. It is a stony ridge, extending North and South, and averaging about one hundred feet in height above the ravines which surround it. It is nearly a mile in length, very narrow at its summit, with steep sides.

"This view is from the foot of the hill, whereon the hottest part of the fight occurred. The north slope of that eminence is seen on the left. In the center, within a sort of basin, into which several ravines converge, is seen the simple monument erected to the memory of Ferguson and others; and in the foreground on the right is shown the great tulip-tree upon which, tradition says, ten Tories were hung.... The monument is a thick slab of hard slate, about three feet high, rough hewn except where the inscriptions are."

When Lossing was there, the single marker commemorated the death of the patriot Major William Chronicle and three of his comrades in the inscription on its north face, and the resting-place of Colonel Ferguson on the south face. It is now much wasted away, and newer stones have been set up, besides the centennial monument provided by public contribution. The site belongs to the National Park Service, and is furnished with a museum containing a diarama of the battle, an electric map, and one of the famous Ferguson rifles.

There is a legend, not officially mentioned. A girl named Virginia Sal, who was Ferguson's mistress, was the first to die on the mountain-top, and is buried with him beneath the stone.

After making his sketches at leisure, Lossing rode back with Mr. Leslie at twilight to spend the night. "On our return, we ascertained that the grandfather of Mr. Leslie, the venerable William McElwees, had just arrived. His company for the evening was a pleasure I had not anticipated. He was one of Sumter's partisan corps, and fought with him at Rocky Mount and Hanging Rock.... Mr. McElwees was eighty-seven years of age when I saw him, yet his intellect seemed unclouded. His narrative of stirring events, while following Sumter, was clear and vivid, and when at a late hour the family knelt at the domestic altar, a prayer went up from that patriot's lips equal in fervid eloquence, both in words and accents, to anything I ever heard from a pulpit."

But before he came to Sumter's rocky battlefields, Lossing must cross the Broad River on his way to the Cowpens, where a battle was fought and won by Dan Morgan on January 17th, 1781, after

Greene had detached him at Charlotte from the main force which marched southward for Cheraw.

"The country over which I passed is exceedingly rough and hilly," he continues. "In some places the road was deep gullied by rains; in others, where it passed through recent clearings, stumps and branches were in the way, endangering the safety of wheel and hoof. Within a mile of the ferry, I discovered that the front axle of my wagon was broken, evidently by striking a stump; but with the aid of a hatchet and strong cord with which I had provided myself, I was enabled to repair the damage temporarily.

"The sun was about an hour high when I reached the eastern bank of the Broad River, a little below the mouth of Buffalo Creek. The house of Mrs. Ross, the owner of the ferry, was upon the opposite side. For more than half an hour I shouted and made signals with a white handkerchief upon my whip, before I was discovered, when a shrill whistle responded, and in a few minutes a fat Negro came to the opposite shore and crossed, with a miserable bateau or river flat, to convey me over. The river, which is there about one hundred and twenty yards wide, was quite shallow and running with a rapid current, yet the ferryman had the skill to pole his vessel across without difficulty.

"I was comfortably lodged at the house of Mrs. Ross for the night, and passed the evening very agreeably in the company of herself and two intelligent daughters. Here I observed what I so frequently saw in the upper country of the Carolinas, among even the affluent planters—the windows without sashes or glass. In the coldest weather these and the doors are left wide open, the former being closed at night by tight shutters. Great light-wood (pine) fires in the huge chimney-places constantly blazing in a measure beat back or temper the cold currents of air which continually flow into the dwellings. This ample ventilation in cold weather is universally practiced at the South. At Hillsborough and Charlotte I observed the boarders at the hotels sitting with cloaks and shawls on at table while the doors stood wide open!

"I was now within fifteen miles of the Cowpens, and at daybreak the next morning started for the interesting locality. This name is derived from the circumstance that some years prior to the Revolution, before this section of country was settled, some persons in Camden (then called Pine-tree) employed two men to go up to the Thicketty Mountain and in the grassy intervals among the hills raise cattle. As a compensation, they were allowed the entire use of the cows during the summer for making butter and cheese, and the steers for tilling labor. In the fall, large numbers of the fattest cattle would be driven down to Camden to be slaughtered for beef. This region, so favorable for rearing cows on account of the grass and fine springs, was consequently called The Cowpens.

"I was informed that the place of conflict was among the hills of Thicketty Mountain, and near the plantation of Robert Scruggs. ... His house is upon the Mill-gap Road, and about half a mile west of a divergence of a highway leading to Spartanburg. Upon the gentle hills on the borders of Thicketty Creek, covered with pine woods, the hottest part of the fight occurred. The battle ended within a quarter of a mile of Scruggs's, where is now a cleared field, in the center of which was a log-house. The field was covered with blasted pines, stumps, and stocks of Indian corn, and had a most dreary appearance.

"In this field and along the line of conflict, a distance of about two miles, many bullets and other military relics have been found. Among other things, I obtained a spur, which belonged to the cavalry of either Washington or Tarleton.

> "Come listen a while, and the truth I'll relate,
> How brave General Morgan did Tarleton defeat;
> For all his proud boasting he forced was to fly,
> When brave General Morgan his courage did try."
> *Revolutionary Song.*

We have now overtaken some of the most colorful men in the whole history of the war; Morgan, William Washington, and John Eager Howard among the Americans, and Tarleton and his Green

Dragoons, who did more to give the British army a bad name than any other corps.

The magnificent Virginia rifleman, Dan Morgan, who topped the Commander-in-chief by an inch and several pounds, had begun as a humble wagoner in the same army under Braddock where Washington served as a mounted aide in 1755. He was a few years younger, but during his British army days he had suffered floggings and a wound which would have wrecked a less powerful physique than his, and he was chronically plagued by rheumatism and sciatica. After a wild youth he had married a gentle, pious woman and settled down on a farm in Berkeley County. In 1775 he left his family and his sober, industrious farmer's life to lead a band of young Virginia sharpshooters to Washington's camp at Cambridge, marching them six hundred miles in twenty-one days.

He served with conspicuous gallantry through the Canadian campaign, Saratoga, Valley Forge, and Monmouth, and then, neglected by Congress, who promoted juniors over his head, and disabled by his rheumatism, he retired to his home in the summer of '79. Although he had had enough of Gates at Saratoga, when the news of the Camden defeat reached him he hurried back to the army, which he then found in pieces roundabout Hillsborough, to offer his services again in what he recognized as dire emergency; and he received a belated promotion to brigadier, in October, while in the Hillsborough camp. The arrival of Greene at Charlotte as Gates's successor must have been very gratifying to Dan Morgan, and Greene at once gave him that detachment of his own with which to threaten the British up-country posts as far as the fort called 96, and to encourage the local militia and mountain men, who were already a little intoxicated with their success at King's Mountain.

Morgan's small force included 400 Maryland Continentals under John Eager Howard, who had been in the war since its beginning, serving first with the Flying Camp at White Plains. After an interval at home because of the death of his father, who owned a large estate near Baltimore, Howard returned to the army and fought at Germantown and Monmouth, before starting South with DeKalb in the attempt which came too late to relieve Lincoln at Charleston. With DeKalb he joined Gates and came to Camden, where he behaved with desperate gallantry and remained to rally the shattered companies after Gates's flight from the field. Cool and clear-headed under fire, he was known for his competence at close quarters with the bayonet, which was shared by the men under his command.

Leading Morgan's cavalry was Colonel William Washington, with about a hundred tough dragoons. He was twenty years younger than the Commander-in-chief, and their exact relationship was a matter of doubt even to the principals, though it appears that their great-grandfathers were brothers. Born and raised in Stafford County, Virginia, not far from Mount Vernon, William nevertheless is not mentioned in George's pre-war diary which faithfully records the family visits and guests during those leisurely years, and he makes his entrance in 1775 as a captain in the regiment of Hugh Mercer, one of George's old friends at Fredericksburg who died from wounds after Princeton. William soon caught the elder Washington's favorable notice, and received minor wounds at both Long Island and Trenton before becoming a captain in a newly formed Virginia cavalry troop in '77. He rode South as a colonel in the spring of 1780 during the attempt to save Lincoln at Charleston, and was luckily on a raid outside the city at its surrender. Having made his way with a handful of men to Charlotte, he was assigned to Morgan there. In character and physique he was a true Washington, powerfully built, a spectacular horseman, modest, soft-spoken, and brave.

He and Tarleton were old enemies who had already met in several skirmishes outside Charleston during the siege, and were now to meet again when Tarleton was ordered up to drive Morgan and prevent him from interfering with British communications by nuisance raids in the vicinity of Cornwallis's base at Winnsboro after the King's Mountain defeat had caused the main British army to fall back from Charlotte and go into winter quarters. Morgan led Tarleton on craftily, leaving his camp-fires still warm behind him, and at the Cowpens posted himself at his leisure in battle order, on ground of his own choosing, served a cooked breakfast to his rested men, and awaited the British attack.

As at Guilford a few weeks later, the disciplined British were thrown into battle after a hard night and a morning march, and as was expected of them they stood withering fire, closed up, and came on again, until it appeared that the Americans were withdrawing from the field, as usual. Then, in their enthusiasm the British infantry broke ranks in headlong pursuit, and the American line suddenly faced about and fired from the hip, with the bayonet ready. Colonel Howard led the bayonet charge, while Washington's cavalry struck on the flank, and that part of the battle ended in wholesale surrender by the British. Colonel Howard is supposed at one time to have held in his hand a bristling bouquet of seven surrendered British swords.

Tarleton with a few horsemen attempted to escape by flight, and William Washington went after them full tilt, outriding most of his troop. Three British officers, Tarleton among them, turned to attack him. Washington's sergeant disabled one of them, and his fourteen-year-old bugler pistoled another in the nick of time, as Washington closed with Tarleton in the personal encounter both had been yearning for. Washington's sabre made a gash in Tarleton's hand, Tarleton fired his pistol at close range, wounding Washington in the knee and killing his horse, and got away.

The British losses at the Cowpens were a fantastic nine-tenths killed, wounded, or captured, along with guns, colors, baggage, and ammunition, for the baggage guards cut the horses loose and rode them from the field, abandoning the wagons. Tarleton's prestige never entirely recovered, though he was present at Guilford Courthouse and remained with Cornwallis till the Yorktown surrender, having retreated with his remnants to the main camp at Winnsboro, where he met with scant sympathy.

There is a story that some time later, while being entertained at his own request in an American household in Carolina, Tarleton spoke contemptuously of William Washington, with a remark that he would like to see him around. To which a spirited patriot belle who was present replied, "If you had looked behind you, Colonel Tarleton, at the battle of Cowpens, you would have had that pleasure!"

Coming on top of Ferguson's disaster at King's Mountain the previous October, the Cowpens defeat cancelled out Camden for good, and Cornwallis found himself confronted with the necessity to deal single-handedly with both Morgan in the mountains and Greene in South Carolina. He chose Morgan first, as the nearer and smaller force, and set out in pursuit, hoping also to regain some of Tarleton's men whom Morgan had taken prisoner. Morgan meanwhile moved by forced marches towards a junction with Greene's main army which was now coming north from Cheraw. And so the great race began.

Leaving Huger and Otho Williams to bring up the main army, Greene had ridden ahead with a small escort, and joined Morgan on the Catawba January 31st. From there, with Cornwallis close behind, Greene and Morgan retreated steadily towards the friendly neighborhood of the Dan River in Virginia. It was a battle of fords, in which the rains and high water of the spring season played a leading part. At Cowan's Ford on the Catawba there was a heavy skirmish in which the Americans were nearly worsted. At Trading Ford on the Yadkin, Morgan's cavalry crossed at midnight, and his infantry followed in bateaux which they secured on the far side, and Cornwallis could not pass the river until the flood subsided. At Guilford Courthouse, which Greene reached for the first time on February 7, five weeks before he fought the battle there, he was joined by Huger, Williams, and Lighthorse Harry Lee, in charge of the rest of his troops from Cheraw.

At a council of war it was decided to avoid an engagement with Cornwallis's superior force and try to beat him to the Dan. It was the same maneuver of calculated withdrawal which George Washington had performed with such success in Jersey in 1776, before he re-crossed the Delaware and threw the Hessians at Trenton and the British at Princeton into fatal confusion. Morgan was by now worn down with fatigue and tormented by his old enemy rheumatism, and he begged leave of Greene to retire. Otho Williams was given command of the light corps which would have been Morgan's. Sorry as he was to lose the old waggoner's experience and popularity with the troops, Greene had chosen wisely, and Williams rose superbly to the occasion.

"The two armies moved in lines almost parallel with each other," Lossing relates, "Greene on the right and Cornwallis on the left. Colonel Williams, with his light corps, took an intermediate road, to watch the movements of the enemy. Lee's partisan legion, which maneuvered in the rear, was often in sight of O'Hara's vanguard. Great vigilance was necessary at night to prevent a surprise, and so numerous were the patrols that each man enjoyed only six hours' sleep in forty-eight. Williams always moved at three o'clock in the morning, so as to get a sufficient distance in advance to partake of breakfast, the only meal they were allowed each day. Cornwallis was equally active, and both armies made the extraordinary progress of thirty miles a day."

Skirmishes were incessant. Lee and Williams with the rear guard often lost touch with Greene and were ignorant of his progress, anxious for his safety. They saw more of O'Hara's van than they did of their own army's rear. The last day below the Dan, February 14th, was sheer melodrama.

"The roads, passing through a red clay region, were wretched in the extreme," says Lossing, "yet the pursued and the pursuers pushed forward rapidly. During the forenoon, only a single hour was allowed by the belligerents for a repast. At noon a loud shout went up from the American host; a courier, covered with mud, his horse reeking with sweat, brought a letter to Colonel Williams from Greene, announcing the joyful tidings that he had crossed the Dan safely at Irwin's Ferry on the preceding day. That shout was heard by O'Hara, and Cornwallis regarded it as ominous of evil. Still he pressed forward.

"At three o'clock, when within fourteen miles of the river, Williams filed off towards Boyd's Ferry, leaving Lee to maneuver in front of the enemy. Williams reached the shore before sunset, and at dark was landed upon the north side. Lee sent his infantry on in advance, and at twilight withdrew with his cavalry, and galloped for the river. When he arrived, his infantry had just passed in boats with safety. The horses were turned into the stream, while the dragoons embarked in bateaux. At nine o'clock, Lieutenant-colonels Lee and Carrington (the quarter-master general) embarked in the last boat, and before midnight the weary troops were deep in slumber in the bosom of Virginia.... after one of the most skillfully conducted and remarkable retreats on record."

It was from here, after a brief period of rest and recruitment, that Greene faced about and met Cornwallis at the time and place of his own choice, for the engagement at Guilford Courthouse, on the 15th of March, 1781.

XI

Cherokee Ford to Hobkirk's Hill

CROSSING the Broad River at Cherokee Ford, Lossing spent a pleasant Sabbath at Yorkville and drove on again early Monday morning "with the impression that not a lovelier village flourishes in the upper country of the South." He had seen his first palmettos in its gardens, and its streets were lined with Pride of India trees bearing clusters of fruit.

"Leaving the great highway to Columbia on the right, I traversed the more private roads in the direction of the Catawba to visit the scenes of valor and suffering in the vicinity of that stream," he continues. "The weather was fine and the roads generally good....

"I crossed the Fishing Creek at sunset; and at the house of a young planter, a mile beyond, passed the night. There I experienced hospitality in its fullest degree. The young husbandman had just begun business for himself and, with his wife and wee bairn, occupied a modest house with only one room. I was not aware of the extent of their accommodations when I asked for a night's entertainment, and the request was promptly complied with. It made no difference to them, for they had two beds in the room, and needed but one for themselves; the other was at my service. The young man was very intelligent and inquiring, and midnight found us in pleasant conversation. They would accept no compensation in the morning; and I left his humble dwelling full of reverence for that generous and unsuspecting hospitality of Carolina, where the people will give a stranger lodging even in their own bedrooms, rather than turn him from their doors.

"My journey of a day from Fishing Creek to Rocky Mount on the Catawba was delightful. The winter air was like a breath of late April in New England; and the roads, passing through a picturesque country, were generally good. Almost every plantation is clustered with Revolutionary associations; for this region, like Westchester County in New York, was the scene of continual partisan movements, skirmishes, and cruelties, during the last three years of the war. Near the mouth of Fishing Creek, which empties into the Catawba two miles above the Great Falls, Sumter suffered defeat [in August, 1780] after partial success at Rocky Mount and Hanging Rock below; and down through Fairfield, Chester, and Richland, too, Whigs and Tories battled fearfully for territorial possession, plunder, and personal revenge.

"Turning to the left at Beckhamville, I traversed a rough and sinuous road down to the banks of the Catawba, just below the Great Falls. The place is wild and romantic. Almost the whole volume of the river is here compressed by a rugged island into a narrow channel between steep, rocky shores, fissured and fragmented as if by some powerful convulsion. There are no perpendicular falls; but down a rocky bed the river tumbles in mingled rapids and cascades, roaring and foaming, and then subsides into comparative calmness in a basin below.

"It was late in the afternoon when I finished my sketch of the Falls, crossed Rock Creek, and reined up in front of the elegant mansion of Mrs. Barkley at Rocky Mount. Her dwelling, where refined hospitality bore rule, is beautifully situated upon an eminence overlooking the Catawba and the surrounding country, and within a few rods of the remains of the old village and the battle-ground. Surrounded by gardens and ornamental trees, it must be a delightful summer residence.... Accompanied by Mrs. Barkley's three daughters and a young planter from 'over the river,' I visited the battle-ground before sunset, examined the particular localities indicated by the finger of tradition...."

We have now arrived with Lossing and Charley in the dramatic partisan territory of South Carolina, where Sumter in the up-country and Marion in the swamps near the coast played their part in the campaign which enabled Greene to wear down the British army and so divide and cripple it as to make inevitable the surrender at Yorktown.

Of the two, Sumter has been even more lost sight of than the man known as the Swamp Fox. Thomas Sumter was unique among the American generals in that he had once seen George III face to face. He was born in Hanover County, Virginia, of very humble parents, two years later than George Washington on the Potomac. Like Washington, he was at Fort Duquesne in '56, and was also with Forbes in the '58 campaign, and yet there is no record of an acquaintance then between him and the mounted, commissioned aide who was to become the American Commander-in-chief. When Sumter went to Williamsburg to see the Royal Governor on Indian affairs in '62, George Washington was already established as a gentleman farmer at Mount Vernon, only appearing in Williamsburg as a Burgess at the Assembly times. Sumter somehow became involved at this time in the determination of three friendly Cherokee warriors to see the King in London. The expedition was sanctioned by the Governor, and as a sergeant in a red coat Sumter sailed with them and an interpreter from Hampton Roads. The interpreter died at sea, and Sumter was left as their bear-leader on what must have been a hilarious tour which included everything from a presentation at the Court of St. James to high-jinks at Vauxhall Gardens. Within the year, a somewhat sophisticated and polished young man of thirty-four, he returned with his charges on a boat which landed them at Charleston.

Apparently his family ties in Virginia were not strong since his father's death, and when on his return there he had been jailed for old debts and escaped again to South Carolina he remained to open a store at a cross-roads near Eutaw Springs. As a successful merchant, a loyal friend, and a sober citizen, he was commissioned justice of the peace, in '67 married a wealthy widow nearly ten years older than he was, and began to acquire property. There was one son, Thomas, Jr., and a daughter who died as a baby.

Sumter, who had actually seen the King and was not perhaps much taken with him, was elected delegate to the first Provincial Congress in '74, and commanded a regiment during the first unsuccessful British attempt on Charleston in '76. He then took part in some unproductive Georgia campaigning and in September, '78, resigned from the army and returned home to salvage his private affairs which had suffered during his absence. His wife, "an amiable, fine-looking woman," affectionately known as Miss Polly, was now an invalid, and either from a fall or a paralytic stroke was never able to walk again, but lived another thirty years confined to a chair in which she was carried about by her devoted household.

By the spring of 1780, when Lincoln was besieged in Charleston, the refugees were slipping out of the doomed city across the Santee ferry near the Sumter house, but Sumter had seen the British beaten at Charleston before and did not leave home, though on a quiet day the siege guns could be heard from there. After the surrender, which must have come as an unpleasant surprise to him, the Sumter family was living at the house he had built for the hot weather in the hills on the north side of the Santee, when Tarleton was sent out on the raid which ended in the massacre of Buford's men at Waxhaw Creek at the end of May. The warning of Tarleton's approach was carried by twelve-year-old Thomas, Jr., in time for his father to conceal himself at a distance. Miss Polly faced the Green Dragoons in her chair, and denied any knowledge of her husband's whereabouts. Enraged by her polite fearlessness, they carried her, chair and all, out on to the lawn while they plundered and burned the house, before riding on to deal with Buford in a way which established their reputation forever.

Four days later Sumter had seen his family safely back to the house near the ferry, and was in the field again, gathering about him a little force of patriots who rendezvoused at Tuckesegee Ford, bringing mill saws, plows, and iron tools of all kinds from which a local blacksmith made swords and bayonets. His workmanship was so fine it was said that the sword points might be forced back through the handle without injury to the blades. In the middle of June the motley corps of refugees, farmers, ex-soldiers, and Indians who were assembled at the Ford elected Sumter their general, and were all sworn to Liberty or Death—the first organized militia after the fall of Charleston the previous month. Word spread of his leadership, and more men came in daily, bringing their own horses and arms. His nickname of the Gamecock came not from an exasperated British officer, but was lovingly bestowed on him by a group of hard-bitten back-country men whose favorite sport of cock-fighting he had interrupted by forcibly inviting them to join the army for a man-sized fight. He was now forty-six, slender and wiry in build, and possessed of that personal magnetism which held his unruly, undisciplined troop together.

In July, Sumter heard of DeKalb's arrival at Hillsborough with the reinforcements intended for Lincoln, and wrote to him, giving an account of the situation in South Carolina, and suggesting a well-thought-out plan of campaign which would cut off the British from their Charleston base by occupying the fords along the Santee behind them, with small American posts. DeKalb was unable to take any action before the arrival of Gates, who was about to supersede him in the Southern command, and Sumter meanwhile undertook to dislodge a small British force at Rocky Mount, which was making troublesome cavalry raids on an already impoverished countryside. They were established on top of a hill on the west bank of the Catawba, in a fortified post consisting of two log houses and a large frame house with loop-holes and reinforced walls, inside a ditch and abatis.

"At an early hour of the day [August 1st, 1780]," says Lossing, "Sumter appeared with his whole force upon the crown of the hill now occupied by the servants' houses of Mrs. Barkley. The British commander, warned of his approach by a Tory, was prepared to receive him, and though the Americans poured several volleys upon the fortification (if it can be called one) they produced but little effect. Having no artillery, they resorted to means for dislodging the enemy seldom used in war.

"Leaping the abatis after three assaults, they drove the garrison into the houses. These, according to Mr. McElwees, who was in the engagement, were situated near the bottom of the slope and were composed of logs. They first attempted to set them on fire by casting burning fagots upon them. Not succeeding in this, an old wagon was procured, and upon it was placed a quantity of dry brush and straw taken from the abatis. These were ignited, and then rolled down against the houses. The British, perceiving their danger, hoisted a flag. Supposing they intended to surrender, Sumter ordered the firing to cease. At that moment a shower of rain extinguished the flames, and the enemy defied him. Having no other means at hand to dislodge or seriously injure the garrison, Sumter withdrew, first to the north side of Fishing Creek, near the Catawba, and then to Landsford where he crossed the river. Seven days afterward he was battling the enemy at Hanging Rock." Sumter lost four men killed, including a Catawba Indian, and ten wounded. The British lost ten killed and the same number wounded.

"I left the family of Mrs. Barkley with real regret," Lossing confesses, for he always seemed to fall in with delightful young ladies, "and pursuing a crooked, steep, and rough road down to the brink of the river, crossed the Catawba upon a bateau at Rocky Mount Ferry, just below the Falls at the mouth of Rocky Mount Creek. The scenery here, and for some miles on my road toward Hanging Rock, was highly picturesque. I was approaching the verge of the Lowlands, the apparent shore of the ancient ocean, along which are strewn huge boulders—the mighty pebbles cast upon the beach when, perhaps, the mammoth and the mastodon slaked their thirst in the waters of the Catawba.

"For several miles the road passed among the erratic rocks and curiously-shaped conglomerates. When within three miles of Hanging Rock, I passed the celebrated Anvil Rock, one of the curiosities of the South. It appears to be a concretion of the soil around, being composed of precisely similar material; or the soil may be disintegrated rocks of similar character. In its sides are cavities from which large pebbles have apparently fallen, and also furrows as if made by rains. Its height above the ground is about twelve feet; its form suggested its name.

"I reached the Lancaster and Camden highway at noon, and on inquiry ascertained that the celebrated Hanging Rock, near which Sumter and his companions fought a desperate battle, was about a mile and a half eastward. Thither I went immediately, notwithstanding the temptation of a good dinner, freely offered, was before me, for I desired to get as far on towards Camden that night as possible. The roads were now generally sandy, and in many places soft and difficult to travel, making progress slow. Along a by-road across the high rolling plain upon which tradition avers the hottest of the battle was fought, I rode to the brow of a deep narrow valley, through which courses Hanging Rock Creek, one of the headwaters of Lynch's Creek, the western branch of the Great Peedee.

"The mingled sound of falling waters and grinding mill-stones came up from the deep furrow while from a small cabin by the roadside, upon the verge of the steep bank, I heard a broken melody. Alighting, I entered the cabin, and there sat an aged Negro dining upon hoe-cake and bacon, and humming a refrain. He was the miller. His hair was as white with the frost of years as his coarse garb was with flour. To my question respecting his family, he said, shaking his bowed head, 'Ah, massa! I lives all alone now; t'ree years ago dey sol' my wife, and she's gone to Mississippi. Hab to bake my own hoe-cake now. But neber mind; needn't work 'less I'm a mind to; 'nough to eat, and pretty soon I die.'

"He told me he was more than eighty years old, and remembered seeing 'de redcoats scamper when Massa Sumter and Jacky McClure pitched into 'em.' Pointing to the celebrated Hanging Rock upon the opposite side of the stream, 'Dar,' he said, 'a heap o' redcoats sleep de night afore de battle, and dar I hid de night arter.' From the venerable slave, whose memory appeared unclouded, I learned the location of several points mentioned in the accounts of the engagement.

"Leaving Charley to dine upon the verge of the stream, I proceeded to Hanging Rock, of whose immensity I had heard frequent mention. It is a huge conglomerate boulder, twenty or thirty feet in diameter, lying upon the verge of the high east bank of the creek, nearly a hundred feet above the stream. Around it are several smaller boulders of the same materials. It is shelving towards the bank, its concavity being in the form of the quarter of an orange paring, and capacious enough to shelter fifty men from rain.

"Near the Hanging Rock, on the western bank of the creek, Lord Rawdon, the British commander in that section, had established a post.... The greater portion were Loyalists, the remainder were regulars.... We have observed that after the assault on Rocky Mount, Sumter crossed the Catawba, and proceeded towards Hanging Rock. He marched early in the morning cautiously, [on August 6th] and approached the British camp in three divisions, with the intention of falling upon the main body, stationed upon the plain at Coles's Old Field. Through the error of his guides, Sumter came first upon Bryan's corps of Loyalists, near the Great Rock, half a mile from the British camp. The Tories soon yielded and fled towards the main body, many of them throwing away their arms without discharging them. These the Americans seized; and pursuing this advantage, Sumter next fell upon Brown's Loyalist corps, which poured a heavy fire upon him from a wood. They also received him with the bayonet. A fierce conflict ensued, and for a while the issue was doubtful. The riflemen with sure aim soon cut off almost all of Brown's officers, and many of his soldiers, and at length his corps yielded and dispersed in confusion. The arms and ammunition procured from the vanquished were of great service, for when the action commenced Sumter's men had not two rounds each.

"Now was the moment to strike for decisive victory; it was lost by the criminal indulgence of Sumter's men in plundering the portion of the British camp already secured, and drinking freely of the liquor found there. Sumter's ranks became disordered; and while he was endeavoring to bring order out of confusion, the enemy rallied.

"Of his six hundred men, only about two hundred could be brought to bear upon the remaining portion of the British, who were yet in some confusion, but defended by two cannons. Sumter was not to be foiled. With a shout, he and his handful of brave men rushed forward to the attack. The enemy had formed a hollow square, with the field-pieces in front, and in this position received the charge. The Americans attacked them on three sides, and the contest was severe for a while. At length, just as the British line was yielding, a reinforcement from Tarleton's legion, returning from an excursion towards Rocky Mount, appeared, and their number being magnified, Sumter deemed a retreat a prudent measure. This was done at meridian, but the enemy had been so severely handled that they did not attempt a pursuit. Could Sumter have brought all of his forces into action in this last attack, the rout of the British would have been complete.

> "He beat them back! beneath the flame
>   Of valor quailing, or the shock!
> He carved, at last, a hero's name
>   Upon the glorious Hanging Rock!"

Hanging Rock today still stands lonely and impressive in a deeply wooded gorge on a winding dirt road from Lancaster, looking much as Sumter saw it. Underneath its tremendous overhang the ashes of a recent camper's fire remain as direct descendants of those left by the British when they went out to answer the alarm. The echoes seem to be still there. It is a place to sit down and think and wonder, and the past comes very close—a place where it is easy to imagine that turbulent spirits might return in search of the peace which now enfolds it.

As Sumter fell back across the Catawba from Hanging Rock, Gates and DeKalb were coming down towards Camden. At Wateree Ford on the 15th Sumter intercepted a British supply train en route to Rawdon's post at Camden, and secured stores of food and clothing, and some prisoners. Two days later he heard of the defeat of Gates and withdrew hastily with his winnings up the Catawba to Fishing Creek near the Great Falls, where he went into camp to rest his men and await further word from Gates. He was of course unaware that Cornwallis had sent Tarleton after the captured wagons and supplies. It was a very hot day, and the Americans were relaxed, bathing in the river, repairing their equipment, dozing in the shade. By some unaccountable carelessness in setting out sufficient pickets, and in heeding the one or two shots which might have given the alarm, Sumter allowed himself to be surprised at Fishing Creek—surprised to such an extent that he himself was asleep under a wagon with his boots off when Tarleton struck. In the confusion and slaughter which followed, Sumter escaped capture only by flinging himself on to a horse without a saddle, hat, or coat, and arrived two days later almost unattended, at Charlotte, which was still crowded with fugitives and wounded from Camden. He lost fifty men in the fighting at the camp, and all the captured stores were retrieved by Tarleton and carried back to the British army. It was just one more disaster in the fatal campaign around Camden in the summer of 1780.

Nevertheless Sumter rallied briskly, independent of Gates's bewildered remnants, and during the next three months until Greene took charge, Sumter's force of mounted volunteers maintained a series of raids in the neighborhood which, except for Francis Marion's little band in the lowland swamps, was all that remained of resistance in South Carolina. "The indefatigable Sumter is again in the field," Cornwallis reported angrily on August 29th to Clinton at Charleston, "and is beating for recruits with the greatest assiduity."

Gates had retired to Hillsborough and Cornwallis had advanced to Charlotte when the news of the British defeat at King's Mountain on October 7th dislocated Cornwallis's plans and compelled him to evacuate Charlotte and go into winter headquarters at Winnsboro, at the end of a disastrous march through autumn rains, during which both Tarleton and Cornwallis were taken ill. From Winnsboro, which the British reached on October 29th, Cornwallis dispatched Tarleton southward after Marion, and assigned Major Wemyss to deal with Sumter, who was operating along the Broad River near the mills which Cornwallis depended on for some of his supplies.

Before joining Cornwallis at Winnsboro, Wemyss had already distinguished himself by brutal behavior in the lowlands when he was sent to establish a garrison at Georgetown; burning, pillaging, and molesting women, till with Ferguson gone he was probably the second best hated man in the British army, after Tarleton. He planned a night surprise on Sumter's camp, and set aside an officer with five dragoons and a guide with the sole object of bagging Sumter personally in his tent. But Wemyss did not count on being severely wounded himself in the arm and knee by the first fire of the pickets, so that his carefully planned attack disintegrated into a reckless charge into the light of Sumter's camp-fires. The Americans were sleeping on their arms that night, and had no trouble to pick off the half-blinded troopers as they came. The seven-man posse reached Sumter's tent, but he dodged out under the back end and hid in the darkness by the riverbank, half-clothed and nearly freezing, till the thwarted British withdrew, leaving their helpless commander and twenty other wounded under a white flag.

When Sumter emerged after daylight to take their paroles, a list of Wemyss's crimes in the Pedee country was found in his pocket, in a record of houses burned and patriots hanged. He cast himself on Sumter's mercy and begged for protection. As a magnanimous gesture to a grievously wounded enemy, Sumter threw the paper in the fire, and allowed all the wounded to be conveyed to Charleston on parole. Wemyss was disabled for life.

Cornwallis next recalled Tarleton from a fruitless pursuit of Marion among the swamps near King's Tree, and sent him after Sumter who was now believed to have intentions against the Tory post at 96. Tarleton hoped for another Fishing Creek, and stalked Sumter for several days, keeping his green coats well out of sight by daylight. Sumter was warned "by a woman on horseback" who took a short cut to his camp at the Blackstocks plantation on the Tyger River—and he decided to make a stand there, where a log house and a log barn, with a thick woods between, could be well defended.

Having lost the advantage of surprise, Tarleton paused on the opposite hill to await his infantry and cannon, but Sumter sent out detachments to attack first, and Tarleton found himself engaged, with his losses mounting. He could make no impression on the garrisoned buildings without cannon, while a murderous fire came from the woods between. He was compelled to order a hasty retreat, without his wounded.

It was towards the end of the fight, when Sumter was on horseback with his men in the woods, that he was struck in the right shoulder by a ball. He "gave no sign of being hurt, it is said, until McKelvey, hearing the trickling of blood on to the dry leaves underfoot, exclaimed, 'General, you are wounded!'

"'I am wounded,' said Sumter. 'Say nothing about it.' Turning to Hampton, he asked the captain to sheathe his sword for him and get a man to lead off his horse, adding, 'Say nothing about it . . . and request Colonel Twiggs to take the command.'"

As darkness came on it began to rain, and with Sumter's usual compassion the British wounded were gathered up and brought into the log houses. But he knew that the improvised fortifications would not withstand another attack and he ordered a withdrawal.

A litter was made of a raw cow-hide hung between two horses to carry him in, and a man remained behind to keep up the watch-fires till all the rest had got quietly away.

Sumter was well aware that he would be disabled for some time to come, and retired with a small escort to a camp about twenty miles from Charlotte. Cornwallis at Winnsboro heard an exaggerated rumor that he was "speechless and past all hope," and wrote Rawdon at Camden, "We have lost two great plagues in Sumter and Clarke. I wish your friend Marion was as quiet." On the same day (November 25, 1780) Sumter, anything but speechless, was writing to Gates, who was then returning to Charlotte where he expected to set up winter headquarters, before Greene's arrival changed his plans Sumter urged him to strike Cornwallis at Winnsboro during Tarleton's continued absence, and finished on a pathetic note: "My hurry and distress I am with my wound will I hope sufficiently apologize for my being laconick, I am without medicine or necessaries of any kind, and feel the want of them much."

Gates sent a prompt reply, medicines, and a probe, but Sumter's camp surgeon had already removed the ball with an ordinary knife, when it was found that a splinter of the back-bone had been carried away. Without anaesthetics or sterile conditions, the agony of such an operation must have been intense. Governor Rutledge of South Carolina paid a visit to his camp, bringing a surgeon from the Continental hospital at Salisbury, who dressed the wound, but Sumter refused to be removed to the hospital for further care. He continued to receive reports from his detachments and his intelligence service, and to keep up a correspondence with Gates, whose inaction must have been very galling to the bed-ridden Gamecock. And here we will leave him for a time, fuming but still efficient, and resume the journey southward.

Lossing apparently did not discover that the Sumter family burying ground can be reached from Stateburg by a dirt road, in the depths of the forest—a place of whispering silence and real bewitchment, with the grey rows of Sumter tombs guarded by the tiny brick chapel which was built for the General's daughter-in-law, the Comtesse Natalie DeLage De Volude, an émigrée from the French Revolution.

From the Hanging Rock Lossing rode on towards Camden and spent the night at the house of a Mrs. Fletcher, and encountered an old man who gave him valuable information on historical localities between there and Camden. The first of these is Clermont, sometimes called Rugeley's, where General Gates had concentrated his army before Camden, and where William Washington surpassed himself in a small affair the following December (1780), while Gates was attempting to reorganize at Charlotte. A body of Tories under Colonel Rugeley was interfering with the American supply wagons, and Colonel Washington was sent out to deal with them.

"They retreated," says Lossing, "and took post at Rugeley's house on the Camden road, which he had stockaded, together with his log-barn. Washington with his cavalry pursued, and at about ten o'clock on the 4th of December appeared at Rugeley's Mill, on the other side of the creek. The Loyalists were strongly posted in the log-barn, in front of which was a ditch and abatis. Having no artillery, Washington could make but little impression upon the garrison, and so he resorted to stratagem. Fashioning a pine-log so as to resemble a cannon, he placed it in such a position near the bridge as, apparently, to command both the house and barn of Colonel Rugeley. He then made a formal demand for surrender, menacing the garrison with the instant demolition of their fortress. Alarmed at the apparition of a cannon, Rugeley sent out a flag, and with his whole force of one hundred and twelve men, immediately surrendered. Poor Rugeley never appeared in arms afterward. Cornwallis in a letter to Tarleton said, 'Rugeley will not be made a brigadier.'

"Soon after leaving Rugeley's I came to a shallow stream which flows out of Gum Swamp, and known in the Revolution as Graney's Quarter Creek. It was thickly studded with gum shrubs and canes, the latter appearing as green and fresh as in summer. It was now about noon, and while I made the accompanying sketch Charley dined upon corn which the generous driver of a team hauling cotton gave me from his store.

"Between this stream and Sander's Creek, within seven miles of Camden, is the place of Gates's defeat. The hottest part of the engagement occurred upon the hill just before descending to Sander's Creek from the north, now, as then, covered with an open forest of pine trees. When I passed through it the underbrush had just been burned, and the blackened trunks of the venerable pines, standing like the columns of a vast temple, gave the whole scene a dreary, yet grand appearance. Many of the old trees yet bear marks of the battle, the scars of the bullets being made very distinct by large protuberances. I was informed that many musket-balls have been cut out of the trees; and I saw quite a number of trunks which had been recently hewn with axes for the purpose. Some pines had been thus cut by searchers for bullets which must have been in the seed when the battle occurred. Within half a mile of Sander's Creek, on the north side, are some old fields, dotted with shrub pines, where the hottest of the battle was fought. A large concavity near the road, filled with hawthorne, was pointed out to me as the spot where many of the dead were buried.

"Sander's Creek is a considerable stream, about two hundred feet wide, and quite shallow at the ford. Though flowing through a swamp like Graney's Quarter, its waters were very limpid. Numerous teams drawing heavy loads of cotton, on their way to Camden, were passing at the time, and the songs and loud laughter of the happy teamsters enlivened the dreary aspect of nature. All the way from Yorkville I passed caravans of wagons with cotton on their way to Camden or Columbia. The teams are driven by Negroes, sometimes accompanied by an overseer. They carry corn and fodder (cornstalks) with them, and camp out at night in the woods, where they build fires, cook their bacon, bake their hoe-cake, and sleep under the canvas covering of their wagons. It is a season of great delight to those who are privileged to haul cotton to market.

"This view is from the north side of the ford. Like the other stream, it is filled with canes, shrubs, and many blasted pines."

At Camden we finally arrive at what should have been the starting point of the Southern tour, for after the loss of Charleston in May of 1780 it was the defeat at Camden the following August which brought the whole war to the Carolinas and Virginia—which, in effect, began a new war linked to the Northern campaigns which had gone before it only by a few transplanted commanding officers and veterans, and by the distant, almost legendary figure of the Commander-in-chief.

It began by being unfortunate in its generals. Lincoln, who surrendered Charleston, we shall come to when Lossing reaches Georgia and again at Charleston. Gates, who fled from the Camden battlefield without waiting to surrender, was responsible for an even greater disaster. For a man whose nickname among the irreverent soldiery was Granny, doubtless because of his spectacles and his portliness (though Knox and Greene would have both outweighed him, and nobody would ever liken either of them to an old lady) Gates created a spectacular amount of trouble.

He began the war at Washington's side as adjutant of the army at Cambridge in 1775. Conceited and ambitious, an undistinguished veteran of the Braddock campaign in the French-Indian War of 1755, where Washington at twenty-three had played a gallant part, Gates always considered that he was better qualified for the post of Commander-in-chief than the man who held that still doubtful honor. It had been the object of the Conway Cabal in the dreadful winter of 1777-78 to replace Washington with Gates. While Washington was enduring the hardships and near despair of Valley Forge with his army, Gates was snug at York, where the Congress was then sitting, pushing his petty intrigues and calumnies against the lonely, impassive man who refused to be dislodged from his duty, though he must many times have longed to lay down his burden on any excuse to return to his beloved Virginia acres. If Washington had quit at Valley Forge, from weariness, weakness, or righteous resentment against men he had believed to be his friends until their treachery came to light, the British, who then held both Philadelphia and New York, would have made short work of the busybodies who were so anxious to take over his job. And if any proof were needed of their incompetence, Gates provided it, with bells on, at Camden less than two years later.

The Cabal fizzled out early in '78, Conway was dropped by the politicians who had somehow affixed his name forever to their schemes, and Gates wrote a remarkable letter to Washington assuming that bygones would simply be bygones, which the magnanimous Washington allowed to happen. Gates was given a post on the Hudson which relieved Headquarters of the embarrassment of his presence there, but his influence, though subterranean, continued to operate at York. Most of the original delegates to the Congress which had framed and signed the Declaration of Independence at Philadelphia were now sitting in their State Legislatures or had simply gone home, and some had died, so that the legislative body at York consisted largely of second-rate men, many of whom had no personal acquaintance with the Commander-in-chief. His scrupulous care never to assume an authority which technically belonged to them, particularly in the matter of appointments, was bad for their egos. And when it became necessary to choose a man to lead an army south to retrieve the loss of Charleston in 1780, they gave it to Gates without even consulting the Commander-in-chief. The result was very nearly the loss of the whole war.

By his Congressional appointment Gates outranked and superseded DeKalb, who before the news of Charleston's surrender reached Washington at his Morristown Headquarters had already started south with a small force of Maryland and Delaware troops, designed merely to reinforce Lincoln at Charleston and act under his command. Like Steuben, DeKalb had promoted himself to the title of Baron, having been born plain Johann Kalb in Bavaria in 1721, which made him a good ten years older than Washington. When he joined the French army at sixteen he became Jean De-Kalb, and by the time the Seven Years' War began in '56 he was a major, and rose to Lieutenant-colonel before it ended. The peace found him of sufficient social standing to marry a beautiful French heiress to whom he was devoted, and after a domestic interval he resumed his self-made career to accompany young Lafayette to America in '77. He was with Washington's army at Valley Forge and Morristown, massive, genial, abstemious, and frugal almost to monkishness in his habits, cheerful in adversity.

In June of 1780 he was on the way with his little force to join Lincoln at Charleston before he heard of its surrender. Until Lincoln could be paroled and exchanged, DeKalb was left the senior officer in command of the Southern Department, which now consisted of his own small corps and a few scattered detachments including William Washington's dragoons, who had not been trapped inside the city. DeKalb did not know quite what to do next. He could hardly take on the British with the handful of men which composed his army, and he camped at Hillsborough, hoping for recruits which did not come in. His men were short of wagons and camp equipment of all kinds, they had to forage daily for food, they were plagued by summer ills, ticks, and mosquitoes. He had had to leave precious artillery behind along the road for want of horses able to draw the guns, and when he moved on to Buffalo Ford on the Deep River in July he had only eight pieces left. "Although I have put the troops on short allowance for bread, we cannot get even that," he wrote. "The design I had to move nearer the enemy to drive them from the Pedee River, a plentiful country, has been defeated by the impossibility of subsisting on the road.... I could hardly depend on any but the Maryland and Delaware regiments of my division and Col. Armand's legion, and all those very much reduced by sickness, discharge, and desertion."

Too little is known about Charles Armand, Marquis de la Rouarie, who seems to have embodied romance like a story-book. He was said to have come out to America because in France he was crossed in love. He was said to have killed his best friend in a duel there over an actress. He had tamed a wolf cub to follow him like a puppy. In person he was handsome and spirited, and led his little corps of dare-devil horsemen with dash and distinction. Its duties at quiet times were to police the camp for deserters, thieves, and strangers without passes. In time of action he was assigned to watch the flanks of the army for fugitives and spies. George Washington was fond of him, and at the end of the war wrote him letters which show something of the same fatherly affection Lafayette had won from the Commander-in-chief.

DeKalb showed no resentment when Gates arrived, urbane and pompous, at the Deep River Camp to take command on July 25th, but received him with ceremony and a continental salute from the little park of artillery. But Gates began at once to assert himself in all the wrong directions. Refusing advice, he laid out his own obstinate route southward and ordered an immediate march, through a disaffected Tory region, infertile, swampy, and already plundered by the enemy, instead of taking a longer way round which would have provided food and forage as they went. Colonel Otho Williams of the Maryland Line, who was the deputy Adjutant-general, ventured to remonstrate with Gates and was swept aside. His narrative of the ensuing march and the resulting disaster at Camden is one of the most valuable first-hand accounts of the war.

"General Gates said he would confer with the *general officers* when the troops should halt at noon," Williams wrote. "Whether any conference took place or not the writer does not know. After a short halt at noon when the men were refreshed upon the *scraps* in their *knapsacks*, the march was resumed. The country exceeded the representation that had been made of it; scarcely had it emerged from a state of sterile nature; the few rude attempts at improvements that were to be found were most of them abandoned by their owners and plundered by the neighbors.... The distresses of the soldiery daily increased. They were told that the banks of the Pedee River were extremely fertile—and so, indeed, they were; but the preceding crop of corn was exhausted, and the new grain, although luxuriant and fine, was unfit for use. Many of the soldiery, urged by necessity, plucked the green ears and boiled them with the lean beef which was collected in the woods, made for themselves a repast, not unpalatable to be sure, but which was attended with painful effects. Green peaches also were substituted for bread, and had similar consequences. Some of the officers, aware of the risk of eating such vegetables, and in such a state, with poor fresh beef, and without salt, restrained themselves from taking anything but the beef itself, boiled or roasted. It occurred to some that the hair-powder which remained in their bags would thicken soup, and it was actually applied.

"On the 3d of August the little army crossed the Pedee River, in bateaux, at Mask's Ferry; and were met on the southern bank by

Lieutenant-colonel Porterfield, an officer of merit who after the disaster at Charleston retired with a small detachment, and found means of subsisting himself and his men in Carolina until the present time.... The expectation, founded on assurances of finding a plentiful supply of provisions at May's Mill, induced the troops again to obey the order to march with cheerfulness; but being again disappointed, fatigued, and almost famished, their patience began to forsake them... when the regimental officers, by mixing among the men and remonstrating with them, appeased murmurs, for which unhappily there was too much cause. The officers, however, by appealing to their own empty canteens and mess-cases, satisfied the privates that all suffered alike.... Fortunately a small quantity of Indian corn was brought into camp; the mill was set to work, and as soon as a mess of meal was ground it was delivered to the men; and so, in rotation, they were all served in the course of a few hours. More poor cattle were sacrificed, the camp-kettles were all engaged, the men were busy, but silent, until each had taken his repast; and then all was again content, cheerfulness, and mirth. It was as astonishing as it was pleasing to observe the transition. The General and field officers were not the first served upon this occasion; nor were they generally the most satisfied....

"Impressed by a sense of difficulties, and perhaps conceiving himself to be in some degree accountable to the army for the steps he had taken, General Gates told Colonel Williams, who acted as deputy Adjutant-general to the Southern army, that he had in a measure been forced to take the route he had done; that General Caswell had evaded every order that had been sent to him, as well by the Baron DeKalb as himself to form a junction of the militia with the regular corps; that it appeared to him that Caswell's vanity was gratified by having a separate command; that he probably contemplated some enterprise to distinguish himself and gratify his ambition, 'which,' said he, 'I should not be sorry to see checked by a rap over the knuckles, if it were not that the militia would disperse....'

"Such evasion of orders... determined Gates to reach his camp in person ... and the deputy Adjutant-general had the honor of attending the General to the headquarters of the commandant of the militia. The reception was gracious, and the General and his suite were regaled with wine and other novelties, exquisitely grateful and exhilarating; but a man must have been intoxicated indeed not to perceive the confusion which prevailed in the camp; tables, chairs, bedsteads, benches, and many other articles of household stuff were scattered before the doors in great disorder. It was understood that General Caswell had discovered, by the death of horses and the breaking-down of wagons, that he was unable to move, and was making an effort to divest himself of his heavy baggage. (If, in these notes, a tenor censorious of General Caswell's conduct appears to the reader, the writer begs that it may not be imputed to any personal prejudice or malicious motive. He never had the honor of seeing the general until this time, and all that he had ever heard of him was favorable to his character as a gentleman and a patriot. A regard to facts, to which the writer thinks he may hereafter be called on to testify on oath, obliges him to state them faithfully as they occurred, or were communicated to him.)"

Richard Caswell, who had been a delegate for North Carolina to the Continental Congress, though not a Signer of the Declaration, remains a somewhat enigmatic figure. He was President of the First Provincial Congress of his State, and was also its first Governor. It will be seen that at Camden his militia threw away their arms and fled, while he himself was the only officer who kept up with Gates in his flight from the field. Yet Caswell went on to be Senator, and again Governor, and was chosen as delegate to the 1787 Convention at Philadelphia, to which he sent a deputy, remaining at home in the State Legislature by choice.

There was never any doubt, however, about Francis Marion, whom Lossing introduces here:

"While Gates was pressing forward towards Camden, Marion with about twenty men and boys was annoying the Tories in the neighborhood of the Pedee. With his ragged command, worse than

Falstaff ever saw, he appeared at the camp of Gates, and excited the ridicule of the Continentals. Colonel Williams in his *Narrative* says of Marion and his men at that time: 'Colonel Marion, a gentleman of South Carolina, had been with the army a few days, attended by a very few followers, distinguished by small leather caps and the wretchedness of their attire; their numbers did not exceed twenty men and boys, some white, some black, and all mounted, but most of them miserably equipped, their appearance was in fact, so burlesque, that it was with difficulty that the diversion of the regular soldiery was restrained by the officers; and the General himself was glad of an opportunity of detaching Colonel Marion, at his own instance, towards the interior of South Carolina, with orders to watch the motions of the enemy and furnish intelligence.'

"Gates too would doubtless have thought lightly of him," Lossing continues, "if Governor Rutledge, who was in the American camp, and knew the partisan's worth, had not recommended him to the notice of that General. Gates listened to his modestly expressed opinions respecting the campaign, but was too conceited to regard them seriously, or to offer Marion a place in his army. While he was in Gates's camp, the Whigs of the Williamsburg (S.C.) district, who had risen in arms, sent for him to be their commander. Governor Rutledge gave him the commission of a brigadier on the spot, and he hastened to organize that brigade which we shall hereafter meet frequently among the swamps, the broad savannahs, and by the watercourses of the South."

The Rutledge brothers, John and Edward, had been delegates from South Carolina to the Philadelphia Congress, and approved the appointment of George Washington as Commander-in-chief, before John returned in the autumn of '75 to Charleston to serve in the Provincial Assembly. Edward, ten years younger, remained in Philadelphia another year, and left his signature on the Declaration. John was elected President, or Governor, of South Carolina, and commander-in-chief of its militia forces, though he never carried arms and had never had a fencing-lesson. With one brief interval he was still Governor when the British fleet arrived for the second attempt to take Charleston, which was successful in May, 1780. During the desperate defence of the city Rutledge was voted dictatorial powers, but before the siege ring closed entirely he was smuggled out on horseback, in the belief that he could be of more moral value to the cause if he remained free to represent the State government and to recruit up-country. He left a coach and horses at Hillsborough where the Legislature of North Carolina was sitting, making that place his nominal headquarters, but he turned up everywhere on his famous white horse called Caesar, making speeches to encourage enlistment, receiving and passing on secret intelligence all the way from Charleston by his private grapevine; conferring, advising, and some thought interfering—but he was the best recruiting sergeant they had, and he often risked capture by the Tories to make his eloquent appeals in one town after another. Sometimes he commandeered supplies from the countryside, bringing in a few wagon-loads of clothing or forage to some hard-pressed camp. In December of 1780 he rode all the way to Philadelphia to beg the wherewithal for the scattered forces which still opposed the British in his captive State. He was said to have a spell-binding voice and personality, and always had the women on his side, though John Adams had complained about his air of "reserve, design, and cunning," at the First Congress. It was more likely just the well-bred poker-face of the Southern aristocrat.

Both Thomas Sumter and William Washington had also communicated with Gates, and had received very little encouragement, for with Armand's handful of horsemen Gates believed that he had no further use for cavalry, although Tarleton was just ahead of him in Rawdon's army at Camden. This neglect may have been the source of Sumter's persistently unco-operative attitude thenceforth, though he was naturally an independent character, and averse to serving under another officer, or to having his corps preempted for co-ordination with some major movement of the main army.

Having deprived himself of Marion, Sumter, and William Washington, Gates had accepted Porterfield's contribution of a hundred Virginia troops, and Caswell's North Carolina militia, whose provisions appeared to be mainly liquid in nature. General Stevens now brought in some Virginia militia in poor condition, and with these combined forces Gates occupied Clermont, also known as Rugeley's, on the 13th of August. What he still did not know was that Cornwallis himself had arrived from Charleston to join Rawdon at Camden.

Young Lord Rawdon, who was the son of the Earl of Moira, was now twenty-six and had seen nearly ten years of service in the British army. As a lieutenant at Bunker Hill he had rallied and held his men after his superior officers had all been disabled, and his rise in rank since then had been rapid. His remarkable military ability was offset by a ruthlessness very like that of Tarleton and Wemyss—he was a tall, dark, ugly man, genial enough to his associates, but a terror to his enemies. With Cornwallis's experience and prestige added to Rawdon's dash and drive, they were the most formidable pair the British army could produce, and up against them was Granny Gates, in his sublime self-assurance which had no better foundation than the Saratoga victory which had been won by two other men.

The Camden engagement was one of those monumental coincidences which occur in history almost as often as they do in bad fiction. No novelist striving for theatrical effects would dare to start two armies towards each other simultaneously, the order to march of each unknown to the other, so that they met unprepared the same night in the middle of a swamp, but that is what happened on August 15th, 1780, outside Camden. Gates knew that Lord Rawdon, as Cornwallis's second in command, was at Camden with a substantial British force. He thought Cornwallis was still at Charleston. Rawdon knew that Gates was blundering towards them through the midsummer Carolina heat with an exhausted, starving army. And Gates's apprehensive staff knew that he had no plan of action, and no way of providing for his men beyond what they could scrape up beside the road from day to day, as he marched deeper into the Carolinas, which were dominated by the British from their bases at Charleston, Georgetown, Wilmington, and Camden.

On August 15th in his camp at Rugeley's Mill—where William Washington was later to stage his successful hoax with the pine-tree cannon—Gates called a council of his officers, not to ask for advice or information, but to read out to them his detailed orders for a night march on Camden. They heard him in speechless horror, apparently paralyzed by his fantastic over-confidence, but once out of his presence, the officers voiced their misgivings.

"Although there had been no dissenting voice in the council," says Otho Williams's *Narrative*, "the orders were no sooner promulgated than they became the subject of animadversion. Even those who had been dumb in council said that there had been no consultation; that the orders were read to them, and all opinion seemed suppressed by the very positive and decisive terms in which they were expressed. Others could not imagine how it could be conceived that an army consisting of more than two thirds militia, and which had never been once exercised in arms together, could form columns and perform other maneuvers in the night, and in the face of an enemy.

"But of all the officers, Colonel Armand took the greatest exception. He seemed to think the positive orders respecting himself implied a doubt of his courage; declared that cavalry had never before been put in the front of a line of battle in the dark; and that the disposition, as it respected his corps, proceeded from resentment in the general on account of a previous altercation between them about horses, which the general had ordered to be taken from the officers of the army to expedite the movement of the artillery through the wilderness. A great deal was said upon the occasion; but the time was short, and the officers generally not knowing or believing any more than the general that any considerable body of the enemy were to be met with out of Camden, acquiesced with their usual cheerfulness, and were ready to march at the hour appointed.

"As there were no spirits yet arrived in camp, and as until lately it was unusual for troops to make a forced march, or prepare to meet an enemy without some extraordinary allowance, it was unluckily conceived that molasses would, for once, be an acceptable substitute, accordingly the hospital stores were broached, and one gill of molasses per man, and a full ration of corn-meal and meat, were issued to the army previous to their march, which commenced according to orders at about 10 o'clock at night of the 15th. (But I must arrest the progress of the narrative to apologize for introducing a remark seemingly so trivial. Nothing ought to be considered trivial in an army which in any degree affects the health or spirits of the troops; upon which often, more than upon numbers, the fate of battles depends. The troops of General Gates's army had frequently felt the bad consequences of eating bad provisions; but at this time, a hasty meal of quick-baked bread and fresh beef, with a dessert of molasses mixed with mush or dumplings, operated so cathartically as to disorder very many of the men, who were breaking the ranks all night, and were certainly much debilitated before the action commenced in the morning."

At the same time that Gates's Council was meeting in Rugeley's log barn, Rawdon and Tarleton at Camden, which was only a collection of log-houses, taverns, and barter-stores, were receiving from Cornwallis orders for an attack on Gates. There is nothing to be gained by rewriting Williams's restrained eye-witness account of what followed, and it is accordingly substituted for Lossing's, to continue:

"Both armies, ignorant of each other's intentions, moved about the same hour of the same night, and approaching each other met about half way between their respective encampments at midnight. The first revelation of this unexpected scene was occasioned by a smart mutual salutation of small arms between the advanced guards. Some of the cavalry of Armand's legion were wounded, retreated, and threw the whole corps into disorder—which recoiling suddenly on the front of the column of infantry, disordered the first Maryland brigade, and occasioned a general consternation through the whole line of the army. The light infantry under Porterfield, however, executed their orders gallantly; and the enemy, no less astonished than ourselves, seemed to acquiesce in a sudden suspension of hostilities.

"Prisoners were taken on both sides. From one of these the deputy Adjutant-general extorted information. He informed that Lord Cornwallis commanded in person about three thousand regular British troops which were in line of march about five or six hundred yards in front. Order was soon restored in the corps of infantry in the American army, and the officers were employed in forming a front line of battle, when the deputy Adjutant-general communicated to General Gates the information which he had from the prisoner. The General's astonishment could not be concealed. He ordered the deputy Adjutant-general to call another council of war. All the general officers immediately assembled in the rear of the line. The unwelcome news was communicated to them. General Gates said, 'Gentlemen, what is to be done?' All were mute for a few moments, when the gallant Stevens exclaimed, 'Gentlemen, is it not too late now to do anything but fight?' No other advice was offered, and the General desired that the gentlemen would repair to their respective commands.

"The Baron DeKalb's opinion may be inferred from the following fact. When the deputy Adjutant-general went to call him to council he first told him what had been discovered. 'Well,' said the Baron, 'and has the General given you orders to retreat the army?' The Baron, however, did not oppose the suggestion of General Stevens, and every measure that ensued was preparatory for action."

Otho Williams's spare, soldierly narrative does not dwell on what must have been an eerie scene—the group of clanking, epaulletted, haggard officers gathered round the flabby figure of their commanding officer, probably lighted by a couple of flares or lanterns, in the midst of a sweltering swamp, with the night noises of disturbed wild life mingling with the confusion attending the formation of a front line by the infantry officers not far away.

Brave, headlong Stevens, a Virginia man, veteran of the Jersey campaigns, survived the impending ordeal to be wounded at Guilford Courthouse the following year, but recovered in time to assist at the surrender at Yorktown. Porterfield had already received a mortal wound during the first exchange of shots in the road, and was missing from the council. DeKalb also was going to his death wound on the field. Gates—nothing ever quite caught up with Gates.

"Frequent skirmishes happened during the night between the advanced parties, which served to discover the relative situations of the two armies, and as a prelude to what was to take place in the morning," Williams continues. "At dawn of day, on the morning of the 16th of August, the enemy appeared in front, advancing in column. Captain Singleton, who commanded some pieces of artillery, observed to Colonel Williams that he plainly perceived the ground of the British uniform at about two hundred yards in front. The deputy Adjutant-general immediately ordered Singleton to open his battery, and then rode to the General, who was *in the rear of the second line,* and informed him of the cause of the firing which he heard. He also observed to the General that the enemy seemed to be displaying their column by the right; the nature of the ground favored this conjecture, for yet nothing was clear.

"The General seemed disposed to await events; he gave no orders. The deputy Adjutant-general observed that if the enemy, in the act of displaying, were briskly attacked by General Stevens's brigade, which was already in the line of battle, the effect might be fortunate, and first impressions were important. 'Sir,' said the General, 'that's right—let it be done.' This was the last order that the deputy Adjutant-general received.

"He hastened to General Stevens, who instantly advanced with his brigade, apparently in fine spirits. The right wing of the enemy was soon discovered *in line,* it was too late to attack them displaying; nevertheless, the business of the day could no longer be deferred. The deputy Adjutant-general requested General Stevens to let him have forty or fifty privates, volunteers, who would run forward of the brigade and commence the attack. They were led forward to within forty or fifty yards of the enemy, and ordered to take trees and keep up as brisk a fire as possible. The desired effect of this expedient—to extort the enemy's fire at some distance, in order to render it less terrible to the militia—was not gained. General Stevens, observing the enemy to rush on, put his men in mind of their bayonets; but the impetuosity with which the enemy advanced, firing and huzzahing, threw the whole body of militia into such a panic that they generally threw down their *loaded* arms and fled in the utmost consternation!

"The unworthy example of the Virginians was almost instantly followed by the North Carolinians; only a small part of the brigade, commanded by Brigadier-general Gregory, made a short pause. A part of Dixon's regiment fired two or three rounds of cartridge. But a great majority of the militia (at least two thirds of the army) fled without firing a shot. The writer avers it of his own knowledge, having seen and observed every part of the army, from left to right, during the action. He who has never seen the effect of a panic upon a multitude can have but an imperfect idea of such a thing. The best disciplined troops have been enervated and made cowards by it. Armies have been routed by it, even where no enemy appeared to furnish an excuse. Like electricity, it operates instantaneously—like sympathy, it is irresistible where it touches.

"But, in the present instance, its action was not universal. The regular troops, who had had the keen edge of sensibility rubbed off by strict discipline and hard service, saw the confusion with but little emotion. They engaged seriously in the affair; and notwithstanding some irregularity, which was created by the militia breaking pell-mell through the second line, order was restored there time enough to give the enemy a severe check, which abated the fury of their assault, and obliged them to assume a more deliberate manner of acting. The Second Maryland brigade, including the battalion of Delawares, on the right, were engaged with the enemy's left, which they opposed with very great firmness. They even advanced upon them, and had taken a number of prisoners, when their companions of the First Brigade (which formed the second line) being greatly outflanked and charged by superior numbers, were obliged to give ground.

"At this critical moment the regimental officers of the latter brigade, reluctant to leave the field without orders, inquired for their commanding officer, Brigadier-general Smallwood, who was not to be found; notwithstanding, Colonel Gunby, Major Anderson, and a number of other brave officers, assisted by the deputy Adjutant-general and Major Jones, one of Smallwood's aides, rallied the brigade and renewed the contest. Again they were obliged to give way; and were again rallied; the Second brigade were still warmly engaged; the distance between the two brigades did not exceed two hundred yards, their opposite flank being nearly upon a line perpendicular to their front.

"At this eventful juncture the deputy Adjutant-general, anxious that the communication between them should be preserved, and wishing that in the almost certain event of a retreat some order might be sustained by them, hastened from the First to the Second brigade, which he found precisely in the same circumstances. He called upon his own regiment, the Sixth Maryland, not to fly, and was answered by the lieutenant-colonel, Ford, who said—'They have done all that can be expected of them; we are outnumbered and outflanked. See, the enemy charge with bayonets.' The enemy, having collected their corps, and directing their whole force against these two devoted brigades, a tremendous fire of musketry was for some time kept up on both sides, with equal perseverance and obstinacy, until Lord Cornwallis, perceiving that there was no cavalry opposed to him, pushed forward his dragoons—and his infantry charging at the same moment with fixed bayonets, put an end to the contest. His victory was complete. All the artillery and a great number of prisoners fell into his hands; many fine fellows lay on the field, and the rout of the remainder was entire. Not even a company retired in any order; everyone escaped as he could.

"If, in this affair, the militia fled too soon, the regulars may be thought almost as blamable for remaining too long on the field, especially after all hope of victory must have been despaired of.

Let the commandants of the brigades answer for themselves. Allow the same privilege to the officers of the corps comprising those brigades, and they will say that they never received orders to retreat, nor any order from any *general* officer, from the commencement of the action until it became desperate. The brave major-general, the Baron DeKalb, fought on foot with the Second brigade, and fell, mortally wounded, into the hands of the enemy—a fate which probably was avoided by other generals only by an opportune retreat."

There we have the bare bones of battle, as seen by a cool-headed veteran who rode to and fro unscathed through the thick of it. Williams does not emphasize that he himself, the deputy Adjutant-general, led the first band of volunteer marksmen from Stevens's regiment, nor mention that Stevens's men had been issued their bayonets only the day before the battle, and were unfamiliar with them as weapons. It was John Eager Howard, the subsequent hero of the Cowpens, who led the Maryland bayonet charge which first checked the British rush. The reader must detect for himself that Williams continually risked his own life by "hastening" on horseback from one part of the field and one commanding officer to another, sustaining and rallying the hard-pressed men by his own reckless example, until the charge of the Green Dragoons completed the slaughter and drove the mangled remains of the Continentals into the swamps. General Smallwood, who "was not to be found" when wanted by his subordinates, was less conspicuous in his absence than Gates and Caswell, but had lost face with his fellow officers when he turned up quietly at Charlotte two days later with one aide and a half dozen followers. He was a red-faced, bad-tempered man, and though his record before Camden was good enough he was always a trial to his associates. He conducted a small party on to Hillsborough at his leisure, and a dispute between him and Gates arose over orders. "Notwithstanding that the disasters of the Southern army, and a sense of common danger, had seemingly obliterated all recollection of former differences and animosities among the officers of the regular corps," says Williams towards the end of his account, "it ought not to be dissembled that such were among the causes which for a time postponed the new organization of the troops. What cause General Gates had to apprehend being superseded in the command of the Southern army may be conjectured by those who have a knowledge of the facts; but what reason General Smallwood could have to hope to become his successor, none who are not grossly imposed upon can possibly imagine. The misunderstanding between these two officers was never, I believe, avowed; but as Gates resumed his command, Smallwood retired from it." And Williams eventually succeeded to Smallwood's command.

The loss of DeKalb was genuinely mourned, and the story of his fall was told and retold around the camp-fires He was unhorsed early in the fight, and received a head wound which stained his white hair with blood, until one of his aides bound it up in his scarlet sash, with spectacular effect. The Baron stood more than six feet tall, and weighed a good two hundred pounds. Sword in hand, roaring encouragement to his unfaltering men, he engaged in personal combat with the enemy, and when he finally fell he was bleeding from eleven separate wounds. He went down just as Tarleton's cavalry charge was coming in, and his devoted aide, DuBuysson, threw his own body over the prostrate Baron, crying out the name and rank of the man he tried to protect, and received in his own back the sabre cuts which might have ended DeKalb's life on the field. Both men were carried into Camden as prisoners, where DeKalb died with his French wife's name on his lips. DuBuysson survived and was exchanged, and served to the end of the war.

"General Gates and Caswell arrived at Charlotte on the night of the action," Williams's *Narrative* goes on. "The ensuing morning presented nothing to them but an open village, with but few inhabitants, and the remains of a temporary hospital containing a few maimed soldiers of Colonel Buford's unfortunate corps, which had been cut to pieces on the retreat after the surrender of Charleston. ... The morning of the 19th was fair, and the officers were assembling about the public square and encouraging one another with hopes of a more favorable course of affairs than had been current for some time past, when they received unquestionable information that Colonel Sumter, whose arrival they looked for every moment, was completely surprised the preceding day (at Fishing Creek) and the whole party killed, captured, or dispersed! Dead or alive, he was censured for suffering a *surprise*.

"No organization nor order had yet been attempted to be restored among the few troops that had arrived in Charlotte; the privates were therefore hastily formed into ranks, and the officers were among themselves adjusting the commands to be taken by them respectively, when the number of supernumerary officers was discovered to be very considerable. Everyone, however, took some charge upon himself.... There was no council, or regular opinion taken respecting this irksome situation. The general idea was that Charlotte, an open, wooded village, without magazines of any sort, without a second cartridge per man, and without a second ration, was not tenable for an hour against superior numbers which might enter at every quarter. Moreover, it was estimated by those who knew the geography of the country that the victorious enemy might be in the vicinity of the place. It was admitted by everyone that no place could be more defenceless....

"Difficulties almost innumerable presented themselves to obstruct a march. Several officers with small parties were known to be on the route from Camden; some refugees might possibly escape from Sumter's detachment; many of the wounded were obliged to be left in the old hospital, dependent entirely on the enemy or on a few of the inhabitants who were unable to retire; were all these to be abandoned?

"Time was never more important to a set of wretches than now; but whether to take it 'by the forelock' as the adage is, or await its more propitious moments, none of us could decisively resolve. Brigadier-general Smallwood, who had quartered himself at a farmhouse a little way from town, appeared at this time approaching the parade in his usual slow pace. As senior officer [Gates having departed for Hillsborough] his orders would have been obeyed, even to setting about fortifying the village; but being informed of Sumter's situation, and concurring in the general sentiment, he leisurely put himself at the head of a party and moved off towards Salisbury. The deputy Adjutant-general and Brigade-major Davidson took the route to Camden in order to direct all they might meet to file off towards Salisbury.

"By noon a very lengthy line of march occupied the road from Charlotte to Salisbury.... Among the rest were six soldiers who had left the hospital with other convalescents; they had all suffered in Buford's unfortunate affair, and had but two sound arms among them—indeed four of them had *not* one arm among them, and two only an arm apiece; each of them had one linen garment. Those officers and men who were recently wounded, and had resolution to undertake the fatigue were differently transported—some in wagons, some in litters, and some on horseback. Their sufferings were indescribable....

"At Salisbury, one hundred and twenty or thirty miles from the scene of the late action, Smallwood took time to dictate those letters which he addressed to Congress, and in which he intimated the great difficulties he had encountered and the exertions he had made to save a remnant of General Gates's army—letters which procured him, it was generally believed in the line, the rank of *major-general*, and which probably prompted the resolution of Congress directing an inquiry into the conduct of General Gates. But many of the officers wrote to their friends from Salisbury, and being chagrined and mortified at not overtaking their commanding general in so long a retreat, expressed themselves with great disgust and freedom."

By the middle of September the whole army had caught up with Gates at Hillsborough, where the North Carolina Legislature was sitting, and where the inhabitants "soon began to experience and complain of the inconvenience of having soldiers billeted among them; and the officers were equally sensible of the difficulty of restraining the licentiousness of the soldiers when not immediately under their observation." Williams therefore withdrew his regiment out of town, distributing the few tents he had among several companies. He encamped on a vacant farm, or rather in the woodland belonging to it, and covered his men with wigwams made of fence-rails, poles and corn-tops, regularly disposed. The tents were chiefly occupied by the officers, but as they were all much worn, wigwams were soon preferred on account of their being much warmer.

"The usual camp-guards and sentinels being posted, no person could come into or go out of camp without a permit. Parade duties were regularly attended, as well by officers as soldiers, and discipline not only began to be restored, but even gave an air of stability and confidence to the regiment, which all their rags could not disguise.... Absolutely without pay, almost destitute of clothing, often with only a half ration, and never with a whole one, without substituting one article for another, not a soldier was heard to murmur after the third or fourth day of their being encamped. Instead of meeting and conferring in small, sullen squads, as they had formerly done, they filled up the intervals with manly exercises and field-sports; in short, the officers had very soon the entire confidence of the men, who devoted themselves to duty and pastime within the limits assigned them.... If any of my friends should inquire why I descend to particulars so minute and unimportant, I answer that I am not writing a history of the Revolution, nor of the proceedings of government; and that it is *not* unimportant for any officer to observe every incident in the life and conduct of a soldier which may in any degree serve to illustrate his disposition."

It is fairly obvious that the men under Colonel Otho Williams's command were somewhat to be envied. As his *Narrative* is not now easily available, it has been allowed to run its course for 1780, without interference from Lossing or editor. Williams was there.

Into this camp at Hillsborough there now came Dan Morgan, as we have seen, with a handful of men, very different from the proud contingent he had led to Cambridge in '75. And a little later William Washington brought in sixty or seventy dragoons retrieved from the Charleston area. With these additions, officered by such veterans as Morgan, Howard, Williams, and William Washington,

Gates's army set out in November to retrace its steps towards Charlotte, Cornwallis having gone into what was known as a "camp of repose" at Winnsboro, leaving garrisons at Camden and Rugeley's. And at Charlotte in December, General Greene took over from Gates.

The defeat at Camden left South Carolina for the second time without a Continental army, as one had already been surrendered at Charleston by Lincoln, and many influential Carolinians gave up the cause as lost, and took protection from the British. For more than three months, until Greene arrived at Charlotte, there was no organized resistance in South Carolina, though Marion and Sumter stayed in their saddles, and Governor Rutledge on the white horse remained a symbol. But there followed the American victory at the Cowpens in January; the long retreat of Greene's army to the Dan, and the return to fight at Guilford, the retreat of the British to Wilmington, their march to the James in Virginia, and the final capture of Cornwallis's army at Yorktown.

Because Hobkirk's Hill was only a few miles from the scene of Gates's defeat, Lossing makes another inconvenient hurdle in time, and comes to the battle which was fought there the following year by Greene and Rawdon (April 24th, '81) about six weeks after the engagement at Guilford when both Rawdon and Cornwallis were present. Having won his pyrrhic victory that day in March, Cornwallis left Rawdon in command at the Camden post and retreated with his battered army to the coast. Greene had on the whole weathered the battle in better shape than the British, and he detached Lee's Lighthorse for the second time to co-operate with Marion on the Santee while he himself moved towards Rawdon. He was not strong enough to attack the Camden post, but hoped for reinforcement from Sumter (who never came in) and eventually from Lee and Marion. Rawdon did not wait for that. He came out and attacked Greene's camp on Hobkirk's Hill, a high ridge overlooking Camden town.

"Upon the table-land of its summit is a beautiful village," Lossing says, "composed of many fine houses, the residences of wealthy inhabitants of that region who have chosen this spot for its salubrity in summer. It was just at sunset when I first looked from this eminence upon the town below and the broad plain around it. Although it was midwinter, the profusion of evergreens gave the landscape the appearance of early autumn. Here was fought one of the memorable battles of our war for Independence; and yonder, stretching away towards the High Hills of Santee, is the plain once red with British legions and glittering with British bayonets. It is a balmy evening; birds are chirping their vespers among the dark green foliage of the wild olives in the gardens, and buds are bursting into blossoms upon every tree. Here upon a bench by the bubbling spring, where General Greene was at breakfast when surprised by Lord Rawdon, we will read and ponder in the evening twilight."

It was a severe skirmish while it lasted, and though a brilliant cavalry charge by William Washington finished it, Greene again had to retreat in good order, with prisoners, and the British withdrew back into Camden, and, says Lossing, "the dead alone occupied the field." Greene was disappointed at the outcome, having hoped for better, and it was after this engagement that he wrote his famous summing up, which might have been applied to the whole war: "We fight, get beat, rise, and fight again."

But Rawdon was sufficiently uneasy at Greene's strength and enterprise to call in his outposts as far as 96 and evacuate Camden, falling down the river towards the British base at Charleston, with the intention of putting a stop to the partisan operations of Marion and Lee along his lines of communication.

"It was almost dark when I rode into Camden and alighted at Boyd's Hotel," Lossing continues. "Here was the end of my tedious but interesting journey of almost fourteen hundred miles with my own conveyance; for learning that I could reach other chief points of interest at the South easier and speedier by public conveyance, I resolved to sell my travelling establishment. Accordingly, after passing the forenoon of the next day visiting the battle-ground on Hobkirk's Hill, sketching the scenery at the spring, and the monument erected to the memory of DeKalb on the green in front of the Presbyterian church in Camden, I went into the market as a trafficker.

"A stranger both to the people and to the business, I was not successful. I confess there was a wide difference in my 'asking' and my 'taking' price. My wagon was again broken, and, anxious to get home, I did not dicker long when I got an offer, and Charley and I parted, I presume with mutual regrets. He was a docile, faithful animal, and I had become much attached to him. A roll of Camden bank-notes soothed my feelings, and I left the place of separation at dawn the next morning in the cars for Fort Motte and Columbia, quite lighthearted "

XII

High Hills to Eutaw Springs

"IT WAS A brilliant, frosty morning when I left Camden to visit the scenes of some of the exploits of Marion and his partisan compatriots," says Lossing. "Soon after crossing the Big Swift and Rafting Creeks, we reached the High Hills of Santee, whereon General Greene encamped before and after the battle at Eutaw Springs [which did not take place until just before Yorktown in the autumn of '81]. They are immense sand hills, varying in width on the summit from one to five miles, and are remarkable for the salubrity of the atmosphere and for medicinal springs. Just at sunrise, while swiftly skirting the base of these hills, with the Wateree Swamp between us and the river on the east, we saw the sharp pencillings of the few scattered houses of Stateburg against the glowing eastern sky. There was the residence of General Sumter after the war, and in his honor the surrounding district was named.

"After skirting the Wateree Swamp some distance, the road passes through a high sand bluff, and then crosses the great morass to the river, a distance of four miles. Beyond that stream, it joins the railway from Columbia. Through the swamp the iron rails are laid upon a strong wooden frame-work, high enough to overtop a cane-brake. The passage is made at a slow rate to avoid accidents. The scenery was really grand, for below were the green canes waving like billows in the wind, while upon either side of the avenue cut for the road towered mighty cypresses and gum-trees, almost every branch draped with long moss. Cluttered around their stately trunks were the holly, water-oak, laurel, and gall-bush, with their varied tints of green; and among these, flitting in silence, were seen the gray mocking-bird and the brilliant scarlet tanager. Here, I was told, opossums and wild-cats abound, and upon the large dry tracts of the swamp wild deers are often seen.

"This little sketch is from the pen of J. Addison Richards, one of our most accomplished landscape painters. The cypress 'knees' as they are called, are here truthfully shown. They extend from the roots of the trees, sometimes as much as two feet above the earth or water, but never exhibit branches or leaves. They appear like smooth-pointed stumps.

"We arrived at the junction station at a little past eight o'clock, and crossing a narrow part of the Congaree Swamp and River, reached Fort Motte Station, on the southern side of that stream, before nine, a distance of forty-four miles from Camden.

"The plantation of Mrs. Rebecca Motte, whose house, occupied and stockaded by the British, was called Fort Motte, lies chiefly upon a high rolling plain, near the Buck's Head Neck, on the Congaree, thirty-three miles below Columbia, the capital of the state. This plain slopes in every direction, and is a commanding point of view, overlooking the vast swamps on the borders of the Congaree. It is now owned by William Love, Esq., with whom I passed several hours very agreeably. His house is built nearly upon the site of Mrs. Motte's mansion, desolated by fire at her own suggestion while occupied by the British.

"The well used by that patriotic lady is still there ... and from it to the house there is a slight hollow which indicates the place of the covered way dug for the protection of the soldiers when procuring water.... This house was built by Mrs. Motte immediately after the close of the war.

"Fort Motte was the principal depot of the convoys between Charleston and Camden, and also for those destined for Fort Granby and 96. The British had taken possession of the mansion, which occupied a commanding position. They surrounded it with a deep trench (a part of which is still visible) and along the interior margin of it erected a high parapet. Mrs. Motte and her family, known to be inimical to the British, were driven to her farm-house upon a hill north of the mansion, and their place was supplied by a garrison of 150 men under Captain McPherson, a brave British officer. The Americans were stationed upon an eminence about a quarter of a mile northeast of the house towards the Congaree, in the direction of McCord's Ferry. A little eastward of the house was an oval mound, when I was there in 1849, about twelve feet in height, and dotted with the stumps of trees recently cut down. This is the vestige of a battery, upon which the assailants planted a field-piece to dislodge the British."

Rebecca Motte was one of the wealthy Brewton family of Charleston, sister to Tory Miles Brewton who sailed for England in 1774 rather than countenance the idea of independence for the colonies. He took with him his family and all his movable treasures, and was never heard of again, his ship apparently having been lost at sea. Ironically, the same issue of the *Gazette* which published the text of the Declaration of Independence carried a notice that his will had been proved and his large estate taken over by his executors, one of whom was Rebecca's husband, Jacob Motte. Jacob died soon after, and Rebecca was living with her three beautiful daughters in Miles Brewton's Charleston mansion when it was occupied as British headquarters in May, 1780. The eldest daughter, Elizabeth, had been lately married to Thomas Pinckney, who had been sent out of the city before its fall and gone to Washington's headquarters in the North, where he was assigned to Gates's staff. He later received a bad wound at Camden, and was taken prisoner there.

Mrs. Motte had her opinion of the British, and is said to have kept her three girls safely locked on the third floor out of sight of her unwelcome guests in the Charleston house, although she herself was for a time required to act as housekeeper for the British commander, General Clinton. She somehow prevailed on him to allow her to leave the city with her family, and took refuge at her plantation on the Congaree. That house too was soon possessed by the enemy, while the Motte ladies retreated again, to the farm-house of her overseer on the opposite hill. It was there that she gave a warm welcome to Harry Lee and Francis Marion, setting forth the best in wine and food which her secret stores allowed, when they arrived with a combined force in the following May, '81, to oust the British garrison. For this *opéra bouffe* affair, we have Lighthorse Harry's own straight-faced narrative in his circumspect *Memoirs*, which are written entirely in the third person. But, like Otho Williams, he was there. "Opposite to Fort Motte, to the north, stood another hill, where Mrs. Motte, having been dismissed from her mansion, resided, in the old farm-house. On this height, Lieutenant-colonel Lee with his corps took post, while Brigadier Marion occupied the eastern declivity of the ridge on which the fort stood.

"Very soon the fort was completely invested; and the six-pounder was mounted on a battery erected in Marion's quarter for the purpose of raking the northern face of the enemy's parapet, against which Lee was preparing to advance. McPherson was unprovided with artillery, and depended for safety upon timely relief, not doubting its arrival before the assailant could push the preparations to maturity. The vale which runs between the two hills admitted our safe approach to within four hundred yards of the fort. This place was selected by Lee to break ground. Relays of working parties being provided for every four hours, and some of the

Negroes from the neighboring plantations being brought by the influence of Marion to our assistance, the works advanced rapidly. Such was their forwardness on the 10th that it was determined to summon the commandant.

"A flag was accordingly dispatched to Captain McPherson, stating to him with truth our relative situation, and admonishing him to avoid the disagreeable consequences of an arrogant temerity. To this the Captain replied that disregarding the consequences he should continue to resist to the last moment.... The large mansion in the center of the encircling trench left but a few yards of the ground within the enemy's works uncovered; burning the house must force their surrender.

"Persuaded that our ditch would be within arrow shot before noon of the next day, Marion and Lee determined to adopt this speedy mode of effecting their object. Orders were issued to prepare bows and arrows with missive combustible matter. This measure was reluctantly adopted; for the destruction of private property was repugnant to the two commandants, and upon this occasion was peculiarly distressing. The house was a large pleasant edifice, intended for the summer residence of the respectable owner, whose deceased husband had been a firm patriot, and whose only marriageable daughter was the wife of Major Pinckney, an officer in the South Carolina Line, who had fought and bled in his country's cause and was now a prisoner with the enemy. These considerations forbade the execution of the proposed measure; but there were others which applied personally to Lieutenant-colonel Lee, and gave a new edge to the bitterness of the scene.

"Encamping near to Mrs. Motte's dwelling, this officer had upon his arrival been requested in the most pressing terms to make her house his quarters. The invitation was accordingly accepted; and not only the Lieutenant-colonel, but every officer of his corps when off duty daily experienced her liberal hospitality, politely proffered and as politely administered.... While her richly spread table presented all the luxuries of her opulent country, and her sideboard offered without reserve the best wines—antiquated relics of happier days—her active benevolence found its way to the sick and to the wounded; cherishing with softest kindness infirmity and misfortune, converting despair into hope, and nursing debility into strength. Nevertheless the obligations of duty were imperative; the house must burn; and a respectful communication to the lady of her destined loss must be made. Taking the first opportunity which offered the next morning, Lieutenant-colonel Lee imparted to Mrs. Motte the intended measure, lamenting the sad necessity, and assuring her of the deep regret which the unavoidable act excited in his and every breast.

"With a smile of complacency this exemplary lady listened to the embarrassed officer, and gave instant relief to his agitated feelings by declaring that she was gratified with the opportunity of contributing to the good of her country, and that she should view the approaching scene with delight. Shortly after, seeing accidentally the bows and arrows which had been prepared, she sent for the Lieutenant-colonel and presenting him with a bow and its apparatus imported from India, she requested his substitution of these as probably better adapted for the object than those we had provided.

"Receiving with silent delight this opportune present, the Lieutenant-colonel rejoined his troops, now making ready for the concluding scene. The lines were manned, and an additional force stationed at the battery, lest the enemy might determine to risk a desperate assault. As soon as the troops reached their several posts, a flag was again sent to McPherson, with an assurance that longer perseverance in vain resistance would place the garrison at the mercy of the conqueror. . . . The British captain received the flag with his usual politeness, but he remained immovable, repeating his determination to hold out to the last.

"It was now about noon, and the rays of the scorching sun had prepared the shingle roof for the projected conflagration. The first arrow struck, and communicated its fire; a second was shot at another quarter of the roof, and a third at a third quarter; this last also took effect, and like the first soon kindled a blaze. Mc-

Pherson ordered a party to repair to the loft of the house and by knocking off the shingles to stop the flames. This was soon perceived, and Captain Finley was directed to open his battery, raking the loft from end to end.

"The fire of our six-pounder soon drove the soldiers down; and no other effort to stop the flames being practical, McPherson hung out the white flag.... He was charged with having subjected himself to punishment by his idle waste of his antagonists' time; and ... frankly acknowledged his dependent situation and declared his readiness to meet any consequence which the discharge of duty conformably to his own conviction of right might produce. Powerfully as the present occasion called for punishment, and rightfully as it might have been inflicted, not a drop of blood was shed, nor any part of the enemy's baggage taken. McPherson and his officers accompanied their captors to Mrs. Motte's, and partook with them of a sumptuous dinner. The deportment and demeanor of Mrs. Motte gave a zest to the pleasures of the table. She did its honors with that unaffected politeness which ever excites esteem mingled with admiration. Conversing with ease, vivacity, and good sense, she obliterated our recollection of the injury she had received; and though warmly attached to the defenders of her country, the engaging amiability of her manners left it doubtful which set of officers constituted these defenders. Requesting to be permitted to return to Charleston on parole, they were accordingly paroled and sent off in the evening to Lord Rawdon, now engaged in passing the Santee at Nelson's Ferry."

Noblesse oblige.

As Lossing on his tour penetrated no further than this point into the swamps which sheltered Francis Marion during his long running fight with the British in the last two years of the war, this is as good a place as any to pause for contemplation of that most picturesque of all the desperate, dauntless partisans who somehow contrived to outguess and outlast the British regulars in the Carolina campaigns.

"Among the bold, energetic, and faithful patriots of the South none holds a firmer place in the affections of the American people than General Francis Marion," says Lossing. "His adventures were full of the spirit of romance, and his whole military life was an epic poem. The followers of Robin Hood were never more devoted to their chief than were the men of Marion's brigade to their beloved leader. Bryant has sketched a graphic picture of that noble band in his SONG OF MARION'S MEN."

In Lossing's time every schoolchild could recite verses like Bryant's about Marion, but as literature they have gone a little out of style. Look back, for no one since then has said it any better:

> "Our band is few, but true and tried,
>   Our leader frank and bold;
> The British soldier trembles
>   When Marion's name is told.
> Our fortress is the good green wood,
>   Our tent the cypress tree;
> We know the forest round us
>   As seamen know the sea.
> We know its walls of thorny vines,
>   Its glades of reedy grass;
> Its safe and silent islands
>   Within the dark morass.
>
> Woe to the English soldiery
>   That little dread us near!
> On them shall light at midnight
>   A strange and sudden fear;
> When, waking to their tents on fire,
>   They grasp their arms in vain,
> And they who stand to face us
>   Are beat to earth again;
> And they who fly in terror deem
>   A mighty host behind,
> And hear the tramp of thousands
>   Upon the hollow wind.

Then sweet the hour that brings release
    From danger and from toil;
We talk the battle over,
    And share the battle's spoil;
The woodland rings with laugh and shout,
    As if a hunt were up,
And woodland flowers are gather'd
    To crown the soldier's cup.
With merry songs we mock the wind
    That in the pine-top grieves,
And slumber long and sweetly
    On beds of oaken leaves.

Well knows the fair and friendly moon
    The band that Marion leads—
The glitter of their rifles,
    The scampering of their steeds.
'Tis life to guide the fiery barb
    Across the moonlight plain;
'Tis life to feel the night-wind
    That lifts his tossing mane.
A moment in the British camp—
    A moment—and away
Back to the pathless forest,
    Before the peep of day.

Grave men there are by broad Santee,
    Grave men with hoary hairs,
Their hearts are all with Marion,
    For Marion are their prayers.
And lovely ladies greet our band
    With kindest welcoming,
With smiles like those of summer,
    And tears like those of spring.

> For them we wear these trusty arms,
> And lay them down no more,
> Till we have driven the Briton
> Forever from our shore."

We noticed Marion briefly as he appeared in Gates's camp before Camden in July, 1780, where his ragged followers excited only amusement in the scarcely less destitute Continentals, and from where he was allowed to depart unregretted to operate in defence of the Whig population in the lowland swamps of the Santee and Pedee Rivers. He had at that time recently escaped capture at the fall of Charleston by a mere coincidence which might be regarded as a miracle, and had since gathered together a little force of friends and neighbors, armed and mounted by their own efforts, who formed as deadly a striking force as a water-moccasin. Their only uniform was a helmet-shaped leather cap decorated with a silver crescent inscribed *Liberty or Death*. Their swords were home-made, and their horses were the tough, scraggy local breed.

His friend Peter Horry, who rode with him on most of his adventures, attempted to write a true account of Marion's life after the war, but the manuscript fell into the hands of the ubiquitous Parson Weems, who himself wrote such a questionable life of George Washington, and Horry afterward claimed that his work had been tampered with by Weems, before publication. Nevertheless, with another forgotten *Memoir* by one of the James brothers who also served with him and survived to become a judge, it forms a colorful source of romantic legend and incredible fact for the only other full-scale biography, compiled by William Gilmore Simms in 1854.

Judge James, writing within living memory of Marion, and consulting with other survivors, had also the advantage of possessing several of Marion's letter-books, which no one else had made use of. It is on his rare little volume, published in 1821, that one can best rely for direct accounts of this extraordinary man. "He was rather below the middle stature of men," James says, "lean and swarthy. He had a countenance remarkably steady; his nose was aquiline; his chin projecting; his forehead was large and high, and his eyes black and piercing. He was now forty-eight years of age; but still even at this age, his frame was capable of enduring fatigue and every privation necessary for a partisan. His wisdom and patriotism will become henceforth conspicuous."

Marion's first notable success after leaving Gates's camp for the lowlands was the rescue of a body of American prisoners and walking wounded which had been taken at Camden and were being marched to confinement at Charleston. He surprised the British escort at Nelson's Ferry and scattered it. From then till the end of the year he skirmished up and down the rivers with British detachments, always avoiding a set battle and always escaping unscathed. In December, 1780, he retired to Snow's Island, where he established a sort of headquarters. Judge James described the camp, having known it well himself:

"This island became henceforth the most constant place of his encampment; a secure retreat, a depot for his arms and ammunition; ... [it] lies at the confluence of Lynch's Creek and the Pedee.... The island is high river swamp, and large, of itself affording much provision and live stock, as did all the Pedee river swamp at that day. In places there were open cultivated lands on the island, but it was much covered by thick woods and cane-brakes; ... and by crossing the river and marching two or three hours Marion could forage in an enemy's country. Reinforcements were now coming in to him daily, and his party began at this time to assume the appearance and force of a brigade. He lay here to receive them, and to repose his men and horses, which ... had passed over at least three hundred and sixty miles in rapid marches and counter-marches, made principally in the night....

"At and near Snow's Island, Marion secured what boats he wanted, and burnt those more remote. To prevent the approach of an enemy he fell upon a plan of insulating as much as possible the country under his command. For this purpose he broke down bridges and felled trees across causeways and difficult passes. As there was no market in those days, and the vicinity of a road was dangerous, the inhabitants aided him much in this design. . . .

"When General Marion himself, or any of his parties, left the Island on an expedition, they almost invariably struck into the woods towards the heads of the larger water courses, and crossed them near their source; and if in haste, they swam over them. Many of the General's trails remained for a long time after, and some are now roads. Where it is said hereafter that General Marion crossed a river, it is not to be understood that he stopped, like Caesar at the Rhine, to build a bridge over it; or that he was provided with the convenient modern apparatus of pontoons, or oftentimes with a common flat; even the last would have been too slow for the usual rapidity of his motions. He seldom waited for more than a single canoe, along-side of which his sorrel horse Ball was usually led into the river, and he floated over like an amphibious animal. The rest of the horses soon learned to follow instinctively. Where a canoe was not to be had, the General swam over frequently on the back of this uncommon horse. No leader, in ancient or modern times, ever passed rivers with more rapidity. His plans were laid, and his movements conducted with the utmost secrecy. After making a movement, his most confidential officers and men have had to search for him for days together, perhaps without finding him. His scouts, when returning, and at a loss, used a loud and shrill whistle as a signal; which could be heard in the night to an astonishing distance.

"His men having been several times unexpectedly led out upon long expeditions without preparation, and suffering for the want of food on such occasions, were in the habit of watching his cook, and if they saw him unusually busied in preparing any of the frugal fare then in use, they also prepared accordingly. The General's favorite time for moving was at the setting sun, and then it was expected the march would continue all night. Before striking any sudden blow he had been known to march sixty or seventy miles, without taking any other refreshment than a meal of cold potatoes and a drink of cold water, in twenty-four hours.

"During this period the men were but badly clothed in homespun, which afforded little warmth. They slept in the open air according to their means, either with or without a blanket. They had nothing but water to drink. They fed chiefly on sweet potatoes, either with or without fresh beef. And they submitted to this without a murmur, but all sighed for salt! for salt! that first article of necessity for the human race. Little do the luxurious of the present day know of the pressure of such a want. Salt was now ten silver dollars the bushel, when brought more than thirty miles from the Waccamaw sea shore, where it was coarsely manufactured. It was harder to get one silver dollar then than ten now; so that on a low calculation, a bushel of coarse bay salt sold at that time for one hundred dollars value of the present day [1821]. As soon as General Marion could collect a sufficient quantity of this desirable article at Snow's Island, he distributed it out in quantities not exceeding a bushel to each Whig family; and thus endeared himself the more to his Whig followers.

"About the beginning of this year (1781) Marion appointed two aides, Thomas Elliott and Lewis Ogier, the first of whom conducted most of his correspondence. He formed a mess, of which Colonel Hugh Horry and Colonel James Postell were inmates, and apparently his principal councillors; Sergeant Davis was the caterer, and supplied his dinners, *such as they were;* heretofore he had seldom anything but meat and sweet potatoes, and often not both of these at a time, but now he had the luxury of rice. He did what was of more consequence than this, he put in requisition all the saws in the country, and all the blacksmiths, and made swords for four troops of militia cavalry. He had so little ammunition this expedient was necessary. He gave the command of this corps to Colonel Peter Horry who had been a captain with him in the second regiment."

Simms, who was a contemporary of Lossing, had access to a manuscript *Memoir* of Peter Horry, as yet unpublished, which supplied some colorful material not contained in James's book. It was apparently written crudely in its author's old age, and contained some unconscious humor which Simms more or less suppressed.

Horry confessed that as a young man he had had a great passion for "the Sex" which led him into frequent difficulties which he set down at some length. It also emerges that Peter Horry stammered, especially at times of anxiety and excitement. This leads to a story of his having been ordered by Marion to await in ambush the approach of a British detachment. The maneuver was successfully carried out, but when Horry tried to give the order to his men to fire, the initial letter defeated him. "F—f—f—*shoot*, damn you, *shoot!*" he exploded, which must have surprised the British as much as the opening volley.

Simms also has the story about the British officer who came to dinner. This starchy young man, sent up from the British post at Georgetown on a mission regarding the exchange of prisoners, was found by Marion's scouts riding around in circles looking for the camp, and was promptly blind-folded according to custom and conducted by intricate paths into the recesses of the island. Here, when his eyes were uncovered, he found himself surrounded by what Simms suggests must have reminded him of Robin Hood and his outlaws. "He was in the middle of one of those grand natural amphitheaters so common in our swamp forests," Simms's narrative runs, "in which the massive pine, the gigantic cypress, and the ever-green laurel, streaming with moss, and linking their opposite arms, group together the most graceful features of Gothic architecture. Through the massed foliage the sunlight came as sparingly as through the painted windows of a cathedral. Scattered round were the forms of those hardy warriors with whom our young officer was yet destined to meet in conflict—strange or savage in costume or attitude—lithe and sinewy of frame—keen-eyed and wakeful at the least alarm. Some slept, some joined in boyish sports; some stood ready for the signal to mount and march. The deadly rifle leaned against the tree, the sabre depended from its boughs. Steeds were browsing in the shade with loosened bits, but saddled, ready at the first sound of the bugle to skirr through brake and thicket.

"The British visitor," Simms goes on, "was a young man who had never seen Marion. The generals whom he was accustomed to see were great of limb, portly, and huge of proportion. Such was Cornwallis, and others of the British army. Such too was the case among the Americans. The average weight of these opposing generals during that war is stated at more than two hundred pounds. The successes of Marion must naturally have led our young Englishman to look for something in his stature even above this average. His astonishment when they did meet was probably not of a kind to lessen the partisan in his estimation. That a frame so slight, and seemingly so feeble, coupled with so much gentleness and so little pretension, should provoke a respect so general and fears so impressive was calculated to compel inquiry as to the sources of this influence."

Doubtless fascinated with his host, the officer accepted Marion's invitation to dine with them, and received another surprise. The meal was served on slabs of bark for plates, and consisted entirely of roast sweet potatoes, with a healthful mixture of vinegar and water to drink. He had probably never met a sweet potato in the mess before, and there was no butter and no salt to help it go down. "But surely," he is said to have said, "this cannot be your usual fare." To which Marion replied with a social smile that it was, indeed, except that on that day, in honor of company, there was a second helping. And the Briton is supposed to have retired from the service, after his return to Georgetown, out of a conviction that such men could never be conquered.

As late as 1953, it was possible to approach Snow's Island in a motor car by a road which ended abruptly at a grassy bank above the black swamp water, on which floated a couple of log canoes. A lumber project was then in possession and its narrow-gauge line leading towards the center of the island made it possible to travel by hand-car on rails which were often under water, about half way to where the immense live oak still stands, under which local tradition says that Marion's tent-fly was stretched. From the end of the rails it was a long, long walk with two guides, in breathless heat which sang with insects, through bamboo and live-oak and under-brush—across the still brown streams of water by perilous fallen logs which bridged the banks, or by more perilous broad jumps, propelled from one strong handclasp across to the other—along a trail perceptible only to the lean, untalkative men who as boys had followed it with their fathers before them—until the great tree was actually there, in its cathedral silence and its tremendous height, remarkable even among its vast brotherhood for its size and, one could easily imagine, for its memories.

Unlike Gates in every way, General Greene when he came South had the good sense and the civility to appreciate Marion, and he wrote to him the day after arriving at Charlotte. "I have not the honor of your acquaintance, but am no stranger to your character and merit.... Your letter of the 22d of last month to General Gates is before me. I am fully sensible your service is hard and sufferings great, but how great the prize for which we contend! I like your plan of frequently shifting your ground. It frequently prevents a surprise and perhaps a total loss of your party. Until a more permanent army can be collected than is in the field at present, we must endeavor to keep up a partisan war, and preserve the tide of sentiment among the people in our favor as much as possible. Spies are the eyes of an army, and without them a general is always groping in the dark, and can neither secure himself nor annoy his enemy. At present, I am badly off for intelligence. It is of the highest importance that I get the earliest intelligence of any reinforcement which may arrive at Charleston. I wish you, therefore, to fix some plan for procuring such information and conveying it to me with all possible dispatch. The spy should be taught to be particular in his inquiries and get the names of the corps, strength, and commanding officer's name—place from whence they came and where they are going...."

He had found the right man for the job, who had had his own system of spies and runners ever since he took the field. The main embarrassment, in Greene's camp as well as Marion's, was the lack of hard money with which to buy such perilous service. Soon after

Greene's withdrawal to Cheraw for the winter, he sent Lee's Legion to join Marion's irregular corps, and the series of raids and skirmishes began which, after a short interval in which Lee joined Greene's great retreat, brought them in May, 1781, to the joint attack on Fort Motte, where we left Lossing, who now resumes the story:

"During the day of the capitulation [at Fort Motte] Greene arrived with a small troop of cavalry, being anxious to know the result of the siege, for he was aware that Rawdon was hastening to the relief of the garrison. Some writers attribute Greene's presence at Fort Motte on this occasion to other motives than here presented. An unsatisfactory correspondence had recently taken place between Greene and Marion, the former having blamed the latter for not furnishing cavalry horses when in his power to do so. Marion, conscious of having been eminently faithful, felt deeply wronged, and tendered the resignation of his command to Greene. The latter soon perceived the injustice of his suspicions, and took this, the first opportunity for a personal interview, to heal the wound. Finding everything secure, he returned to his camp, then on the north side of the Congaree, after ordering Marion to proceed against Georgetown and directing Lee with his Legion to attack Fort Granby, which was a point of departure for the wilderness of the Cherokee country, and was located thirty-two miles above Fort Motte near the present city of Columbia. . . .

"The morning after my arrival at Columbia was very inclement. A cold drizzle which iced everything out of doors made me defer my visit to Fort Granby until noon, when, seeing no prospect of abatement, I procured a conveyance and crossing the great bridge over the Congaree rode to the home of James Cacey, Esq., the Fort Granby of the Revolution, two miles below. It is a strong frame building two stories in height, and stands upon an eminence near the Charleston road, within three-fourths of a mile of Friday's Ferry upon the Congaree. It overlooks ancient Granby and the country around. Several houses of the old village are there, but the solitude of desolation prevails, for not a family remains. Mr. Cacey was a hopeless invalid, yet he was able to give me many interesting reminiscences connected with that locality, and I passed an hour very pleasantly with him and his family.

"Mr. Friday, the father-in-law of Mr. Cacey, and his brother were the only Whigs of that name in the state and often suffered insults from their Tory kinsmen. Mr. Friday owned mills at Granby, and also a ferry called by his name; and when the British fortified that post the garrison supplied themselves with flour from his establishment. He gave the British the credit of dealing honorably, paying him liberally for everything they took from him—flour, poultry, cattle, etc. On one occasion, when Friday was called to the fort to receive his pay, Colonel Maxwell, the commandant of the garrison, said to him, 'Mr. Friday, I hope you are as clever a fellow as those of your name who are with us.' 'No!' shouted his Tory uncle who was standing near. 'He's a damned rebel, and I'll split him down!' at the same time rushing forward to execute his brutal purpose. Colonel Maxwell protected the patriot, but dared not rebuke the savage Tory, for fear of offending his comrades.

"The dwelling of Mr. Cacey was originally built by some gentlemen of Pine-Tree [Camden] as a store-house for cotton and other products of the country, whence they were sent upon flat-boats down the river to the seaboard. When the chain of [British] military posts from Camden to Charleston was established [after the

Charleston surrender in May, 1780] this building, eligibly located, was fortified and called Fort Granby. A ditch was digged around it; a strong parapet was raised; bastions were formed; batteries were arranged; and an abatis was constructed. The garrison consisted of three hundred and fifty men, chiefly Loyalists, with a few mounted Hessians, under the command of Colonel Maxwell, a refugee from the eastern shore of Maryland. He was neither brave nor experienced, and the want of these qualities of the commandant being known to Lee, he felt no hesitation in attacking him in his strong position.

"Detaching a small troop of cavalry under Captain Armstrong, to watch the movements of Rawdon, Lee pushed forward with his usual celerity to the investment of Fort Granby. Only a few days earlier, Sumter had made a demonstration against Fort Granby but finding it too strong for his small arms, had retired and marched to attack the British post at Orangeburg fifty miles below. Lee arrived in the vicinity of the fort on the evening of the fourteenth of May, 1781 [2 days after surrender of Fort Motte], the day on which Sumter took possession of Orangeburg; and in the edge of a wood, within six hundred yards of the fort, he began the erection of a battery. A dense fog the next morning enabled him to complete it before they were discovered by the garrison."

When the fog lifted, and Lee opened fire with his cannon and musketry, Colonel Maxwell was willing to negotiate, and before noon on the 15th of May the American flag went up over one of the bastions. The captive garrison was marched with an escort to Rawdon's camp and permitted to retire to Charleston on parole from there. They left cannon, ammunition, salt, and liquor in Lee's possession, besides an almost bloodless victory. A message went to Greene, who was close on the retreating Rawdon's heels, and he came into Lee's camp the same evening. Their reunion was enlivened within the next twenty-four hours by the news of Rawdon's further withdrawal from Nelson's Ferry, and of Sumter's success at Orangeburg. May 17th, 1781, was something of a holiday in the American camp, before Greene moved out westward towards the British post of 96, and Lee set out for Augusta to join Pickens there. Pickens, like Marion and Moultrie, was a veteran of the Cherokee wars, and had been operating independently as a partisan with a small body of militia.

Lossing found that Cacey's house near Columbia bore "honorable scars made by the bullets of Lee's infantry; and in the gable towards the river between the chimney and a window is an orifice formed by the passage of a six-pound ball from Lee's cannon. In one of the rooms are numerous marks made by an ax when cutting up meat for the use of the garrison; and an old log-barn near, which stood within the entrenchments, has also many bullet scars."

The house has gone now, and no one remembers what happened there. In 1953 the site was marked only by the ruins of its brick chimney in a bramble patch on a dirt road outside Columbia. There was a boulder with a metal plaque, erected by the D.A.R. in 1925, when the house still stood—"*Captured by Lee, May 15th, 1781,*" it reads in part. *Reoccupied by Rawdon, July 1, 1781. Reoccupied by Greene, July 4, 1781.*"...A local query about the house brings only a vague reply—"It was taken down—"

At Columbia Lossing encountered a gentleman from the 96 district who discouraged him from attempting the journey of seventy-nine miles to where a pleasant village called Cambridge was all that remained of the wild little stockaded post which was the furthest western garrison of the British occupation of South Carolina. It was held by a handful of men under a New York Loyalist named Cruger, an energetic and capable officer, who when he heard of Greene's approach so strengthened his fortifications that he could defy the American force, and settled down to withstand a siege. He held out for twenty-seven sanguinary days, in spite of attempts to cut off his water supply and to fire into his redoubt from a log tower above it. Then Rawdon's approach from Charleston with reinforcements compelled Greene to withdraw. Lossing adds a footnote here:

"The wives of Lieutenant-colonel Cruger and a Loyalist Major Greene were at a farm-house in the neighborhood of 96 when the Americans arrived. General Greene soon quieted their fears, and as they preferred to remain where they were to joining their husbands in the beleaguered town, he placed a guard there to protect them. This kindness Mrs. Cruger reciprocated on the day when the Americans left, by informing some light troops of Greene's, who had been out scouting and were passing by the farm-house towards the post, of the termination of the siege and the direction taken by General Greene in his retreat. Without this timely information they would have been captured."

Greene had intended to retreat as far as Charlotte, depending on the movements of the enemy, but when he learned that Rawdon was preparing to abandon 96 altogether and join up with an additional British force coming up to meet him from Charleston under Colonel Alexander Stewart, with the idea of scattering the forces of Marion and Sumter and regaining the posts the partisans had taken but were unable to occupy and hold for lack of men to form garrisons, Greene prepared to pursue him. He sent Lee to gain the front of the British army before it could reach Friday's Ferry again, and dispatched messages to Sumter and Marion, ordering them to similar action, and fixing as a point of future rendezvous between them and the main army a rest camp to be established by him in the High Hills of Santee.

"It is related," says Lossing in another of his dry, tantalizing footnotes, "that the message to Sumter from Greene was conveyed by Emily Geiger, the daughter of a German planter in the Fairfield District. He prepared a letter to Sumter, but none of his men appeared willing to attempt the hazardous service, for the Tories were on the alert as Rawdon was approaching the Congaree. Greene was delighted by the boldness of a young girl, not more than eighteen years of age, who came forward and volunteered to carry the letter to Sumter. With his usual caution, he communicated the contents of the letter to Emily, fearing she might lose it on the way. The maiden mounted a fleet horse, and crossing the Wateree at the Camden Ferry pressed on towards Sumter's camp. Passing through a dry swamp on the second day of her journey, she was intercepted by some Tory scouts. Coming from the direction of Greene's army, she was an object of suspicion, and was taken to a house on the edge of the swamp and confined in a room. With proper delicacy, they sent for a woman to search her person. No sooner was she left alone, than she ate up Greene's letter, piece by piece. After a while, the matron arrived, made a careful search, but discovered nothing. With many apologies Emily was allowed to pursue her journey. She reached Sumter's camp, communicated Greene's message, and soon Rawdon was flying before the Americans toward Orangeburg. Emily Geiger afterward married Mr. Thurwits, a rich planter on the Congaree. The picture of her capture here given I copied from the original painting by Flagg, in the possession of Stacy Potts, of Trenton, New Jersey."

Lossing left Columbia in the cars early on Monday morning, and reached Orangeburg, fifty-one miles distant, by half-past nine. The weather was now delightful, he tells us, and as usual he soon found a companion. "A dreamy haziness was in the atmosphere, and the air was as mild as early June. Leaving my baggage at the railway station, I strolled over that village and vicinity for an hour, with a gentleman from Columbia, who was familiar with its historic localities. The village, which was settled as early as 1735, is beautifully situated upon a gently rolling plain, near the banks of the Edisto, which is here skirted with swamps, and contains about four hundred inhabitants. There are several elegant dwellings standing upon each side of the broad street extending from the railway to the heart of the village, all shaded by lofty trees. It is about eighty miles west of Charleston, and being the seat of justice is regularly laid out.

"The old jail, which the British fortified while they occupied the place, was built of brick in 1770, and stood upon the crown of a gentle hill, a few yards northwest of the old courthouse, which is yet standing. The courthouse is a frame building, and was used as a blacksmith's shop when I was there.... This edifice exhibited several bullet marks, the effect of Sumter's assault in 1781.

"Orangeburg was one of the chain of military posts established by the British after the fall of Charleston in May, 1780. The jail was fortified and garrisoned by about seventy militia and a dozen regulars. Sumter, when marching to join Greene according to orders before Hobkirk's Hill, conceived a plan for capturing Fort Granby and therefore did not re-enforce his general. He began the siege successfully, but learning that Rawdon had ordered the evacuation of Orangeburg, he left Colonel Taylor with a strong party to maintain the siege at Fort Granby while he should strike the garrison at Orangeburg before it could retire. By a rapid march he reached Orangeburg on the morning of the 11th of May (1780) and after one or two volleys the garrison surrendered themselves unconditional prisoners of war. Paroling his prisoners, Sumter hastened back towards Fort Granby; but before his arrival

Lee had invested and reduced it, allowing the most favorable terms. Sumter was incensed at the conduct of Lee, for he felt that Lee had not only snatched from him the laurels he had almost won, but that Lee had hastened the capitulation and allowed favorable terms in order to accomplish the surrender before Sumter could arrive. No doubt the garrison would have surrendered unconditionally, if besieged a day or two longer. Sumter sent an indignant letter of complaint to Greene, enclosing his commission. Greene, knowing his worth, returned it to him with many expressions of regard, and Sumter, sacrificing private resent for the good of the cause, remained in the army.

"On the day after Rawdon's arrival at Orangeburg (having evacuated Camden and 96) he was joined by Lieutenant-colonel Alexander Stewart, with the regiment which Rawdon had ordered up from Charleston. The retirement of Greene to the High Hills of Santee, and the rendezvous there of the several corps of Marion, Lee, and Sumter, indicating a temporary cessation of hostilities, Lord Rawdon proceeded to Charleston and before long embarked for England, for the purpose of recruiting his health.

"The command of all the British troops in the Southern field now devolved upon Colonel Stewart. That officer soon left Orangeburg and encamped on the Congaree, near its junction with the Wateree. The two armies were only sixteen miles apart by airline, but two rivers rolled between, and they could not meet without making a difficult circuit of seventy miles. Stewart's foraging parties soon spread over the country, and Marion was detached from Greene's camp in the High Hills towards the Combahee Ferry, and [Colonel] Washington across the Wateree to disperse them. Many brisk skirmishes ensued. In the meantime, Greene was reenforced by a brigade of Continentals from North Carolina, and determined with his augmented strength to attack again.

"He left the Hills on the 22d of August (1781), crossed the Wateree at the Camden Ferry and made rapid marches to Friday's Ferry on the Congaree. There he was joined by General Pickens with the militia from 96 and a body of South Carolina state troops.

On hearing of Greene's approach, Stewart decamped from Orangeburg and pitched his tents at Eutaw Springs, forty miles below, vigorously pursued by the Americans."

When he had sketched the courthouse at Orangeburg, which was the only remaining relic of the Revolution there, Lossing hired a horse and gig to visit Eutaw Springs, near the south bank of the Santee. No one at Orangeburg seemed to know quite where it was or how far away. The price of the gig was dependent on the distance it travelled, which was estimated at the livery-stable as twenty-five or thirty miles. It proved to be nearer forty each way. Lossing left Orangeburg at 11 o'clock on the morning of January 26, in 1849. The day was so warm that he found the shade of the pine forests very refreshing, and his spirits as usual were high. "My horse was fleet, the gig light, the road level and generally fine," he records with satisfaction, "and at sunset I arrived at the house of Mr. Avinger (Vance's Ferry Post Office) thirty miles distant. About fourteen miles from Orangeburg I crossed the Fourhole Swamp, upon a narrow causeway of logs and three bridges. The distance is about a mile, and a gloomier place cannot well be imagined. On either side was a dense undergrowth of shrubs, closely interlaced with vines; and above, draped with moss, towered lofty cypresses and gums. This swamp derives its name from the fact that the deep and sluggish stream, a branch of the South Edisto, which it skirts, disappears from the surface four times within this morass. Plunging into one pit, the water boils up from the next; disappearing again in the third, it reappears in the fourth, and then courses its way to the Edisto. These pits are about half a mile apart, and are filled with remarkably fine fish, which may be taken with a hook and line at the depth of thirty feet.

"At two o'clock I passed one of those primitive schoolhouses built of logs, which the traveller meets occasionally in the South. It stood in the edge of a wood, and in front was a fine Pride-of-India tree, under which the teacher sat listening to the efforts of half a dozen children in the science of orthography. The country is very sparsely populated, and many of the children, living four or five miles away from the schoolhouse, are conveyed on horseback by the Negro servants. I stopped a moment in conversation with the pedagogue, who was a Vermonter, one of those New England people described by Halleck as

'Wandering through the Southern countries, teaching
  The ABC from Webster's Spelling-book;
Gallant and godly, making love and preaching.'

He appeared satisfied with his success in each vocation, and hinted that the daughter of a neighboring planter had promised him her heart and hand. When obtained, he intended to cultivate cotton and maize instead of the dull intellects of other people's children.

"I passed the night at Mr. Avinger's, and very early in the morning departed for Eutaw, ten miles distant. I was now upon the Congaree road, and found the travelling somewhat heavier than upon ways less used. About three miles from Avinger's I passed Burdell's plantation where the American army encamped the night before the battle of Eutaw. It was another glorious morning, and at sunrise I was greeted with the whistle of the quail, the drum of the partridge, the sweet notes of the robin and bluebird, and the querulous cadences of the cat-bird, all summer tenants of our Northern forests. They appeared each to carol a brief matin hymn at sunrise, and were silent the remainder of the day. I saw several mocking-birds, but they flitted about in silence, taking lessons, I suppose, from their Northern friends, to be sung during their absence. Occasionally a wild turkey would start from a branch, or a filthy buzzard alight by the wayside, until, as I came suddenly upon a watercourse a wild fawn that stood lapping from the clear stream wheeled and bounded away among the evergreens of the wood.

"At about eight o'clock I arrived at the elegant mansion of William Sinkler, Esq., upon whose plantation are the celebrated Eutaw Springs. It stands in the midst of noble shade-trees, half a mile from the highway, and is approached by a lane fringed with every variety of evergreen tree and shrub which beautify Southern scenery in winter. I was courteously received by the proprietor; and when the object of my visit was made known, he ordered his horse and accompanied me to the springs and the field of battle, which are about half a mile eastward of his mansion.

"The Springs present a curious spectacle, being really but the first and second apparition of the same subterranean stream. They are a few rods north of the forks of the Canal and the Monck's Corner roads, at the head of a shallow ravine. The first spring is at the foot of a hill, twenty or thirty feet in height. The water bubbles up, cold, limpid, and sparkling in large volumes, from two or three orifices, into a basin of rock-marl, and flowing fifty or sixty yards descends, rushing and foaming, into a cavern beneath a high ridge of marl covered with alluvium and forest trees. This marl appears to be a concretion of oyster shells, and is said to be excellent fertilizer when crushed to powder. In this vicinity many bones of monsters, like the mastodon, have been found.

"After traversing its subterraneous way some thirty rods, the stream reappears upon the other side, where it is a louder stream, and flows gently over a smooth rocky bed towards the Santee, its course marked by tall cypresses draped with moss. The whole length of the Eutaw Creek in all its windings is only about two miles. Where it first bubbles from the earth there is sufficient volume to turn a large mill-wheel, but the fountain is so near the level of the Santee at Nelson's Ferry, where the Eutaw enters, that no fall can be obtained; on the contrary, when the Santee is filled to the brim, the waters flow back to the springs.

"This is a view of the reappearance of the stream (or lower spring) from the marl ridge thirty feet in height. It is probable that a subterranean stream here first finds its way to the surface of the earth.

"Just at the forks of the road on the side towards the springs was a clump of trees and shrubbery which marked the spot where stood a strong brick house, famous as the citadel of the British camp, and a retreat for some of the warriors in the conflict at the Eutaw. Let us sit down here, in the shadow of a cypress by the bubbling spring, and consider the event when human blood tinged the clear water of the Eutaw, where patriots fought and died."

The flooding of a large area of the Santee shores for the Santee-Cooper Dam had recently brought the waters of two artificial lakes perilously close to historic landmarks. But the site of the battle of Eutaw Springs, and Fort Watson were preserved in their mysterious, beautiful landscape of live oaks hung with moss.

XIII

Eutaw Springs to Pond Bluff

GREENE had been beaten in every battle he had attempted since he came to the South. And yet the British had been so severely punished in each engagement that now they were falling back towards the coast, abandoning post after post in the chain which had a year ago reached from Charleston to the wilderness at 96. In Georgia they still held Savannah and Augusta—in South Carolina they occupied Georgetown and Charleston, which was Greene's next concern.

On the night of September 7th (1781) he was at Burdell's Plantation within seven miles of Stewart's camp at Eutaw Springs. He had at last received some skimpy reinforcements. Marion was there, and Harry Lee, and Otho Williams, William Washington, Pickens, and the Hamptons. Sumter was still playing his lone hand, complaining of his Blackstocks wound, and Pickens had united some of Sumter's men with his own command.

Stewart had for cavalry only a Tory troop, for Tarleton was with Cornwallis in Virginia, but unlike the British force at King's Mountain, the Cowpens, and 96, Stewart's army was composed largely of British regulars, including the famous Buffs under the command of Major Majoribanks. It was perhaps the most evenly matched conflict of the war, and both armies had already suffered from the hot weather and sickness.

The battle was long and devious, lasting nearly four hours under an autumnal sun, with the issue more than once in doubt, and there were many moments of individual glory. Once more it is possible to substitute a more concise account of the day for Lossing's, and this one is from Simms's Life of Marion, which drew on contemporary stories:

"The British center began to give way from left to right," he says, "when a bayonet charge led by Williams had thrown the British left into disorder, and the fire of the Marylanders, poured in at the proper moment, completed their disaster. Their whole front yielded, and the shouts of the Americans declared their exultation, as at a victory already won. Unquestionably, the day was theirs. The enemy had fled from the battle. But a new one was to begin, in which victory, at present so secure, was taken from their grasp.

"In the effort to prevent the enemy from rallying, and to cut him off from the brick dwelling into which Sheridan had thrown himself, obeying the commands of Stewart, as soon as the necessity became apparent, the greatest loss of the Americans was sustained. Majoribanks still held his ground, with his entire battalion, in the thick woods which skirted Eutaw Creek, and so well covered was he that in an attempt to penetrate with his cavalry Colonel Washington became entangled in the thicket, was wounded, and fell into the hands of the enemy, while his men suffered severely from the enemy fire, and his troop was routed. A second time they were brought to the charge, but with no better success than before. Majoribanks still maintained his position, watching the moment when to emerge from the thicket with the best prospect of safety to himself and hurt to the Americans. He was soon to have an opportunity.

"The British line had yielded and broken before the American bayonet. The latter pressed closely upon their heels, made many prisoners, and might have cut them off and, by isolating Majoribanks forced him to surrender, but for one of those occurrences which so frequently in battle change the fortunes of the day. The course of the fugitives led them directly through the British encampment. There everything was given up for lost. The tents were all standing, the commissaries had abandoned their stores, and the numerous retainers of the army were already in full flight for Charleston. When the pursuing Americans penetrated the encampment, they lost sight of the fugitives in the contemplation of various objects of temptation which to a half-naked and half-starved soldiery were irresistible. The pursuit was forborne; the Americans fastened upon the liquors and refreshments scattered among the tents; and the whole army with the exception of one or two corps then fell into confusion.

"Yet so closely had the British been pursued to the shelter of the house, and so narrow was their escape, that some of the Americans had nearly obtained entrance with them. It was only by shutting the door against some of their own officers that they made it secure against the pursuers; and in retiring from the house, now a citadel, the Americans only found safety by interposing the bodies of the officers thus made captive at the entrance between themselves and the fire from the windows....

"The British tents had done what the British arms had failed to do. Victory was lost to the Americans. Scattered throughout the encampment, the soldiers became utterly unmanageable. The enemy, meanwhile, had partially recovered from their panic. The party of Sheridan were in possession of the house. Another party held possession of the palisaded garden. Coffin was active with his remnant of cavalry and Majoribanks still held a formidable position in the thicket on Eutaw Creek. From the upper windows of the house the musketry of Sheridan traversed the encampment, which the Americans now trembled to leave lest they should suffer from the fire. Every head that emerged from a tent was a mark for their bullets.

"Aware by this time of the extent of his misfortune, Greene ordered a retreat, which Hampton's cavalry was commanded to cover. In the execution of this duty Hampton encountered the British cavalry. A sharp action ensued; the latter fled, and in the ardor of pursuit the American horse approached so near to the position of Majoribanks as to receive a murderous fire, which prostrated one-third of their number and scattered the rest. Before they could again be brought together, Majoribanks, seizing upon the chance afforded by a temporary clearing of the field, emerged from the wood at a moment which enabled him to put a successful finish to the day. Two six-pounders which had been abandoned by the British had been turned upon the house by the Americans; but in their eagerness they had brought the pieces within the range of fire from the windows. The artillerists had been shot down; and in the absence of the American cavalry Majoribanks was enabled to recover the guns. Wheeling them under the walls of the house, he took a contiguous position, his own being almost the only portion of the British army still in a condition to renew the action.

"The Americans yielded the ground about the house, but were promptly rallied in the skirts of the wood. The British were too much crippled to pursue; and the respite was gladly seized upon by the Americans to plunge headlong into the neighboring ponds, to cool the heat and satisfy the intense thirst occasioned by the burning sun of a Carolina September. Both sides claimed the victory, and with equal reason. In the first part of the day it was clearly with the Americans. They had driven the enemy from the field, in panic and with great loss. They were in possession of five hundred prisoners, nearly all of whom they retained. They had taken two out of the five pieces of artillery which the British had brought into the action; and something more to boast, considering the proverbial renown of the British with this weapon, it was at the point of the bayonet that they had swept the enemy from the ground.

"The British took shelter in a fortress from which the Americans were repulsed. It is of no consequence to assert that they might have taken it. They might—it was in their power to do so —but they did not; and the promptitude with which the British availed themselves of this security entitles them to the merit which they claim. We are constrained to think that the business of the field was strangely bungled by the Americans in the sequel. This may have arisen from the carnage made at this period among their officers, particularly in the persevering but futile endeavors of the latter to extricate the soldiers from the tents. Under cover of a contiguous barn, the artillery presented the means of forcing the building and reducing the garrison to submission. The attempts made at this object, by this arm of the Americans, were rash, badly counselled, and exposed to danger without adequate protection. The British were saved by this error, by the luxuries contained within their tents, by the spirited behavior of Coffin and the cool and steady valor of Majoribanks."

A particular pathos clings to the gallant Major Majoribanks, who even as his stand under the walls of the house saved the day for the British received a mortal wound. He died beside the road as the army retreated on Charleston, and was buried there, alone, where his headstone can be found today.

The sequel to William Washington's wound and captivity was a romantic one. His horse had been killed under him, and while he was pinned by its fall he received a bayonet thrust which disabled him. He was carried into Charleston as a prisoner of war, and during his convalescence he resumed the acquaintance of a Miss Elliott, begun before the siege, "a young lady," says Harry Lee, "in whom concentered the united attractions of respectable descent, opulence, polish, and beauty." In the spring of 1782 he married her, and never went back to Virginia, choosing to live instead on her ancestral estate at Sandy Hill. He also bought a house on the Battery in Charleston which still bears his name, and by this marriage left a son and a daughter.

Greene retired to his favorite rest-camp site on the High Hills of Santee, where he remained until November 18th, reorganizing his worn-out troops and nursing the sick and wounded who were in a deplorable condition, as he reported to Congress in October: "and numbers of our brave fellows who have bled in the cause of their country have been eat up with maggots and perished in that miserable situation. Hospital stores and medicines have been exceedingly scarce; not an ounce of bark have we in the department at this time. But fortunately the cold weather is coming on, and the malignity of the fevers begins to abate.... To afford the sick and wounded all the relief in my power, I visited the hospitals from camp to Charlotte." Greene was still encamped in the High Hills when he received the glorious news of Cornwallis's surrender at Yorktown. But like the Commander-in-chief, he recognized that there was still work to be done.

As there were no permanent fortifications at Eutaw Springs, Lossing found not a vestige of the camp or the battle except a few scattered bricks from the house which the British had used as shelter. But his host Mr. Sinkler showed him a gold watch which one of his Negroes had found ten years before while making holes with a stick to plant cotton seed in the field where William Washington was brought down. The hands were almost destroyed by rust, but otherwise the watch was well preserved.

"Guided by one of Mr. Sinkler's servants, I crossed the Eutaw Creek near his house," Lossing continues, "and rode down to Nelson's Ferry about a mile and a half distant. At its entrance into the Santee the bateau of the ferryman was moored, and almost filled its narrow channel. Beneath the moss-draped trees upon the bank of the river some Negro women were washing clothes, and when they found themselves portrayed in my drawing in all the dishabille of washing-day, they wanted to arrange their dresses and caps and be sketched in a better plight. Time was too precious to allow compliance, for I wished to get as far towards Orangeburg that evening as possible. Promising to improve their toilet when I got home, I closed my port-folio, and, taking the reins, hastened back towards Vance's Ferry.

"Nelson's Ferry, here portrayed, was an important locality during the Revolution. It was the principal crossing-place of the Santee for travellers or troops passing between Camden and Charleston, and as such commanded the attention of the British after they captured the latter city in May, 1780. A redoubt was cast up there upon the North side of the Santee, and garrisoned by a small detachment."

General Marion's shabby little band had not been kindly received in Gates's camp before Camden, it will be recalled, and from there he had gone back to the swamps of the low country to follow his solitary genius of small deadly raids while Gates blundered on into defeat. With Marion were the two Horry brothers, Peter and Hugh, who like their leader were inspired partisan fighters. When Marion heard of Gates's disaster at Camden he withheld the news from his men, "fearing its effect upon their spirits," Lossing explains. "That night (August 18th, '81) his scouts advised him of the approach to Nelson's Ferry of a strong British guard with a large body of prisoners from Gates's army. Though much inferior in numbers, he resolved to attack them. Just before daylight he detached Colonel Hugh Horry with sixteen resolute men, to occupy the road at Horse Creek Pass, in a broad swamp, while with the remainder he should fall upon the enemy's rear.

"The maneuver was successfully performed at dawn on the 20th, and the brave partisan wrote the following dispatch to Colonel Peter Horry, who was at that moment detached and operating against the British at Georgetown: 'On the 20th inst. I attacked a guard of the 63d and Prince of Wales's Regiments, with a number of Tories, at the Great Savannah near Nelson's Ferry; killed and took 22 regulars and 2 Tories prisoners, and retook 150 Continentals of the Maryland Line; one wagon and a drum; one captain and a subaltern were also captured. Our loss is 1 killed; and Captain Benson is slightly wounded on the head.'"

At Vance's Ferry where he had lodged with Mr. Avinger the night before and had hired the horse and gig, Lossing crossed the

Santee in a bateau and drove five miles up the other side to Wright's Bluff Post-Office, where there was "an ancient tumulus, almost fifty feet in height, and now covered with trees. Upon the top of this mound the British erected a stockade; and in honor of Colonel Watson, under whose direction it was built, it was called Fort Watson. Its elevated position, and its close proximity to the water, made it a strong post, yet not sufficiently impregnable to resist the successful assault of Marion and Lee in April, 1781."

Again we are tricked by geography, for Fort Watson was undertaken the month *before* Fort Motte and Fort Granby, both of which came first on Lossing's itinerary. And we will take Harry Lee's account, first-hand, in preference to Lossing's. It begins with his reunion with Marion on Greene's orders, after Guilford Courthouse had sent Cornwallis limping down to Wilmington, while he had dispatched Colonel Watson to the lowland swamps to catch Marion. Having established his post on the Indian mound above the Santee, and left his baggage there with a small garrison under a Captain McKay, Watson continued towards Georgetown in search of Marion, who was therefore able with Lee to cut in behind him and attack McKay. And at Fort Watson Major Hezekiah Maham emerges a moment into the spotlight with his famous tower, and retires again, into ill health and parole, and is dead at fifty.

"Determined to carry this post without delay," Lee's *Memoirs* run, "Marion and Lee sat down before it early in the evening; not doubting from the information received that the garrison must soon be compelled to surrender, for want of water, with which it was supplied from an adjacent lake, and from which the garrison might be readily and effectually secluded. In a very few hours the customary mode of supplying the post with water was completely stopped; and had the information received been correct, a surrender of the garrison could not have been long delayed. The ground selected by Colonel Watson for his small stockade was an Indian mount, generally conceived to be the cemetery of the tribe inhabiting the region; it was at least thirty feet high, and surrounded by table land. Captain McKay, the commandant, saw at once his inevitable fate, unless he could devise some other mode of procuring water, for which purpose he immediately cut a trench secured by abatis from his fosse to the river, which passed close to the Indian mount.

"Baffled in their expectation, and destitute both of artillery and intrenching tools, Marion and Lee despaired of success; when Major Maham, of South Carolina, accompanying Marion, suggested a plan, which was no sooner communicated than adopted. He proposed to cut down a number of suitable trees in the nearest wood, and with them to erect a large strong oblong pen, to be covered on the top with a floor of logs, and protected on the side opposite to the fort with a breast-work of light timber. To the adjacent farms the dragoons were despatched for axes, the only necessary tool, of which a sufficient number being soon collected, relays of working parties were allotted for the labor; some to cut, some to convey, and some to erect. Major Maham undertook the execution of his plan, which was completely finished before the morning of the 23d, effective as to the object, and honorable to the genius of the inventor. The besieged was, like the besieger, unprovided with artillery, and could not interrupt the progress of the work, the completion of which must produce immediate submission.

"A party of riflemen, being ready, took post in the Maham tower the moment it was completed; and a detachment of musketry, under cover of the riflemen, moved to make a lodgment in the enemy's ditch, supported by the Legion infantry with fixed bayonets. Such was the effect of the fire from the riflemen, having thorough command of every part of the fort from the relative supereminence of the tower, that every attempt to resist the lodgment was crushed. The commandant, finding every resource cut off, hung out the white flag."

Maham's tower—built at night, within rifle-shot of the fort, topping the stockade. McKay surrendered to it, and was removed with his garrison and stores to the camp on the High Hills, while Lee and Marion rode on together to fresh triumphs at Fort Motte and Fort Granby. They must have found each other rather a novelty—the thin, sardonic, shabby man from the Carolina countryside, and the spectacular Virginia colonel of dragoons, brought up in a Potomac mansion.

Lossing remained at Fort Watson only long enough to make his sketch, and returned to Vance's Ferry to resume his journey towards Orangeburg, where he was entertained by a Mr. McAnce. "There I met an elderly lady who had been very intimate with the wife of General Marion for several years before her death," he relates. "She informed me that Mrs. Marion, whose maiden name was Videau, one of the Huguenot families, was much younger than the General. She was a large woman, weighing a year or two before her death, 230 pounds. My informant had visited her at her residence, built by the General at Pine Bluff on the Santee, near Eutaw Springs. Miss Videau brought wealth to her husband, and their dwelling was always the abode of liberal hospitality.

"This mansion was demolished a few years before my visit to Eutaw Springs and vicinity, and this drawing was made from a minute description given me by a gentleman with whom I rode in the mailcoach from Augusta to the Ninety-mile Station, on the Great Central Railway in Georgia. His brother had resided there for many years, and he was perfectly familiar with its appearance. At the station I made the sketch, and my informant pronounced it an excellent representation of the residence of General Marion."

The legends surrounding Francis Marion are all fascinating, and not least the matter of his marriage, which did not take place until after the war, in 1786. We can turn here to the discreet Judge James, whose contemporary account of the matter is unexceptional·

"His plantation in St. John's lay within a mile of the marches and countermarches of the British and was subject to every species of wanton waste and depredation. One half of his Negroes were taken away, and the other half must have been faithful or they would not have remained. He had ten workers left, but plantation utensils, clothes for his people, were all to be purchased without a cent of money. He expected to receive half pay, but even in this was disappointed. At a session of the legislature shortly after, a garrison was established at Fort Johnson, and he was appointed commander, with a salary of about £500. Yet in spite of his recent and meritorious services, this moderate appointment became a butt at which they who are forever seeking popularity by recommending curtailments in useful and even necessary expenditures soon levelled their shafts. His spirit could not easily brook such treatment, but his debts made it prudent to submit.

"At this juncture, his merit and high reputation had made a favorable impression on the heart of Miss Mary Videau, one of his relations. She was observed to be fond of hearing his achievements spoken of in terms of high approbation; some of the General's friends noticed it, and gave him a hint. He paid his addresses to her and was well received. They were soon after married, and he resigned his command at the fort. She brought him a handsome fortune, and as there was no great disparity, either in their years or disposition, she made him an excellent wife. She was in countenance the exact counterpart of the General. She partook in all his amusements, accompanied him in his journeys, and in his absence could not be better pleased than by hearing his praises. In short, nothing could have made this matrimonial connexion more happy, but its being more fruitful. They never had an heir. The General built a comfortable house of a single story, with one sitting-room, but many chambers; its materials were of the most durable kind of cypress, but it received no coat either of paint or varnish. Here his friends were received with a hearty welcome and good cheer, and the stranger with kind hospitality His planting interest was judiciously managed, and his property increased yearly...."

The mystery remains, however, of a stubborn local tradition that Marion married a shrew—a story which can be heard today from the residents of his neighborhood, and which is given credence even in the official Guide to South Carolina, is that her moods were so intimidating to the one-time warrior that when he approached his house after an absence it was his habit to throw his hat in at an open window—and if it was pitched right back at him he would retire prudently from the premises till things had simmered down.

The idea of General Marion living out his always lonely life dominated by an over-fond but bad-tempered woman double his weight is both funny and pathetic. It would seem he was the last man in the world to marry for money. And yet he could have been very tired, and longing for a home he could take pride in, and for comforts due the people who depended on him. And he might not have known about her temper till after the wedding. Not everyone could be as lucky as George Washington, who along with a fortune got enduring mutual love and a devoted, courageous, tactful wife when he married the wealthy widow Custis.

XIV

Branchville to Savannah

THE railway journey from Orangeburg to Augusta was extremely monotonous in scenery and incident. At Branchville, on the banks of the Edisto, where the railway from Charleston connects, the immobility into which the passengers were subsiding was disturbed by the advent among us of a 'turban'd Turk' in full Oriental costume. His swarthy complexion, keen eye, flowing black beard, broad turban, tunic, and trowsers, made him the 'observed of all observers' and kept the passengers awake for an hour, for curiosity was too busy to allow drowsiness. 'Whence I came and whither I go, ye know not' were as plain as a written phylactery upon his imperturbable features, and I presume the crowd who gathered around him in the street at Augusta knew as little of his history and destiny as we. It is pleasant sometimes to see curiosity foiled, even though

> "It came from heaven—it reigned in Eden's shades—
> It roves on earth and every walk invades;
> Childhood and age alike its influence own;
> It haunts the beggar's nook, the monarch's throne;
> Hangs o'er the cradle, leans above the bier,
> Gazed on old Babel's tower—and lingers here.
> —CHARLES SPRAGUE

"The scenery by the wayside alternated between oozy swamps embellished with cypresses, cultivated fields, and extensive forests of oak and pine, garnished occasionally by a tall broad-leaved magnolia. The country was perfectly level through Barnwell District, until we passed Aiken into Edgefield, and turned towards Silver Bluff on the Savannah River, when we encountered the sandhills of that region. These continued until we reached the termination of the road at Hamburg, on the northern bank of the Savannah, opposite Augusta. There we were packed into huge omnibuses and conveyed to the city across Schultz's bridge. The village had been named by a German who called it Hamburg in honor of the free city of that name in his native land. He also built the noble bridge across the Savannah at that place. It was sunset—a glorious sunset, like those at the North in September—when we reined up at the United States Hotel. A stroll about the city of Augusta by moonlight that evening, with a Northern friend residing there, was really delightful; for the air was balmy and dry, and the moon and stars had nothing of the crisp, piercing and glittering aspect which they assume in a clear January night in New England.

"Early on the following morning we rode [back] over to Hamburg, and ascended to the summit of Liberty Hill, a lofty sand bluff three fourths of a mile from the river. Flowers were blooming in the gardens on its brow; and over its broad acres green grass and innumerable cacti were spread. The view from this eminence was charming. At our feet lay the little village of Hamburg, and across the shining Savannah was spread out in panoramic beauty the city of Augusta—the queen of all the inland towns of the South. Like a sea in repose, the level country extended in all directions; and city, river, forest, and plain were bathed in the golden haziness which characterizes our Indian summer at the North. From that point the eye could survey the whole historic arena around Augusta, where Royalists and Republicans battled, failed, and triumphed during our war for Independence. While the spirit is charmed with associations awakened by the gleanings of sensuous vision, let us for a moment open the tome of history and give inquiring thought free wing."

At Augusta we must again turn backward in time, to before the fall of Charleston in May, 1780, before either Gates or Greene came South. Richard Howe of North Carolina was in command of the Southern Department, when the British expedition under Colonel Archibald Campbell—not to be confused with Sir William Campbell who was the Royal Governor at Charleston in 1775—sailed from Sandy Hook in December '78, with orders from Clinton to begin a new Southern campaign by capturing Savannah and attacking Charleston overland, from behind. Clinton had recently evacuated Philadelphia for his New York headquarters, meeting Washington at Monmouth on the way, and he was perhaps discouraged about the American Commander-in-chief. The British army didn't seem to be making much headway in Pennsylvania and Jersey. Clinton had a plan to take the war away from Washington, and fight it with Washington's seconds, at too great a distance for the Commander-in-chief's mysterious magnetism and leadership to operate. He was also fighting it with his own seconds, which left him at some disadvantage still, for he himself must keep Washington pinned down in the New York area until sufficient progress had been made to warrant his own arrival on the Southern scene.

The Deep South had been fairly quiet since the first British failure at Charleston in '76, apart from local strife between Whig and Tory, and the sentiment of Georgia particularly was predominately Tory. South Carolina, of course, with John Rutledge as its Governor, was patriot in feeling, and had proved it against a British fleet. When Charles Lee returned North in the autumn of '76, with Charleston saved, he had left Robert Howe of North Carolina as senior in command in the South. Howe was not universally popular, and his right to command was called in question by a number of people, until he insisted upon fighting a duel with his chief opponent, the irascible Gadsden of Charleston—a duel at which everybody fired in the air and belated apologies were duly made.

Robert Howe is not an easy man to comprehend. His father was a well-to-do rice planter on the Cape Fear River, and Robert was educated in England. He married young and was soon estranged and separated from his wife. He was a man of the world, about Washington's age, and had done distinguished service at the time of

Dunmore's depredations around Norfolk in '76. His plantation home near Wilmington had been ravaged by the British. He seems to have had a weakness for the bottle, not unique in either army. "Where is Howe, with his nose? Has he left off his port?" Greene wrote Knox from the Carolinas in '81, when Howe had been superseded in the Southern command and was apparently performing his duties satisfactorily to Washington in the army on the Hudson.

It was Robert Howe, therefore, who awaited the arrival of Campbell's fleet in the Savannah River, under a further threat of British reinforcements from Florida led by Augustine Prevost. Howe lost Savannah to Campbell and Prevost, in January of '79, but Lossing's vexatious route of travel brought him first to Augusta, which was taken almost without a fight a month *later*.

As the threat to the South had been perceived by Congress, General Lincoln was already on his way with an army to Charleston. Lincoln was a Massachusetts man, who had joined Washington at Cambridge with a regiment of militia in the first year of the war. He had been severely wounded at Saratoga, and the wound was still open and troublesome when he was appointed to the Southern command in the autumn of '78. Lack of proper healing left him lame for life, but did not diminish his spirit or patriotism. He was corpulent and benign, a deacon of the church, a devoted husband and father. Though his first independent command was to become a series of disasters ending in the loss of Charleston, it was generally recognized that he had done his best in appalling circumstances, and his courage was never questioned. General Knox was always his friend, and it was Lincoln, paroled and exchanged, who sat a horse at Washington's side to receive the surrendered sword of Cornwallis at Yorktown.

He established a headquarters at Purysburg on the South Carolina side of the Savannah River in January, '79, and Robert Howe joined him there with his defeated army from Savannah as did Isaac Huger, one of the valiant South Carolina brothers, and William Moultrie, veteran of the first Charleston battle. A great deal of bloody skirmishing to and fro during the spring and summer failed to dislodge the British from Georgia, and left Lincoln holding desperately to Charleston until he lost it to Clinton the following year, as we shall see when Lossing arrives there.

Meanwhile Augusta remained in the possession of the British, with a brief interval, until the summer of '81. Its commandant was a Loyalist named Brown, who was a native of the place and took revenge on all his Whig acquaintances and enemies. Its defences were two forts, named for Cornwallis and Grierson, on the riverbank, which withstood several attempts by small militia parties, until Greene arrived in the neighborhood on his way to 96 and sent Lighthorse Harry Lee to join Andrew Pickens in an attempt to force the British out of it and down to Savannah.

Trailing glory from his recent success at Fort Granby, Lee arrived outside Augusta on the 21st of May, '81, and made short work of Fort Grierson. "The Americans now turned their attention to Fort Cornwallis," Lossing's account runs. "They were without artillery, except the old iron-piece in possession of Clarke, and Finley's grasshopper (a small cannon mounted on legs instead of wheels), and their rifles had but little effect on the fort. Lee suggested the erection of a Maham tower, which was used to such an effect at Fort Watson. This was done, under cover of an old frame house which stood directly in front of the present Episcopal church. This procedure made Brown uneasy, and on the night of the 28th he sent out a detachment to drive the Americans from their labor. After a severe skirmish, the enemy were driven into the fort at the point of the bayonet. On the succeeding night a similar attempt was made, with the same result. The tower was completed on the 1st of June, and for its destruction Brown used every effort in his powers. Sallies were made under cover of night, and some severe conflicts ensued. He tried stratagem, and failed in that. He opened a communication with a house in front of the tower, and placed a quantity of powder in it. He then sent a Scotchman, under the cloak of a deserter, who advised the Americans to burn that old house, as it stood in their way. Had they done so, the explosion of the powder might have destroyed the tower. Lee suspected the man and had him confined. Brown finally applied a slow match and blew up the house, but the tower was unharmed.

"On the 31st of May Brown was summoned to surrender. He refused, and that night a six-pounder, brought from Fort Grierson, was placed in battery on the tower. Towards noon, riflemen stationed upon it opened a gruelling fire upon the garrison, which was continued throughout the day. The guns of the fort were soon unmanned by the rifle balls, and the six-pounder dismounted them. The garrison dug vaults within the fort to save themselves from the murderous fire of the assailants, and thus the siege went on until the morning of June 4th, when a general assault was agreed on. While the Americans were forming for attack, Brown perceived the maintenance of his post to be impossible, and sent out a flag offering to make a conditional surrender to Pickens and Lee. The day was spent in negotiations, and early the next morning the garrison marched out and laid down their arms, and Brown and his fellow-prisoners were paroled to Savannah [already in American hands] under a sufficient guard, who marched down the river on the Carolina side. Pickens and Lee soon hastened to the aid of Greene, who was then investing 96. In this siege of Augusta, the Americans had 16 killed, and 35 wounded; 7 of them mortally. The loss of the British was 52 killed; and 334, including the wounded, were made prisoners of war. The British never had possession of Augusta after this event.

"It was towards noon when we descended Liberty Hill, looked in upon the slave-market at Hamburg (the first and last I ever saw) and crossed Schultz's bridge [again] to Augusta. After dinner I visited the site of Fort Cornwallis... also the site of Fort Grierson, of which no vestiges remain. The rivulet is still there, and the marshy lagoon on the brink of the river; but the 'gulley' mentioned in the local histories was filled, and houses and gardens covered the site of the redoubt and its ravelins.

"I left Augusta on the evening of the 25th, with real regret, for the beauty of the city, ornamental with water-oaks, wild olives, holly, palmettoes, magnolias, and other evergreens; the gardens blooming; the orange-trees budding in the bland air, and the courtesy of the citizens whom I met wooed me to a longer tarry. But home, sweet home, beckoned me away, and at eight o'clock I entered a mail-coach with a single fellow-passenger, for a ride of 52 miles to the Ninety-Mile Station on the Great Central Railway. I had a pleasant companion while he kept awake, and we whiled away the tedious night hours by agreeable conversation until we reached Waynesborough, where we exchanged horses and the mails. After leaving the village I endeavored to sleep. My companion complained that he never could slumber in a coach; and I presume his loud snoring always keeps him awake, for in ten minutes after leaving the post-office his nasal pipes were chanting base to the alto of the coach-wheels.

"We breakfasted at sunrise at a log-house in the forest, and arrived at the railway on the upper border of Severn County at eleven o'clock, where we dined, and at one departed for Savannah. Swamps, plantations, and forests, with scarcely a hill, or even an undulation, compose the monotonous scenery. While enjoying the pleasing anticipation of an early arrival in Savannah, our locomotive became disabled by the breaking of a piston-rod. We were yet forty miles from our goal, in the midst of a vast swamp, ten miles from any habitation near the road. The sun went down; the twilight faded away; and yet we were immovable. At intervals the engineer managed to start his steed and travel a short distance, and then stop. Thus we crawled along, and at eleven o'clock at night we reached the Thirty-Mile Station, where we supped at the expense of the railway company. At our haltings we started lightwood fires whose blaze amid the tall trees draped with moss, the green cane-brakes, and the dry oases garnished with dwarf palmettoes produced most picturesque effects. A hand-car was sent down to Savannah for another engine, and at six o'clock in the morning we entered that city. I breakfasted at the Pulaski House, a large building fronting upon Johnson Square, amid whose noble trees stands a monument erected by the citizen of Savannah to the memory of General Greene and the Count Pulaski."

Although Yorktown lies far behind us, the war came last of all to Virginia, when the British had failed everywhere else. Their plan of conquest from the southward almost succeeded, however, and was averted only by a series of small advantages gained by small forces like Marion's, which might so easily have been not quite enough. The British did take Georgia and the Carolinas—but it cost them too much. By the time Cornwallis came to the James he was already spent, while Lafayette, awaiting him there, was young and fresh and confident, and had the whole weight of the Northern command, including the French, behind him. The end result was Yorktown, and the later evacuation of the garrisons below it.

When Archibald Campbell with his seaborne force from New York came up the Savannah River at Christmas time in '78, Howe was at Savannah with the exhausted remnants of a force which had recently failed in an expedition against the British post in Florida, a disaster partly due to the persistent unwillingness to serve under his command of leaders of other American forces which should have co-operated with him. Malaria did the rest.

Clinton's plan was for Prevost to march up from Florida and join Campbell, who would land troops at the mouth of the river, and both move on Savannah. Campbell arrived first, but Prevost was also known to be on the way, and Savannah began panicky preparation for defence, while Howe sent hastily to Lincoln at Charleston for reinforcements. Like Gates at Camden, Howe underestimated the British force which approached him, and called a council when it seemed already too late to do anything but fight. Campbell had landed, though Prevost had not yet come in.

"From the landing-place, which was the nearest the ships could approach," says Lossing, "a narrow causeway with a ditch on each side led through a rice-swamp six hundred yards to firm ground. The 71st regiment of Royal Scots led the van across the causeway, and was attacked by some Americans. Captain Cameron and two of his company were killed and five were wounded. The Highlanders were made furious, and rushing forward drove the Americans into the woods.

"More clearly to understand the nature of the attack, defence, and result, it is necessary to know the position of the town at that time. It is situated on a high bluff of forty feet altitude, and then, as now, was approachable by land on three sides. From the high ground of Brewton's Hill on the east a road crossed a morass upon a causeway, having rice-fields on the north side and a wooded swamp on the south of it. From the south it was approached by the roads from White Bluff and the Ogeechee Ferry; and from the westward by a road and causeway over the deep swamps of Musgrove's Creek, where rice-fields extend from the causeway to the river on the north.

"After Campbell had formed his army on Brewton's Hill (where he landed) he moved forward and took a position within eight hundred yards of the American front, where he maneuvered in a manner to indicate that he intended to attack the center and left. This was at three o'clock in the afternoon. This movement was only a diversion in favor of a body of infantry commanded by Sir James Baird, who, under the guidance of an old Negro named Quamino Dolly, withdrew unperceived and by a by-path through the swamp were gaining the Americans' rear. To this by-path Walton had called Howe's attention in the morning; but knowing its obscurity the General did not think it worthy of regard. Baird and his party reached the White Bluff and attacked Walton's Georgia brigade on the flank and rear. Walton was wounded and taken prisoner along with a large portion of his command.

"At the same moment Campbell moved forward and attacked the Americans in front. The patriot line was soon broken, and perceiving the growing panic and confusion Howe ordered a retreat over the causeway across Musgrove's swamp, west of the town. Already the enemy were there in force, to dispute the passage. By great exertions the American center gained the causeway and escaped without loss. The right flank also retreated across, but suffered from an oblique enfilading fire; while to Colonel Elbert with the left the passage was closed after a severe conflict. He and his troops attempted to escape by the rice-fields, but it being high water in the creek, none but those who could swim succeeded, and these lost their guns and accoutrements. Many were drowned and the remainder were taken prisoners.

"While the British were pursuing the Americans through the town towards Musgrove's Creek, many citizens who had not been in the battle were bayoneted in the streets; but when the action was over, life and property were spared. Campbell's humanity and generosity as a man were equal to his skill and bravery as a soldier, and the active terrors of war in the city ceased with the battle. Like credit cannot be given to Commodore Parker [not Sir Peter, who figured at Charleston in '76]. For want of other quarters the prisoners were placed on board of ships, where disease made dreadful havoc daily during the succeeding summer. Parker not only neglected the comforts of the prisoners, but was brutal in his manner. The bodies of those who died were deposited in the marsh mud, where they were sometimes exposed and eaten by buzzards and crows.

"Deep sadness brooded over Savannah that night, for many bereaved ones wept over relatives slain or mortally wounded. About one hundred Americans were either killed in the action or drowned in the swamps, and thirty-eight officers and four hundred and fifteen privates were taken prisoners. The private soldiers who refused to enlist in the British army were confined in prison ships; the Continental officers were paroled to Sunbury (which was now in the possession of General Prevost). Those few who escaped across Musgrove's swamp retreated up the Savannah and joined Howe who, with the center, fled as far as Cherokee Hill, eight miles distant, and then halted." These were the few who eventually reported to Lincoln, at his headquarters at Purysburg, south of Charleston. And from Purysburg Howe was ordered north, where Washington was disposed to give him another chance.

The spring and summer of '79 passed in bitter little skirmishes, and Lincoln was still covering Charleston when the French Admiral D'Estaing was ordered up from the West Indies to assist him in an attempt to retake Savannah in September. Lincoln sent Count Pulaski ahead with his mounted legion, and himself accompanied the main force, arriving at Miller's Plantation outside Savannah on the 16th.

Among the several foreign adventurers who distinguished themselves in the American war—Steuben, DeKalb, Armand, Pulaski—the Polish count leaves a gallant memory. Like DeKalb he gave his life to the adventure, but he seems to have been destined from childhood for tragedy. While he was still a boy, his father was put to death in one of the bloody little Polish rebellions, in which young Pulaski also took part. Defeated in an attempt to abduct the King of Poland from his carriage in Warsaw, Pulaski escaped to the Turkish army, an outlaw, with his estates confiscated. Later at Paris in 1777 he encountered Dr. Franklin, who was representing the new republic there, and caught the prevailing American fever which also brought Lafayette and DeKalb across the Atlantic. Pulaski offered his services to Washington, who gave him a small cavalry force, which did good service in the Jerseys while the army was at Middlebrook. He was stationed near Headquarters and was famous for his tricks of horsemanship, which several reckless Americans were hurt trying to copy—with his horse at full gallop, Pulaski would discharge his pistol, toss it into the air, catch it by the barrel and hurl it ahead of him as if at an enemy; and then still galloping, would free one foot from the stirrup, bend to the ground and recover the pistol with one sweep and wheel precisely into line with the troop, it was that last touch which defeated the others—they could never come out even.

In the picturesque if faded uniform of a Polish hussar, Pulaski was a colorful figure at Headquarters, and they missed him after he went South in '79.

When Lincoln arrived outside Savannah in October, he found that D'Estaing had already recklessly granted a truce to Prevost, who claimed time to consider the terms of surrender. It was a fatal concession. Prevost used the time to strengthen his fortifications, while Maitland brought up reinforcements from the British post at Beaufort.

"It was now perceived that the town must be taken by regular approaches, and not by assault," says Lossing. "To that end all energy was directed. The heavy ordnance and stores were brought up from the landing place of the French, and on the morning of the 23rd of September ('79) the combined armies broke ground. The French frigates, at the same time, moved up to within gunshot of the town, and compelled the British ships to take shelter under the guns of the battery. Night and day the besiegers applied the spade, and so vigorously was the work prosecuted that in the course of twelve days 53 pieces of battery cannon and 14 mortars were mounted.

"Prevost, cautious and skillful, did not waste his strength in opposing the progress of the besiegers by sorties, but reserved all for the decisive moment. On the morning of the 4th of October, the batteries being all completed and manned, a terrible cannonade and bombardment was opened upon the British works and the town. The French frigate *Truite* also opened a cannonade from the water. Houses were shattered, some women and children were killed or maimed, and terror reigned supreme. Families took refuge in the cellars, and in many a frame the seeds of mortal disease were planted while in those damp abodes during the siege. There was no safety in the streets, for a moment. Day and night an incessant cannonade was kept up from the 4th until the 9th; but while many houses were injured, not much impression was made upon the British works. . . .

"Another promised victory was now before the besiegers, and almost within their grasp, when D'Estaing became impatient. He feared the autumn storms, and the British fleet which rumor said was approaching. A council was held, and when his engineers informed him that it would require ten days more to reach the British lines by trenches, he informed Lincoln that the siege must be raised forthwith, or an attempt be made to carry the place by storm. The latter alternative was chosen, and the work began on the morning of the following day. To facilitate it, the abatis were set on fire that afternoon by the brave Major L'Enfant and five men while exposed to heavy volleys of musketry from the garrison, but the dampness of the air checked the flames and prevented the green wood from burning.

"Just before dawn on the morning of the 9th about 4500 men of the combined armies moved to the assault in the midst of a dense fog and under cover of a heavy fire from all the batteries. They advanced in three columns, the principal one commanded by D'Estaing in person, assisted by General Lincoln. Fog and darkness allowed D'Estaing and Lincoln to approach very near the Spring Hill redoubt before they were discovered. Terrible was the conflict at this point just as the day dawned. The French column led to the assault, and were confronted by a blaze of musketry from the redoubt and by a crossfire from the adjoining batteries. Whole ranks were mowed down like grass before the scythe. D'Estaing was wounded in the arm and thigh early in the action and was carried to his camp....

"While the carnage was occurring at the Spring Hill redoubt, Huger and Pulaski were endeavoring to force the enemy's works on different sides of the town; Huger with his party waded almost half a mile through rice-fields, and assailed the works on the east. They were received with a sharp fire of cannon and musketry, and after losing twenty-eight men retreated. Pulaski at the same time, with about two hundred horsemen, endeavored to force his way into the town a little eastward of the Spring Hill redoubt. At the head of his troops he had passed the abatis, banner in hand, and was pressing forward, when a small cannon shot struck him in the groin and he fell to the ground. His first lieutenant seized the banner, and for a few minutes kept the troops in action; but the iron hail from the seamen's batteries and the field artillery, traversing the columns of the assailants in all directions, compelled the whole force of the combined armies to yield, and they retreated to the camp. Back through the smoke, and over the bodies of the dead and dying, some of Pulaski's soldiers returned, and found the expiring hero and bore him from the field.

"Already the French had withdrawn, and the Continentals under Lincoln were retreating. At ten o'clock, after about five hours hard fighting, the combined armies displayed a white flag, and asked a truce in order to bury the dead. Prevost granted four hours and during that interval D'Estaing and Lincoln consulted in relation to further operations. The latter, although his force was greatly diminished by the action just closed, wished to continue the siege; but D'Estaing, whose loss had been heavy, resolved on immediate departure. The siege was raised, and on the evening of the 18th of October the combined armies withdrew. Lincoln and his little army hastened back to Charleston, where we shall meet them again, besieged, and made prisoners of war."

Pulaski died on board an American brig on the way to Charleston by sea, and was buried on St. Helena's Island, by his devoted friend and lieutenant, Charles Litomiski.

It is not to belittle the French navy's invaluable aid to the Revolutionary cause, to notice that this was not the first time that D'Estaing had sailed away to his West Indian base while an American commander implored him to remain. Only the year before, he had left Sullivan fuming at Newport and gone back to the Islands to refit after his fleet had suffered damage in a storm off the coast of Rhode Island. And after contributing enormously to Washington's success at Yorktown in '81, Admiral De Grasse refused to coöperate further in a proposed American assault on captive Charleston, which Washington tried to urge upon him.

"The result of the siege of Savannah was a deathblow to the hopes of the South," Lossing continues, "and never since the beginning of hostilities had such gloom gathered over the prospects of the future, or so much real distress prevailed in Georgia. Indescribable were the sufferings of the people of Savannah, particularly the families of the Whigs. The females were exposed to daily insults from the soldiery, and many, reduced from affluence to poverty, unable to bear the indignities heaped upon them, travelled away on foot, some of them without even shoes on their feet, and took refuge in the Carolinas.

"There are but few remains of Revolutionary localities about Savannah. The city has spread out over all the British works; and where their batteries, redoubts, ramparts, and ditches were constructed, public squares are laid out and adorned with trees, or houses and stores cover the earth. Not so with the works constructed by the French engineers during the siege in the autumn of 1779. Although the regular forms are effaced, yet the mounds and ditches may be traced for many rods near the margin of the swamp southeast of the city.

"These remains are in the southeastern suburbs, about half way between the Negroes' Cemetery and the residence of Major William Bowen, seen towards the right of the picture. The banks have an average height, from the bottom of the ditch, of about five feet, and are dotted with pines and chincapins or dwarf chestnuts, the former draped with moss. The ground is an open common, and although it was midwinter when I was there, it was covered with green grass bespangled with myriads of little flowers of stellar form."

It was not until July, 1782, that Anthony Wayne entered the town with a force which had marched from Yorktown after the surrender and engaged in some stirring guerrilla warfare with both British detachments and some Creek Indians which had been incited to reinforce the Savannah garrison. But after an occupation of three and a half years, the British evacuated Savannah, accompanied by the usual forlorn horde of Loyalist families and slaves. Some of the refugees went to Charleston, where the British flag still flew, some to the West Indies, and some as far as New York.

XV

Port Royal to Wilmington

A LIGHT haziness began to overspread the sky, which deepened towards evening, and descended in gentle rain when I left the city of Savannah at eight o'clock in a steam-packet for Charleston. We passed the lights at Fort Pulaski at half past eight, and an hour later breasted the rising waves of the Atlantic. I soon discovered the 'use of basins' and at an early hour turned into my berth to prevent a turning out of my supper.

"During the night we passed through Port Royal entrance, touched at Beaufort, stuck in the mud in the channel between Ladies' and St. Helena Islands, and at daylight emerged again into the Atlantic through St. Helena's Sound. The breeze was hourly stiffening, and every landlubber on board preferred the berth to breakfast, until we approached Charleston bar, when the wind died away, the sun gleamed through the breaking clouds, and upon the bosom of long, heaving swells, we were wafted into Charleston harbor. We landed at one o'clock, and dined at two, and at three I called upon the Rev. Samuel Smythe, D.D., with a letter of introduction; with whom I passed the remainder of the afternoon in visiting places of interest upon the banks of the Cooper River, above the city. To the kind courtesy of Dr. Smythe I am indebted for much of the pleasure, interest, and profit of my visit at Charleston and vicinity."

Like Dunmore in Virginia, Lord William Campbell, the Royal Governor at Charleston, took to a British warship in the harbor in the autumn of 1775, while Washington was at Cambridge holding

Boston under siege. Campbell had married an American wife, who was Sarah Izard of Charleston, sister of Ralph, one of the richest men in the province. She soon followed him and they sailed for Jamaica. The Provincial Council then took charge of the city and began to fortify the harbor.

A more distinguished group of citizens have seldom assembled for the defence of a city. Colonel William Moultrie, who was a veteran of the Cherokee wars in the '60's, two years older than Washington who also had an Indian-fighting record on the Pennsylvania frontier, was assigned to build a fort on Sullivan's Island large enough to accommodate a thousand men. Early in 1776 its construction was under way. Moultrie built it of palmetto logs and the sand of the island it stood on, plus a few iron bolts and timbers; rectangular in form with a bastion at each corner, connected by double walls 16 feet apart filled in with sand. The gun platforms inside were 10 feet below the top, of heavy oak timbers.

At Charleston we must return to the very beginning of the war, before Washington lost New York and began the long New Jersey retreat which ended at Trenton on Christmas Day, 1776—before even the Declaration of Independence had been written. On May 3d of that year a British fleet under Admiral Sir Peter Parker, bearing an army to join the one being conveyed from Boston by sea under the command of General Clinton, assembled off Cape Fear and proceeded to Charleston. Charles Lee, who was assigned by Congress to proceed from New York to direct the defence of South Carolina, was already a conspicuous figure in the new American army. He was an English soldier of fortune, who had served in Portugal, in Poland, and in Turkey, and was said to be highly regarded by Frederick the Great. In person Lee was the opposite of Washington in every possible way. He was an emaciated, irascible man with a biting wit, arrogant, vain, but slovenly, excitable sometimes to the verge of insanity, and was accompanied always by a troupe of ill-mannered, bad-tempered dogs whose society he said he preferred to human companionship. Later in the war Lee's jealousy and open criticism of Washington were to cause enormous trouble and anxiety, but at the time he went to Charleston his prestige and rank were second only to Washington's.

The Fort, as it was called in Charleston, was still unfinished when General Lee arrived from the north, and he had little use for it. He was concerned about a line of retreat for the men stationed there, and ordered a bridge of boats to be constructed. There weren't enough boats available, and empty hogsheads with planks laid across them proved impracticable. Lee was very upset about this, and felt that in case of attack the garrison would have to be sacrificed. "For my part," says Moultrie briefly in his *Memoirs*, "I never was uneasy on not having a retreat, because I never imagined that the enemy could force me to that necessity." And exasperating as his attitude may have been to Lee, General Moultrie was right. Lossing's account of the first attempt on Charleston by the British follows, somewhat curtailed.

"On the 4th of June the fleet appeared off Charleston bar, and several hundred land troops took possession of Long Island, which lies east of Sullivan's Island and is separated from it only by a narrow creek. All was now activity among the patriots. The militia of the surrounding country obeyed the summons of Governor Rutledge with great alacrity, and flocked to the town. These, with the regular troops of South Carolina, made an available force of between 5 and 6000 men...

"In the city, Governor Rutledge pursued the rigorous course of martial law. Valuable stores on the wharves were torn down, and a line of defences was made in their places. The streets near the water were barricaded, and on account of the scarceness of lead, many window-sashes of that material were melted into bullets. He pressed into service 700 Negroes with tools, who belonged to Loyalists; and seized for the moment the money and papers of the lukewarm....

"At half-past ten on the morning of the 28th of June, Sir Peter Parker on board his flag-ship made the signal for attack. His fleet immediately advanced, and with springs on their cables anchored in front of Fort Sullivan. At the moment of anchoring, the Fort poured a heavy fire upon them, and each vessel returned the compliment by delivering a broadside upon the little fortress, but with almost harmless effect on the spongy palmetto logs. It was a little before eleven o'clock when the action began, and terrible to the people of Charleston, who looked upon the contest from balconies, roofs, and steeples, was the roar of 300 cannons. To the little garrison the peril seemed great, yet they maintained their fire with precision and coolness."

The battle raged all day, and at the end of it the Americans were still there, and the carnage on the British ships had been horrifying. Lord William Campbell, who had come back with the fleet to reclaim his post as Governor, was killed, and Sir Peter Parker received a wound in the breeches which was too severe to be funny. Sharp-shooters had pinned down the land troops put ashore by Clinton on Long Island. The fibrous palmetto logs did not splinter or break. The cannon balls simply sank into them, and the grape-shot did not ricochet. The return fire towards the ships from the Fort was slow and accurate, with the flag-ship as the favorite target. "Mind the Admiral," Moultrie admonished his gun-crews. "Mind the fifty-gun ships." Meaning, get them. And they suffered most.

Attempting a flanking movement, some ships ran aground in the shoals and were helpless under the American fire. The decks were slippery with blood. But powder was running low in the Fort and its guns fell silent for long intervals. Towards nightfall a violent thunderstorm joined in the noise and drove the citizen spectators indoors. At eleven o'clock that night Parker's crippled armada slipped their cables and withdrew to Five Fathom Hole, except one ship, the *Actaeon*, which remained aground. When the garrison at the Fort fired on her early the next morning, she replied stoutly, but was eventually abandoned by her crew. Clinton made one more effort to land a force on Sullivan's Island and attack the Palmetto Fort, and again was obliged to give up and retire. It was here at Charleston that Cornwallis first set foot briefly, on American soil, with which he was destined later to become so familiar. But this time the British had failed.

"This discomfiture occurred at a time when the British were desirous of making the most favorable impression here and in Europe," Lossing points out, "for Lord Howe [the Admiral] was then on his way to New York as a commissioner to settle all disputes or as a commander to prosecute the war. His course was to be determined by circumstances. This was the first time that the Americans had encountered a regular British fleet. The fact that it had been terribly shattered and driven to sea was very humiliating to the vanquished, and at the same time encouraging to the victors, at a moment when a brilliant act like this was of immense value to the Republican cause.

"On the morning after the battle the British fleet left Charleston harbor and proceeded to Long Island to recruit. Almost every vessel was obliged to remain for that purpose. On the 30th of June General Clinton, with Cornwallis and the troops, escorted by the *Solebay* frigate with Sir Peter Parker on board, sailed for New York with a heavy heart...

"For three years after the repulse of the British from Charleston, South Carolina enjoyed comparative quiet while the war was raging at the North. Yet her sons were not idle listeners to the roar of cannons in New England, New York, and Pennsylvania, but flocked thither in hundreds, under brave leaders, to do battle for their common country. The patriots of that war were not divided by sectional interests. There was no line of demarkation over which men hesitated to pass.

"I visited Sullivan's Island on the day of my departure from Charleston and sauntered for an hour upon the beach where the old Palmetto Fort once stood. Nothing of it now remains but a few of the logs embedded in the drifting sand. The modern Fort Moultrie is not a large, but a well-constructed fortification. The island is sandy, and bears no shrub or tree spontaneously except the Palmetto, and these are not seen in profusion. On the northwestern side of the island are the remains of an old causeway or bridge, extending to the main, nearly upon the site of a bridge of boats which was used during the battle in 1776. It was constructed after that conflict, at the cost of Christopher Gadsden, and was called Gadsden's Bridge. The British, when they afterward possessed Charleston, used it to pass over to their lazaretto, which they erected on Sullivan's Island. This lazaretto was upon the site of the present Episcopal church in Moultrieville. A part of the old brick wall was yet standing when I visited the spot in 1849."

On December 4, 1778, Charleston's comparative immunity was broken by the arrival of General Lincoln, on his way to Savannah, which Robert Howe had recently lost to the British. Lincoln chose Thomas Pinckney of Charleston as his chief aide, and having established headquarters at Purysburg he was joined there by Moultrie and by Robert Howe's defeated army from Savannah. Meanwhile Sir Archibald Campbell at Savannah had been reinforced by Prevost's force from Florida, and while Lincoln moved towards Georgia Prevost prepared to attack Charleston from the landward side, where the city was quite defenceless.

Francis Marion was now in command of the garrison at the Charleston fort named for Moultrie in memory of the victory of '76, and Governor Rutledge brought in some milita from Orangeburg. Moultrie retreated from Purysburg into Charleston ahead of Prevost and took command there, as Lincoln was by then so far advanced on the road to Savannah that it was necessary for him to turn about and try to overtake Prevost from behind. Between the stubborn defence within the city, and the approach of Lincoln's army from the south, Prevost prudently withdrew after some skirmishing, and except for the establishment of a post at Beaufort under Colonel Maitland, the second British attempt on Charleston had proved a failure.

With Maitland's troops at Beaufort, Purysburg was no longer any good to Lincoln as a base, and he retired to Sheldon to wait for the summer heat to subside and to prepare for an autumn campaign against the British in Georgia. In September with D'Estaing he made the unsuccessful attack on Savannah, from where the French withdrew to the West Indies again, and by the end of the year

Lincoln was back in Charleston, which he found full of smallpox. His army dwindled as enlistments ran out, and rumors of conditions on the prison ships at Savannah also discouraged the patriot spirit, which was at a low ebb in the South when in February, 1780, both Clinton and Cornwallis arrived with another fleet, under Admiral Arbuthnot, to try again by sea and land together.

Lincoln's first thought was to evacuate until he could collect a better army up-country and then come back and throw Clinton out. But Governor Rutledge and other influential Charlestonians urged a defence of the city, and Clinton's leisurely behavior about landing his men led to a hope that fortifications and reinforcements might be secured in time. Clinton had had a long, rough voyage from New York, during which he had lost most of his horses. He put troops ashore on John's Island, thirty miles below Charleston, and sent some ships to blockade the harbor, but did not attack at once.

For seven weeks both sides carried forward preparations for a siege, and confidence grew among the Americans, who even dreamed of help from the Spanish in Cuba as Clinton began to close in. On the 29th of March he threw a force across the Ashley River and began his approach by parallels. On April 10th, with British frigates in the harbor and only one avenue of escape remaining open, which led to where Isaac Huger was posted at Monck's Corner, Clinton summoned the town to surrender. Although the Monck's Corner road was still available for his evacuation, Lincoln yielded again to Charlestonian appeals, and decided to sit it out.

On the 13th Clinton began firing into the streets. The citizens took to their cellars and there were few casualties, but some damage was done to the buildings, and fires were started. At midnight Lincoln called a belated council of his officers and asked them to "consider" the situation and dismissed them again. In the meantime, having seized horses for his dragoons from the countryside, Tarleton struck at Huger and completely routed the force at Monck's Corner. William Washington and Huger escaped separately on foot into the swamps, to fight another day. But now the last road out of Charleston was in British hands. Supplies were cut off, and conditions for the civilians under fire became deplorable. The terms of capitulation which Lincoln then insisted on offering to Clinton were refused, for the British were in a position to storm the city.

Clinton's alternative ultimatum was harsh, and Lincoln refused it, and the firing began again. "It was a fearful night in Charleston," says Lossing. "The thunder of 200 cannon shook the city like the power of an earthquake, and the moon, then near its full, with the bright stars, was hidden by the lurid smoke. Shells were seen coursing in all directions, some bursting in mid air, others falling upon houses and in the streets, and in five different places the flames of burning buildings simultaneously shot up from the depths of the city. 'It appeared,' says Moultrie's account, alluding to the bomb-shells, 'as if the stars were tumbling down. The fire was incessant almost the whole night; cannon balls whizzing and shells hissing continually among us; ammunition chests and temporary magazines blowing up; great guns bursting, and wounded men groaning along the lines; it was a dreadful night!' The cannonade was continued all the next day and part of the night, and many Americans were killed by the passage of balls through the embrasures of their batteries. Sand-bags were freely used for protection, but these were swept away, until at several points the besieged were obliged to abandon their works and withdraw. Arbuthnot now prepared to bombard the town from the water, and the batteries at Fort Johnson and Wappoo hurled round shot into the streets."

At two o'clock on the morning of the 11th day of May a delegation of citizens requested Lincoln to accept Clinton's terms, and before dawn the guns were quiet. Articles of capitulation were agreed to, and at noon on the twelfth the Continental troops marched out and laid down their arms after a desperate defence of about forty days. The British at once took possession of the town.

"The fall of Charleston and loss of Lincoln's army paralyzed the Republican strength at the South," Lossing says, "and British commanders confidently believed that the finishing stroke of the war had been given. Lincoln suffered the infliction of unsparing censure, because he had allowed himself to be thus shut up in a town; but had he repulsed the enemy, or the siege been raised, as at one time contemplated, the skill and wisdom of his course would have exceeded all praise.

"Clinton and Arbuthnot sailed for New York on the 5th of June, leaving Cornwallis in chief command of the British troops at the South."

Thus we have come full circle on the crazy chronology of Lossing's journey; as the fall of Savannah brought Lincoln south, so the fall of Charleston brought Gates south; and the defeat of Gates at Camden brought Greene south. The battle of Guilford Courthouse, between Greene and Cornwallis, so crippled the British force that it retired to Wilmington, North Carolina, to recover, and from there marched to the James in Virginia to join Arnold and Phillips; which brought Cornwallis to Yorktown and surrender, though the British continued to hold Charleston and New York for another two years.

General Moultrie surrendered in Charleston with Lincoln, but several invaluable officers for one reason or another were not taken in the city, and were able to keep resistance alive till the tide turned. Governor Rutledge, more or less against his will, was smuggled out on his white horse before the ring closed, and proved a useful and energetic rallying-point for the militia of both Carolinas. William Washington and Isaac Huger recovered a part of their scattered forces after the fight at Monck's Corner, reorganized, and joined the army which carried on the war under Greene. And the theatrical coincidence which saved Francis Marion from capture occurred during the early part of the siege. Simms's version of that familiar story is given here:

"It was the good fortune of the state that Francis Marion was not among those who fell into captivity in the fall of Charleston," he says. "He had marched into the city from Dorchester, when his active services were needed for its defence; but while the investment was in progress, and before it had been fully completed, an event occurred to him, an accident which was no doubt very much deplored at the time, by which his services, lost for the present, were subsequently secured for the country. Dining with a party of friends at a house in Tradd Street, the host with that mistaken hospitality which has too frequently changed a virtue to a vice, turned the key upon his guests to prevent escape till each individual should be gorged with wine.

"Though an amiable man, Marion was a strictly temperate one. He was not disposed to submit to this too common form of social tyranny; yet not willing to resent the breach of propriety by converting the assembly into a bull-ring, he adopted a middle course, which displayed equally the gentleness and firmness of his character. Opening a window, he coolly threw himself into the street. He was unfortunate in the attempt; the apartment was on the second story, the height considerable, and the adventure cost him a broken ankle. The injury was a severe and shocking one, and for the time totally unfitted him for service. He left the city in a litter, while the passage to the country still remained open, in obedience to an order of General Lincoln for the departure of all idle mouths, 'all supernumerary officers, and all officers unfit for duty.' Marion retired to his residence in St. John's parish. Here, suffering in mind and body, he awaited with impatience the progress of events, with which however much he might sympathize he could not share. His humiliation at this unavoidable but melancholy inaction may be imagined from what we know of his habits and patriotism...."

After the city surrendered, Marion's position became precarious in the extreme, as he was too well known not to go unaccounted for. Simms's narrative continues: "Still suffering from the hurts received in Charleston, with bloody and malignant enemies all round him, his safety depended on his secrecy and obscurity alone. Fortunately he had friends among all classes who did not permit themselves to sleep while he was in danger. Their activity supplied the loss of his own. They watched while he slept. They assisted his feebleness. In the moment of alarm, he was sped from house to house, from tree to thicket, from the thicket to the swamp. His hair-breadth escapes under these frequent exigencies were no doubt among the most interesting adventures of his life, furnishing rare material, could they be procured, for the poet and romancer. Unhappily, while the chronicles show the frequent emergency which attended his painful condition, they furnish nothing more. We are without details. These the reader must supply from his own resources of imagination. He must conjecture for himself the casual warning brought to the silent thicket by the devoted friend, the constant woman, or the humble slave; the midnight bay of the watchdog, or the whistle of the scout; or the sudden shot, from friend or foe, by which the fugitive is counseled to hurry to his den. What humble agents have been commissioned by Providence to save a life that was destined to be so precious to his country's liberties!"

Naturally in these circumstances Marion's ankle never healed properly, and he limped for the rest of his life. The house in Tradd Street, with the very window he jumped from, is still pointed out in Charleston.

While he still had to be lifted by his servant up and down from the saddle, he made his way towards DeKalb, who was coming south too late to help Lincoln. The Horrys and other patriot neighbors adhered to him on the way, and the scene at Gates's camp occurred.

The occupation of Charleston was far from being the amiable affair which the British General Howe's sojourn in Philadelphia became, or even Clinton's long residence in New York. At Charleston Clinton took the Miles Brewton house for his headquarters, obliging Brewton's widowed sister, Mrs. Motte, who occupied it, to remain as his housekeeper. After Clinton despatched Cornwallis upcountry and himself returned to New York, the city was governed by a Colonel Balfour, who had been one of Howe's cronies and was better suited to garrison life than the hardships of the field. He lacked Howe's lazy good humor, while embodying all Howe's vices. Established in his turn at the Brewton house, he took great pleasure in arresting and confining prominent citizens who refused the British oath of allegiance, and exiled a shipload of them, including Gadsden and Edward Rutledge, to a St. Augustine prison, where the health of many of them was permanently wrecked. Conditions in the cellar of the Exchange building in Charleston, where prisoners of both sexes were crowded together, were truly appalling. General Moultrie was retained in charge of a prison camp for troops at Snee Farm, outside Charleston, in relative comfort. The final outrage committed by Balfour was the tragic execution of the patriot Colonel Hayne for an alleged violation of his parole—"to make an example"—Hayne being also trapped within a personal feud between Rawdon and Balfour.

The news of the Yorktown surrender found Greene at his camp in the High Hills of Santee, to which he had retired after the battle at Eutaw Springs the previous month. Rutledge was there with him, anxious to re-establish a state government in South Carolina. There were soon hopeful rumors that the British might evacuate Charleston at once and concentrate at Savannah, but these came to nothing. Leaving Sumter at Orangeburgh and Marion on the Santee, Greene broke camp and moved southward across the Edisto to the vicinity of Dorchester, where supplies were for once more plentiful. It was now the turn of the British garrison to go short. Leslie succeeded to the command in Charleston, and while his rule was less severe than Balfour's, the citizens necessarily suffered along with the soldiery, as the American forces drove in the British foraging parties and cut off the flow of food and necessaries from outside the city.

In July, '82, the American army was encamped around Ashley Hall and Middleton plantations, awaiting the certain evacuation of Charleston by sea, which was, however, delayed until December. During the long interim Leslie's lenience allowed the return of American officers under safe conducts to healthier surroundings, and the Americans withheld their fire from British food and watering parties venturing out of the beleaguered city. General Greene's pretty Kitty had arrived in camp in March of that year, making the long journey from Rhode Island, with a visit to the Washingtons in Philadelphia on the way. In June Greene wrote to his former Adjutant, Otho Williams, who had returned to his Maryland home in broken health: "I have just returned from a ride with Mrs. Greene, who rides on horseback. She is very much your friend, and laments your absence from the army.... Our Family is much as formerly; Pearce and Pendleton as polite as ever; Morris, as careless, Burnet, as cross; and Shubrick, as impudent. Morris is courting, but at a distance too much, I fear, to get the citadel. Poor fellow, he is now unwell at Mrs. Elliott's. Washington [William] is married, and fats upon the rice swamps...."

Morris, we are happy to record, succeeded. And William Washington had married the daughter of that same Mrs. Elliott who seems to have mothered all the army.

General Moultrie, who rode in the parade on the great day when Charleston was at last recovered from the British, gives an eye-witness account of that moving scene: "The evacuation took place in the following manner: Brigadier General Wayne was ordered to cross the Ashley River, with 300 light infantry, 80 of Lee's cavalry, and 20 artillery, to move down toward the British lines. General Leslie, who commanded in the town, sent a message to General Wayne, informing him that he would next day leave the town, and for the peace and security of the inhabitants, and of the town, would propose to leave their advanced works next day at the firing of the morning gun; at which time General Wayne should move on slowly, and take possession; and from thence to follow the British troops into town, keeping at a respectful distance (say about 200 yards); and when the British troops after passing through the town gates, should file off to Gadsden's Wharf, General Wayne was to proceed into town, which was done with great order and regularity, except now and then the British called to General Wayne that he was too fast upon them, which occasioned him to halt a little. About 11 a.m. the American troops marched into town and took post at the State House.

"At 3 o'clock General Greene conducted Governor Matthews and the Council, with some others of the citizens into the town. We marched in, in the following order: an advance of an officer and 30 of Lee's dragoons; then followed the Governor and General Greene; the next two were General Gist and myself; after us followed the Council, citizens, and officers, making altogether about fifty; 180 cavalry brought up the rear. We halted in Broad Street, opposite where the South Carolina Bank now stands (1802). There we alighted, and the cavalry discharged to quarters. Afterwards everyone went where they pleased, some in viewing the town, others in visiting their friends.

"It was a grand and pleasing sight, to see the enemy's fleet (upwards of 300 sail) laying at anchor from Fort Johnson to Five Fathom Hole, in a curved line, as the current runs; and what made it more agreeable, they were ready to depart from the port. The great joy that was felt on this day, by the citizens and the soldiers, was inexpressible; the widows, the orphans, the aged men and others, who, from their particular situations were obliged to remain in Charleston, many of whom had been cooped up in one room of their own elegant houses for upwards of two years, whilst the other parts were occupied by the British officers, many of whom were a rude, uncivil set of gentlemen. Their situations, and the many mortifying circumstances occurred to them in that time, must have been truly distressing. I cannot forget that happy day when we marched into Charleston with the American troops; it was a proud day to me, and I felt myself much elated at seeing the balconies, the doors and windows crowded with the patriotic fair, the aged citizens, and others, congratulating us on our return home, saying, 'God bless you, gentlemen! You are welcome home, gentlemen!' Both citizens and soldiers shed tears of mutual joy."

So, as it had pretty well begun there in the first encounter in 1776, the war pretty well ended at Charleston too, though the same ceremony was not enacted at New York until a year later. Lossing's journey also was coming to its end, in the lovely Southern city on the sea.

In May, 1791, in the third year of his first administration, George Washington paid a visit to Charleston during the course of a tour of the Southern States. Travelling without his wife, and accompanied by a single aide, it was his habit to refuse private hospitality and make the best of whatever accommodation occurred along his route. But in Charleston, where he had allowed himself a week's stop-over, he was persuaded to make use of the Heyward house in Church Street, owned by one of the Signers, then living at his plantation on the Combahee. Washington was much taken by the Charleston belles, as appears in the sparse little diary he had resumed after a wartime interval:

"Tuesday, 3d," he wrote. ".... Was visited about 2 o'clock by a great number of the most respectable ladies of Charleston—the first honor of the kind I had ever experienced and it was as flattering as it was singular...."

"Thursday, 5th. Visited the works of Fort Johnson, James Island, and Fort Moultrie on Sullivan's Island; both of which are in ruins, and scarcely a trace of the latter left, the former quite fallen. Dined with a very large company at the Governor's, and in the evening went to a concert at the Exchange, at which there were at least 400 ladies, the number and appearance of which exceeded anything of the kind I had ever seen...."

"Friday, 6th. Viewed the town on horseback by riding through most of the principal streets. Dined at Major Butler's and went to a ball in the evening at the Governor's, where there was a select company of ladies."

In all the records of his Charleston entertainment, one name is conspicuous by its absence—Francis Marion. We find Pinckney, Moultrie, Horry, Izard, Rutledge, William Washington—but Marion, living at Pond Bluff with his wife, did not take the short ride into Charleston to make the acquaintance of his one-time Commander-in-chief. Too shy, too shabby, or because of some unknown slight or illness or accident—his absence remains a mystery.

"On the morning of the day when I departed from Charleston," Lossing's story of his Southern tour concludes, "the sun came up from the sea bright and unclouded, and I could not have wished for a lovelier day to visit places of note in Charleston and vicinity. I had already been out to the Lines, and to the old ship-yard and magazines on Cooper River. The scars of the former are still visible in several places upon the Neck, and a remnant of the 'horn work' survives the general wreck of the military works about Charleston. It was just at sunset when we passed through a beautiful avenue of live oaks draped with moss to view the ruins of the magazines and officers' quarters among thick shrubbery and tangled vines near the banks of the river about four miles above the city. A little to the northwest of these ruins is an ancient burial-ground, on the verge of a deep morass. The tall trees, pendent moss, silent ruins, and deep shadows hovering over the scene, gave the place a tinge of romance, thrilling and sad.

"At three o'clock the next afternoon I left Charleston for home, in a steam-packet bound to Wilmington, bearing with me many memories of the War for Independence at the South, and filled with pleasing recollections of a journey among the inhabitants of that sunny land where I had enjoyed the hospitality and kindness of true Republicans, keenly alive to the reflected glory of their patriot fathers.

"The waters of the harbor were unruffled by a breeze, and I anticipated a delightful voyage to Cape Fear; but as the city and fortifications receded, and we crossed the bar to the broad bosom of the Atlantic, we found it heaving with long, silent undulations, the effects of the subsiding anger of a storm. Sea-sickness came upon me, and I went supperless to my berth, where I remained until we were fairly within the mouth of the Cape Fear on the following morning. The low, wooded shores of Carolina approached nearer and nearer, and at eight o'clock we landed at the ancient town of Wilmington.

"I contemplated spending a day at Wilmington, but circumstances requiring me to hasten homeward, I was there only during the hour while waiting for the starting of the railway cars for the North. I had but little opportunity to view the town, where Republicanism was most rife on the sea-board of North Carolina both before and after the Revolution."

Wilmington was occupied by the British from January, 1781, until after Yorktown, when its commandant retired into Charleston. The chief excitement there was the arrival of Cornwallis after the battle of Guilford Courthouse. After eighteen days' recuperation, he marched out northward towards Virginia, and defeat.

"The railway from Wilmington to Weldon, on the Roanoke," Lossing resumes, "passes through a level pine region, where little business is done except gathering of turpentine and the manufacture of tar. It was a dreary day's ride, for on every side were interminable pine forests, dotted with swamps and traversed by numerous streams, all running coastward. We crossed the Neuse at Goldsborough, and the Tar at Rocky Mount, and at sunset we passed Halifax near the falls of the Roanoke and arrived at Weldon at dark.

"The morning was uncomfortably warm; the evening was damp and chilly; and when we arrived at Richmond the next morning, two hundred and forty miles north of Wilmington, a cold rain was falling and everything was encrusted with ice. I tarried a day at Richmond, another at Washington City, and on the 4th of February I sat by my own fireside in the city of New York, after an absence of about eleven weeks, and a journey of almost three thousand miles. There my long and interesting tour ended, except an occasional journey of a day to some hallowed spot in its vicinity. God, in his Providence, dealt kindly with me, in all that long and devious travel, for I did not suffer illness for an hour, and no accident befell me on the way."

Index

Actaeon, 285
Adams, John, 38-39, 47-48
  quoted, 37, 39-41, 210
Adams, Samuel, 40, 46
Aiken, South Carolina, 267
Albany, New York, 70, 71, 76, 121
Alexandria, Virginia, 37, 85, 88-89
Amboy, New Jersey, 11
American Revolution
  as civil war, 7
  concept of, 5, 8
Amherst, Lord Jeffrey, 7
Anderson, Major, 217
André, Major, 109, 112
Annapolis, 62, 65-67
Anvil Rock, 192
Appleton, quoted, 8, 33
Aquia Creek, 88, 91-92
Arbuthnot, Admiral, 103, 288, 290
Arlington House, 82-83
Armand, Colonel Charles, Marquis de la Rouarie, 205, 210, 212
Armstrong, Captain, 244
Arnold, Benedict, 6, 36, 65, 76, 104-105, 108-112, 121, 154-155, 290
Arnold, Mrs. Benedict (Peggy Shippen), 36, 111-112
Arnold Tavern, Morristown, 73
Articles of Capitulation, 148
Ashley Hall, 293
Augusta, Georgia, 245, 254, 267, 269-270
  siege of, 271
Avinger, Mr., 250-251

Bacon Rebellion, 124
Baird, Sir James, 274
Balfour, Colonel, 292-293
Baltimore, 18, 28, 62-66
Barkley, Mrs, 187, 191-192
Bassett, Burwell, 151
Baum, Captain, 28
Beaufort, North Carolina, 277, 282, 287
Beckhamville, Virginia, 187
Berkeley, Lady, 127
Berkeley, Sir William, 119, 124
Bethlehem, Pennsylvania, 65
Birmingham, New Jersey, 22-23
Blackstocks Plantation, 198, 254
Blair, James, 126-127
Blandford, Virginia, 155
Bordentown, New Jersey, 12, 24
Boston, 31, 37, 44, 103, 135, 283
Botetourt, Lord, 89, 127
Bowen, Major William, 280
Bowling Green, Virginia, 97-98
Braddock, General, 37-38
Branchville, South Carolina, 266
Brandywine, 51, 63, 65, 174
Brewton, Miles, 228, 292
Brewton's Hill, 274
Bridge's Creek, 93
Broad River, 186, 197
Brown, Colonel Thomas, 194, 270-271
Bryant, William Cullen, quoted, 233-235
Buffalo Ford, 205
Buford, Colonel, 160, 189, 219, 221

Bunker Hill, 9, 44-45, 211
Burdell's Plantation, 254
Burgoyne, General, 7, 45, 52, 70
Burnet, Major, 167, 294
Burr, Aaron, 78
Butler, Richard, quoted, 134-135
Byrd, William, II, 114
Byrd, William, III, 110-111, 112-113
Byrd, Mrs William, III (Mary Willing), 112-113

Cacey, James, 242-243, 245
Cambridge, Massachusetts, 37, 40-41, 180, 203, 269
Cambridge, South Carolina, 245
Camden, South Carolina, 6, 11, 104-105, 109, 156, 160, 166, 170-172, 179, 183, 196, 202-203, 210-213, 218-221, 223-225, 229, 235-236, 260, 290
Camden Ferry, 247, 249
Campbell, Colonel Sir Archibald, 103, 161, 175, 268-269, 273-275, 287
Campbell, Lord William, 282-283, 285
Cape Fear, 283, 297
Carolinas, the, 24, 100, 104, 202, 212, 273
  climate of, 178
  (*See also* North Carolina; South Carolina)
Carpenters' Hall, Philadelphia, 45-46
Carrington, Lieutenant-colonel, 185
Carter, Anne, 162
Carter, John, 76
Caswell, General Richard, 170, 207-208, 211, 218-219
Catawba River, 172-173, 183, 186-187, 190, 192, 194, 196
Cerberus, 53
Charles City Courthouse, 110-111, 115-116
Charleston, 6, 15, 102-105, 122, 151, 167, 181, 189-190, 202, 204, 210-212, 223-224, 235-236, 241, 244, 247, 254, 258, 268-270, 275, 279-287, 292, 296
  evacuation of, 293-297
  fall of, 289-290
  occupation of, 292-293
  siege of, 288-289
Charleston *Mercury*, 86
Charlotte, 156, 160, 170, 199, 218, 220-221, 223, 246
Charlottesville, 155
Chastellux, Marquis de, 111, 113
  quoted, 32, 100, 113-114
Chatham, Lord, 7
Cheraw, South Carolina, 104, 109, 160, 162, 172, 242
Cherokee Ford, 186
Chester, Pennsylvania, 144
Chickahominy River, 117-118
Chronicle, Major William, 176
City Point, 154
Clermont, South Carolina, 211
Cleveland, Colonel, 175
Cleveland, Grover, 97
Clinton, General Sir Henry, 6, 15, 17, 25, 52-53, 102-103, 148, 151, 197, 229, 268, 270, 273, 283, 285-286, 288-290, 292
Clinton, Governor, 56
Cochran, Dr. John and Mrs., 79
Coffin, Captain John, 256, 258
Coke, John, 119, 122-124
Cole's Old Field, 194
Colfax, Captain, 72
Columbia, South Carolina, 225-227, 242, 245, 247
Combahee Ferry, 249
Concord, Massachusetts, 38, 105, 129
Concord Bridge, 37
Congaree River, 227-229, 242, 246, 249
Continental Congress, 8, 18, 36, 38, 45-46, 48-50, 62-64, 105, 107, 129, 149, 152, 209-210
Conway, Thomas, 203
Conway Cabal, 203

INDEX

Cornwallis, General Lord Charles, 4, 6-7, 14-15, 18, 25, 28-29, 51-53, 77, 102-105, 111, 119-120, 122, 134, 140-141, 143, 145-148, 150-151, 155, 159-160, 164-166, 168-169, 172, 183-185, 196-199, 211, 213-214, 217, 223, 240, 254, 259, 269, 273, 286, 288, 290, 298
   quoted, 197, 199-200
Cornwallis, Lady (Jemina Tullekens Jones), 15, 150
Cornwallis, Fort, 270-271
Cornwallis's Cave, 141
Cosway, Maria, 116
Coventry, Earl of, 29
Cowan's Ford, 183
Cowpens, the, 6, 104-105, 177, 179, 182-183, 218, 223
   British losses at, 182
Crosswicks, 11-12, 28
Cruger, Lieutenant-colonel, 245-246
Cruger, Mrs, 246
Cunningham, Anne Pamela, 85-86
Custis, George Washington Parke, 82-83, 92-93, 148
   quoted, 150-151
Custis, Mrs. (Mary), 83
Custis, John Parke, 44, 82, 136, 151
Custis, Martha (see Washington, Martha)
Custis, Nelly, 44, 82

Damas, French Adjutant-general, 147
Dan River, 183-184, 223
Dandridge, Dorothea, 131
Declaration of Independence, 9, 48, 105, 130, 139-140, 204, 208-209, 228
Deep River, 160, 168, 205
De Grasse, Admiral, 135, 143-144, 280
De Kalb, Baron Jean, 6, 104-105, 180-181, 190, 196, 204-205, 207, 214-215, 218-219, 225, 276-277, 292
Delaware River, 14-22, 35, 81, 183

D'Estaing, Admiral, 275, 277-280
Deux Ponts, Comte de, quoted, 144
De Volude, Comtesse Natalie De Lage, 200
Dismal Swamp, 153
Donop, Colonel, 28
Dorchester, South Carolina, 293
Du Buysson, Colonel, 219
Dunmore, Lord, 88-89, 105, 127-129, 153-154, 269, 282
Duquesne, Fort, 188

Edisto River, 250, 266
Elkton, Maryland, 60-62
Ellet, Mrs., quoted, 33
Ellicott, Andrew, 69
Elliott, Miss, 258
Elliott, Mrs, 294
Elliott, Thomas, 238
Eltham, Virginia, 151
Eutaw Creek, 253, 255-256, 259
Eutaw Springs, South Carolina, 104-105, 188, 226, 250-252, 253, 254, 259

Ferguson, Patrick, 105, 174-177
Finley, Captain, 232
Fishing Creek, 186-187, 196, 220
Florida, 273, 287
Flucker, Lucy (see Knox, Mrs. Henry)
Forbes, Governor, 188
Ford, Judge, 72, 74-75
Ford, Mrs., 72-73
Ford, Lieutenant-colonel, 217
Ford mansion, Morristown, 73
Four-hole Swamp, 250
France, 9
Franklin, Benjamin, 46, 48
   quoted, 80
Frederick, Maryland, 171
Fredericksburg, Virginia, 88, 91-92, 94-95, 129, 181
Frenchtown, Maryland, 61
Friday's Ferry, 246, 249

INDEX

Gadsden, Christopher, 268, 287, 293
Gadsden's Bridge, 287
Gates, General Horatio, 6, 37, 104-105, 109, 156, 159, 166, 170-172, 180-181, 196-197, 199-215, 218-221, 223, 241, 260, 290, 292
Gee's Bridge, 157
Geiger, Emily, 246-247
George III, 7-8, 188-189
Georgetown, South Carolina, 212, 242, 254
Georgia, 103, 202, 254, 268, 273, 280
German mercenaries, 9
(*See also* Hessians)
Germantown, Pennsylvania, 51-52
Gist, General, 151, 295
Goldsborough, Virginia, 298
Granby, Fort, 228, 242-244, 247
Graney's Quarter Creek, 200-202
Grant, General, 15, 29
quoted, 28
Graydon, Colonel, 17
Great Bridge, 153-154
Great Britain, 8, 29
Great Falls, 187, 196
Green Spring Plantation, 119, 121-122
Greene, General Nathaniel, 6, 24, 33, 104-105, 109, 121, 151, 158-163, 165-166, 169-172, 180, 183-185, 188, 196-197, 199, 203, 223-224, 226, 241-242, 244-250, 254, 270-272, 290, 293-295
quoted, 165-167, 242, 258-259, 269, 294
Greene, Mrs. Nathaniel (Kitty), 121, 166-167, 246, 293-294
Greene, Nathaniel, Jr., 33
Greensborough, North Carolina, 158-159
Gregory, Brigadier-general, 216
Grierson, Fort, 270-271
Grymes, Lucy, 162
Guilford Courthouse, 4-5, 104-105, 158-161, 167, 183

battle of, 163-166, 182, 185, 215, 223, 290
Gum Swamp, 200
Gunby, Colonel, 217
Gwyn's Island, Virginia, 88

Hackensack, 13
Hamburg, Georgia, 267, 271
Hamilton, Alexander, 24, 70-72, 78, 121
courtship of, 74-76
quoted, 77
Hamilton, Mrs. Alexander (Betsey Schuyler), 69-72, 74-78, 94, 121
Hampton, Virginia, 153, 198, 254, 256
Hancock, John, 37-41
Hand, Colonel, 23
Hanging Rock, 5, 177, 187, 192-196
Hanover Court House, 98-100
Harrison, Sarah, 126-127
Harrison, William Henry, 115
Harvard University, 127
Hayne, Colonel, 293
Head of Elk, 61, 65, 144
Henry, Patrick, 46-47, 99-100, 105-108, 129-131, 140, 155
quoted, 106-107
Hesse-Cassel, Landgrave of, quoted, 29
Hessians, 9, 13, 18-19, 23-30, 35, 51, 145, 183, 244
High Hills of Santee, 224, 226, 246, 249, 258-259, 263, 293
Hillsborough, North Carolina, 156-158, 170, 180, 190, 205, 210, 218, 220-222
Hobkirk's Hill, 223-224
Holly, Mrs., 69
Hopkinson, Francis, 12
Horry, Colonel Hugh, 238, 260, 292
Horry, Colonel Peter, 235, 238-239, 260, 292
Horse Creek Pass, 260
Houdon, 86
Howard, Colonel John Eager, 171, 179-182, 218, 222

INDEX

Howe, Admiral Lord, 286
Howe, Robert, 103, 268-269, 273, 275, 287
Howe, General Sir William, 7, 14-15, 25, 28-29, 45, 50-53, 102-103, 160, 292
   description of, 52
Hudson River, 151, 203
   forts on, 13
Huger, Isaac, 171, 183, 269, 279, 288, 290
Hummingbirds, 113-114
Humphreys, David, 149

Irwin's Ferry, 184
Izard, Ralph and Sarah, 282

Jackson, Andrew, 96
Jamaica, 283
James, Judge, 235
   quoted, 235-238, 264-265
James River, 117-118, 120, 122-123, 223
Jamestown, North Carolina, 168
Jamestown, Virginia, 4, 102, 118, 122-125, 127
Jamestown Island, 122-124
Jefferson, Martha (see Randolph, Mrs. Thomas Mann)
Jefferson, Thomas, 48, 105, 109-110, 115-116, 131, 140, 155-156
Jefferson, Mrs. Thomas (Martha Skelton), 115-116, 156
Johnson, Fort, 264, 289
Johnson, Thomas, 41
Jones Bridge, 156
Jones, Major, 217
Jones, Jemina Tullekens (see Cornwallis, Lady)
Jones, John Paul, 131

Keith's farmhouse, 17
Kenmore, 96-97
Kennet Square, 60-61

King's Mountain, 105, 172, 175-176, 180, 181, 183, 197, 254
King's Tree, 198
Kip's Bay, 14
Knox, General Henry, 6, 20, 24, 31-34, 58, 203, 269
   description of, 32-33
   quoted, 30-32, 34
Knox, Mrs Henry (Lucy Flucker), 14, 31-34, 69
Knyphausen, Baron William von, 24, 29

Lafayette, General, 6, 24, 58, 63-65, 104-105, 119-120, 134-135, 145, 155, 205, 273
   and Washington, 64-65
Lafayette, George Washington, 64
Lancaster, Pennsylvania, 35
Lancaster, South Carolina, 192, 195
Lee, General Charles, 17, 37, 39-41, 102, 268, 283-284
Lee, Lighthorse Harry, 148, 161-162, 183-185, 223, 229-236, 242, 244-245, 248, 254, 270-271, 294-295
   quoted, 162, 164-165, 175, 258, 261-263
Lee, Mary Fitzhugh, 83
Lee, Richard Henry, 46-48, 107, 130, 140
Lee, Robert E., 83, 162
Lee, William Ludwell, 124
Leesylvania, 162
L'Enfant, Major, 278
Leslie, General, 104, 293-294
Lewis, Fielding, 95, 97
Lewis, Mrs. Fielding (Betty Washington), 95-97
Lexington, Massachusetts, 38, 105
Lexington, South Carolina, 169
Liberty Hill, 267, 271
Lincoln, General, 103-105, 148, 181, 189-190, 202, 204, 223, 269-270, 273, 275-279, 287-292
Litomiski, Charles, 279

Livingston, Governor, 71
Livingston, Mrs, 79
Long Island, New York, 286
Loring, Mrs., 52-53
Lossing, Benson, 7, 10, 12, 48, 50, 85-86, 102, 142-143, 146, 199, 223, 232, 269
   quoted, 3-5, 7-12, 14, 16, 26, 31, 35-36, 45-49, 53-54, 56, 60-69, 71-75, 78-85, 87-88, 91-94, 97-101, 107-111, 114-120, 122-125, 131-132, 138-139, 141-142, 153-160, 168-169, 172-174, 176-179, 184-188, 190-195, 200-202, 208-209, 223-235, 242-253, 259-260, 263-264, 266-267, 270-275, 277-282, 284-287, 289-290, 296-298
Ludwell, Philip, 119, 127
Lynch's Creek, 193, 236

McClure, Colonel, 193
McConkey's Ferry, 16, 30
McCord's Ferry, 228
McHenry, Colonel, 17
McKay, Captain, 261-263
McKean, President, 149
McKelvey, Captain, 198
McPherson, Captain, 228-232
Maham, Major Hezekiah, 261-263
Maham towers, 262-263, 270
Maitland, Colonel, 277, 287
Majoribanks, Major, 254-258
Manhattan (*see* New York)
Marion, General Francis, 4, 6, 89, 102, 104, 166, 188, 196-197, 199, 208-209, 211, 223, 229-230, 232-242, 254, 260, 261-265, 287, 290-293, 296
Marion, Mrs. Francis (Miss Videau), 263-265
Martinsville, North Carolina, 159
Mask's Ferry, 206
Mattapony River, 97, 98
Matthews, Governor, 295
Maxwell, Colonel, 243-244

May's Mill, 207
Meherrin River, 157
Mercer, General Hugh, 181
Middlebrook, New Jersey, 32, 70, 277
Middleton Plantation, 293
Monck's Corner, South Carolina, 252, 288, 290
Monmouth, New Jersey, 14
   battle of, 6, 53, 58, 65, 70, 180, 268
Monroe, James, 23, 24
Monticello, 109, 115, 155-156
   restoration of, 156
Morgan, General Daniel, 104-105, 169, 171-172, 177-181, 183-184, 222-223
Morris, Colonel, 167
Morris, George P, quoted, 80-81
Morris, Robert, quoted, 62
Morristown, New Jersey, 29, 50, 70-76, 162, 166, 204
Morrisville, Pennsylvania, 35
Motte, Elizabeth, 228-229
Motte, Fort, 6, 225, 227-229, 242, 244
Motte, Jacob, 228
Motte, Mrs. Rebecca, 227-232, 292
Moultrie, Colonel William, 102, 245, 269, 283, 287, 293-294
   quoted, 284-285, 289, 294-295
Moultrie, Fort, 286-287
Mount Vernon, 38, 42-43, 82-88, 94-95, 136, 144-145, 151, 162
   restoration of, 86
Musgrove's Creek, 274-275

Nantucket, 168
Nelson, Scotch Tom, 139
Nelson, Thomas, II, 140
Nelson, Governor Thomas, III (Jr.), 131, 136, 138, 139-141
Nelson, William, 138, 141
Nelson's Ferry, 236, 253, 259-260
New Brunswick, 13, 15, 28, 81
New Garden Meeting-house, 160, 163, 165, 168
New Jersey, 13, 15, 20-21, 50, 63, 268

INDEX

New Kent Courthouse, 145
New London, Maryland, 61
New Town, Pennsylvania, 26, 28
New Windsor, New York, 76
New York, 6-7, 10, 13, 18, 50, 52-53, 103, 143, 151, 203, 268, 281, 283, 286, 290
Newark, 13
Newport, Rhode Island, 13, 17, 103, 280
Norfolk, Virginia, 109, 130, 153-154, 269
North, Lord, 7
North Carolina, 208, 210, 268
Nut Bush Post Office, 157

Occoquan, Virginia, 86-88
Ogier, Lewis, 238
O'Hara, General Charles, 146-148, 150, 164, 166, 184
Orangeburg, South Carolina, 244, 247-250, 293
Oxford, North Carolina, 157

Paine, Thomas, 22, 46
  quoted, 22-23
Pamunkey River, 98
Parker, Admiral Sir Peter, 102, 283-286
Parker, Commodore, 275
Peale, Charles Wilson, 6, 38, 81, 121
Pedee River, 205-206, 208
Pendleton, Edmund, 41
Pennsylvania, 14, 16-17, 20, 22, 268
Petersburg, Virginia, 109, 155-156
Philadelphia, 6, 12-13, 18, 28-29, 35-36, 45-52, 54, 63, 111-112, 149, 152, 165, 203, 292
  capture of, 102-103
Philadelphia Convention of 1787, 208
Phillips, General, 104, 154-155, 290
Pickens, General Andrew, 245, 249, 254, 270-271

Pinckney, Thomas, 229-230, 287
Pluckemin, New Jersey, 33
Pocahontas, 123
Poe, Edgar, 64
Poe, Mr. and Mrs., 63-64
Pohick Church, 87, 89
Pope's Creek, 92
Porterfield, Lieutenant-colonel, 207, 211, 214-215
Port Royal, 282
Portsmouth, Virginia, 120
Postell, Colonel James, 238
Potomac River, 6, 68, 82, 83, 84, 88, 91, 92
Powhattan, 118, 124
Prevost, General Augustine, 269, 273, 277, 287
Princeton, 13, 15, 29, 82, 183
Pulaski, Count, 272, 276-279
Pulaski, Fort, 282
Purysburg, South Carolina, 275, 287
Putnam, General Israel, 28, 37-38, 41
  quoted, 62-63

Queen Anne, Maryland, 67-68

Raleigh Tavern, Williamsburg, 5, 131
Rall, Colonel, 23-29
Randolph, Thomas Mann, 156
Randolph, Mrs. Thomas Mann (Martha Jefferson), 156
Randolph-Peachy house, Williamsburg, 136
Rappahannock River, 92
Rawdon, Lord, 104, 193, 196, 198, 210-211, 213, 223-224, 242, 244-248
Richards, J. Addison, 227
Richmond, Virginia, 97-102, 105-110, 129, 154-155, 298
Roanoke River, 156-157
Rochambeau, Count de, 7, 105, 113, 134, 136, 143-144, 147, 150
Rockefeller, John D., Jr., 97, 133

INDEX

Rocky Mount, North Carolina, 177, 187, 190, 195
Rugeley, Colonel, 200
Rugeley's, 200, 211, 213, 223
Rutledge, Edward, 209, 293
Rutledge, John, 199, 209-210, 223, 268, 284, 287-288, 290, 293

St. Augustine prison, 293
St. Clair, General, 27, 151
St. Helena's Island, 279
St. John's Church, Richmond, 105, 107-109
St. Mary's, Maryland, 62
St. Simon, Marquis de, 134-135
Salisbury, North Carolina, 169-170, 199, 221
Sander's Creek, 201-202
Sandy Hook, 268
Santee River, 189-190, 223-224, 226, 246, 250, 252-253, 260, 293
Saratoga, New York, 52, 180, 269
Savannah, 6, 254, 268-269, 273, 276-277, 290
  capture of, 103, 105
  evacuation of, 281
  siege of, 280
Savannah River, 267, 269, 275
Scammell, Colonel, 145-146
Schimmelpfennig, Captain von, 28
Schultz's bridge, 267, 271
Schuyler, Angelica, 70, 76
Schuyler, Betsey (*see* Hamilton, Mrs. Alexander)
Schuyler, Philip, 37, 41, 69-71, 76
Scotland Wharf, 127
Selden, John A., 111
Shelby, Colonel, 175
Sheldon, South Carolina, 287
Sherwood Forest, 116-117
Shippen, Peggy (*see* Arnold, Mrs. Benedict)
Simcoe, Colonel, 109-110
Simcoe's Rangers, 109, 155

Simms, William Gilmore, 236, 238-239
  quoted, 240, 255-258, 290-292
Singleton, Captain, 215
Sinkler, William, 251, 259
Skelton, Bathurst, 115
Skelton, Martha (*see* Jefferson, Mrs. Thomas)
Smallwood, Brigadier-general, 217-221
Smith, Captain John, 118
Smythe, the Rev. Samuel, 282
Snee Farm, 293
Snow's Island, 236-238, 240
Solebay, frigate, 286
"Song of Marion's Men," Bryant, 233-235
South Carolina, 11, 188-190, 209, 223, 245, 254, 268, 283, 286, 293
Sprague, Charles, quoted, 266
Spring Hill redoubt, 278-280
Stark, Colonel, 24
Stateburg, South Carolina, 226
State House, Philadelphia, 46, 49-50
Staten Island, 15
Staunton, Virginia, 155
Stephen, General, 19
Steuben, General, 6, 58, 104, 109, 119, 122, 134
Stevens, General, 211, 214-216, 218
Stewart, General Alexander, 104-105, 151, 246, 249-250, 254
Stirling, General, 27
Stuart, Colonel, 164, 166
Stuart, Gilbert, 6
Sullivan, Fort, 284-285
Sullivan, General John, 23-24, 280
Sullivan's Island, 283-286
Sumter, General Thomas, Jr., 4-6, 104, 166, 187-199, 210-211, 220-221, 223, 226, 244, 246-249, 254, 293
Sumter, Mrs. Thomas, 189
Sunbury, North Carolina, 275
Susquehanna River, 61
Swan Tavern, Yorktown, 142

INDEX

Tarleton, Colonel Banastre, 25, 100, 105, 108-109, 155, 160-161, 166, 179, 181-183, 189, 194, 196-200, 210-211, 213, 254, 288
Tarleton's Dragoons, 103, 160, 180, 189, 218-219
Taylor, Colonel, 247
Taylorsville, 16
Thatcher, Dr., quoted, 149-150
Thicketty Mountain, 179
Thomson, Charles, 46-48, 165
Tilghman, Colonel Tench, 72, 149
Tracy, Sarah, 86
Trading Ford, 169, 183
Trenton, New Jersey, 6, 11, 13-14, 29, 35, 283
    battle of, 23-28, 30, 63, 102, 183
    march on, 18-23
Troublesome Creek, 165-166
Truite, frigate, 278
Trumbull, John, 116
Tuckesegee Ford, 172, 190
Tyler, James, 115-117

Valley Forge, 6, 14, 53-54, 56-59, 63, 70-71, 180, 203
Vance's Ferry Post Office, 250, 259-260
Varnum, General, 58
Videau, Miss (*see* Marion, Mrs Francis)
Virginia, 36-38, 46-47, 65, 104, 109, 115, 127, 130-131, 143, 184-185, 202, 273, 290, 298
Virginia Convention of 1775, 105, 130
    of 1776, 130, 140
Virginia *Gazette*, 129, 228

Waccamaw, 238
Wakefield estate, 92, 96-97
Wappoo, 289
Ward, General Artemus, 37-38, 40-41
Warren, Mercy, 54
    quoted, 47

Washington, Augustine (half-brother of George), 96-97
Washington, Betty (sister of George), (*see* Lewis, Mrs Fielding)
Washington, Bushrod (nephew of George), 42, 85
Washington, George, 4, 6-7, 13, 18-27, 32-33, 36-37, 50, 70-72, 76, 89, 102, 104-107, 113, 115, 130, 134-135, 143, 172, 183, 188, 203-205, 268, 283-284, 296
    birthplace of, 92-93, 96-97
    chosen commander in chief, 39-41
    descriptions of, 14, 37
    and Lafayette, 64-65, 205
    at Morristown, 71-73
    mother of, 93-97
    quoted, 17-18, 41-42, 76-77, 79-80, 89, 95-96, 144-145, 148-149, 296
    at Valley Forge, 56-59, 203
    at Yorktown, 146-148, 150
Washington, George Augustine, 95
Washington, John (grand-nephew of George), 83, 85-86
Washington, John Augustine (Jack) (brother of George), 17, 42, 85
Washington, Lawrence (half-brother of George), 84
Washington, Martha, 14, 38, 42-43, 54, 57, 59, 71-73, 79, 115, 135-136, 151-152, 166, 265
    quoted, 44
Washington, Mary (mother of George), 93-97
Washington, Colonel William (cousin of George), 24, 171, 179, 181-182, 200, 210-212, 222, 224, 249, 254-255, 258-259, 288, 290, 294
Washington, William Augustine (nephew of George), 97
Washington City, 67-68, 78, 91, 298
    burning of, 69
Washington's Crossing, 16
Wateree Ford, 196

Wateree Swamp, 226, 247, 249
Watson, Colonel, 261-262
Watson, Fort, 253, 261, 263
Watson, John, quoted, 51-52
Waxhaw Creek, 189
Wayles, John, 115
Wayne, General Anthony, 6, 104, 119-122, 134, 151, 281, 294
Waynesborough, 121
Webster, Colonel, 164, 166
Weems, Parson, 87, 89-90, 235
Weldon, North Carolina, 298
Wemyss, Major, 197-198, 211
West Indies, 275, 280-281
West Point, 76, 79, 109, 112
Westham, 110
Westover Plantation, 109-114
Whitemarsh, Pennsylvania, 53
William and Mary College, 126-127
Williams, Colonel Otho, 166, 170-171, 183-184, 206-207, 218, 222, 254, 294
    quoted, 170-171, 206-207, 209, 212-222

Williamsburg, 4-5, 47, 88-89, 98, 105, 109, 113-114, 119-120, 127-136, 145, 154-155
    restoration of, 97, 133
Williamsburg, South Carolina, 209
Willing, Mary (*see* Byrd, Mrs. William, III)
Wilmington, North Carolina, 104, 165, 212, 223, 290, 297-298
Winnsboro, South Carolina, 170, 181, 199
Wirt, Mr., quoted, 107
Wright's Bluff Post Office, 261
Wythe, George, 135-136

Yadkin River, 169-170, 183
York, Pennsylvania, 51, 63, 203-204
York River, 138-139
Yorktown, Virginia, 4, 6-7, 102, 104-105, 119-120, 134-136, 138-152, 188, 223, 273, 280
    siege of, map, 147
    surrender of, 259, 269, 290, 293
Yorkville, 186